"Christianity is incomprehensibl[e] ... clusion upon reading *From Plat[o]* ... ... to the continuing relevance of Plato's dialogues for today's world, Louis Markos takes us both to Plato himself and to key Christian Platonists, instilling in us the same longing for truth, goodness, and beauty that animated Plato and his Christian heirs through the centuries. Here is a book that will inspire you to ascend the rising path and find the higher purpose for which you were born."

Hans Boersma, Saint Benedict Servants of Christ Professor of Ascetical Theology, Nashotah House Theological Seminary

"This is an urgently needed book. That educated persons too often have no knowledge of Plato is a real disaster. With his usual flair and concision, Markos brings forward Plato's greatest insights and describes their reception in the Christian tradition, as well as their rejection by Hobbes and Nietzsche. May the Christian retrieval of the best of Plato—joined by his student Aristotle—commence in earnest!"

Matthew Levering, James N. and Mary D. Perry Jr. Chair of Theology, Mundelein Seminary

"We need this book because we cannot understand ourselves unless we understand the tradition of thought that has shaped the West, including the church. One of the key thinkers at the root of our culture is Plato. His influence on Christian writers has been immense, yet he is little known and greatly misunderstood today. Louis Markos does us a great service in this accessible and fascinating book, which functions as an introduction to the thought of Plato and an assessment of his influence on major Christian writers from the church fathers to C. S. Lewis."

Craig A Carter, research professor of theology at Tyndale University, Toronto

FROM PLATO TO CHRIST

How Platonic Thought Shaped the Christian Faith

Louis Markos

Academic

An imprint of InterVarsity Press
Downers Grove, Illinois

InterVarsity Press
P.O. Box 1400, Downers Grove, IL 60515-1426
ivpress.com
email@ivpress.com

InterVarsity Press® is the book-publishing division of InterVarsity Christian Fellowship/USA®, a movement of students and faculty active on campus at hundreds of universities, colleges, and schools of nursing in the United States of America, and a member movement of the International Fellowship of Evangelical Students. For information about local and regional activities, visit intervarsity.org.

Scripture quotations, unless otherwise noted, are from the Holy Bible, Authorized King James Version.

Cover design and image composite: David Fassett
Interior design: Daniel van Loon
Images: crosses and monograms: © Adobest / iStock / Getty Images Plus
    Plato illustration: © ZU_09 / DigitalVision Vectors / Getty Images

ISBN 978-0-8308-5304-5 (print)
ISBN 978-0-8308-5305-2 (digital)

Printed in the United States of America ♾

InterVarsity Press is committed to ecological stewardship and to the conservation of natural resources in all our operations. This book was printed using sustainably sourced paper.

Library of Congress Cataloging-in-Publication Data
A catalog record for this book is available from the Library of Congress.

P	25	24	23	22	21	20	19	18	17	16	15	14	13	12	11	10	9	8	7	6	5	4	3	2	1
Y	37		36		35		34		33		32		31		30		29		28		27		26		25		24		23		22		21

For my brother George

With memories of many late-night talks about

God, man, and the universe

CONTENTS

PREFACE

By titling this book *From Plato to Christ* I do not mean to suggest that it can only be profitably read by Christians. I hope it will be read by people of all religious backgrounds, or no religious background, who share my (and Plato's) love for beauty, hunger for goodness, and passion for truth. I do, however, mean to suggest that the works of Plato can be most profitably read on two simultaneous levels: as works of genius in their own right and as inspired writings used by the God of the Bible to prepare the ancient world for the coming of Christ and the New Testament. Plato, to my mind at least, is the greatest of all philosophers—the culmination of the best of pagan (pre-Christian) wisdom, a wisdom that challenges the mind as much as it fires the imagination and that leaves the soul yearning for more. Though he lacked the direct (or special) revelation afforded to Moses, David, Isaiah, John, and Paul, Plato was nevertheless inspired by something beyond the confines of our natural world. Along with such Greco-Roman sages as Aeschylus, Aristotle, Cicero, and Virgil, Plato glimpsed deep mysteries about the nature of God and man,[1] the earth and the heavens, history and eternity, virtue and vice,

---

[1]True to the legacy of the classical literature and philosophy that I will be discussing in this book, I will be using traditional English grammar throughout: that is to say, I will use *he, him,*

and love and death that point forward to the fullness of the Judeo-Christian worldview.

I am aware that such a reading of Plato and his work may seem bizarre at best and anti-intellectual at worst to the modern, post-Enlightenment mind, but we should not forget that many of the finest thinkers of the past—men like Origen, Augustine, and Erasmus—held just such a view of Plato and his fellow proto-Christians. The very reason that Aristotle and Virgil could serve as forerunners and guides to the two greatest repositories of medieval Catholic learning (the *Summa theologiae* and the *Commedia*) was because Aquinas and Dante understood that their pagan mentors had access to a wisdom that transcended their time and place. Though they believed that man was fallen both in body and in mind, they also believed that man was created in God's image and still retained the mark of his Creator. True, our reason, conscience, and powers of observation were corrupted by the fall, but they still operated and could afford us limited knowledge of the Good, the True, and the Beautiful.

Indeed, so sure was Boethius that fallen man retained, under the wider umbrella of God's grace, the capacity to grope after that which is real (see Acts 17:27) that he attempted, in his *Consolation of Philosophy*, to embody Christian ethical principles while yet strictly confining himself to the wisdom achieved by such pagan thinkers as Plato and Aristotle. Chaucer, author of the third great repository of medieval Catholic learning (*Canterbury Tales*), clearly believed Boethius's attempt was successful, for his *Knight's Tale* strikes the same literary-philosophical stance: pointing forward to the fuller Christian revelation while limiting its characters to beliefs accessible to the pre-Christian world. And most of those beliefs Chaucer borrowed directly from a book he translated into Middle English: the *Consolation of Philosophy*.

Let me be clear: I shall be treating Plato as a bona fide source of wisdom. Though I shall in no way abdicate my responsibility to

---

and *his* as the gender-inclusive pronouns and *man*, *men*, and *mankind* to refer collectively to the human race.

measure, test, evaluate, and critique, my primary posture vis-à-vis Plato will be that of a student learning at a master's feet. Plato was a genius, a vessel through whom much beauty, goodness, and truth was ushered into our world. He was neither flawless nor free from error, but he shone a light that we would do well to attend to—especially if we desire to move up the rising path toward those things that are really real and truly true.

If we read Plato in this spirit, then I believe we will be changed by what we read. We will come to see our world and the next through different eyes; we will reevaluate the worth of things that we once thought dear and perhaps even alter the trajectory of our lives. Plato's dialogues are fun, and the great master is not above tweaking the noses of his readers, but let no one think that they are mere pastimes for idle college students (or professors!). Plato is about serious business, and we should be as well.

Though Plato helped teach the Western world that knowledge is something that should be sought for its own sake rather than as a utilitarian method for achieving power and wealth—a teaching foundational to all liberal arts institutions—he did not consider philosophy to be merely an end in itself. Philosophy properly pursued and wrestled with should lead to a higher and greater end—the contemplation of what Plato called the Good and later Christian theologians called (after Plato) the Beatific Vision. The purpose of Plato's dialectic is not to teach us to play mental games but to propel us forward on the road to greater wisdom and insight. Though Plato the pre-Christian did not know that Truth is ultimately a Person (see John 14:6), he sought it as tenaciously and passionately as Solomon or John or Paul. Let us do the same.

THE PATH AHEAD

My dialogue with Plato's dialogues begins with a close look at the influence that Socrates, the sophists, and the Presocratics exerted on the thought and practice of Plato. Socrates, for all his passion and genius, was, I will argue, the kind of thinker who was better at asking questions than providing answers—the ideal type of thinker, that is, to inspire his star pupil to take up the mantle of his master and move forward toward the formulation of answers. The Presocratics, on the other hand, paved the way for Plato by laying down a riddle for which Plato would provide, in the pre-Christian world, the most original and influential solution.

After the first chapter, which includes a quick overview of Plato's early Socratic dialogues, I put my full focus on the great dialogues of Plato's middle period, including *Republic, Symposium, Phaedrus, Phaedo,* and *Timaeus*. It is in these dialogues that Plato's mature voice is heard in all its beauty and majesty and where his most lasting ideas find their fullness of expression. As *Republic* is his best and most fully realized work, I devote all of chapter two to following Plato as he explores the nature of justice both in the individual and in the governments that individuals construct. I focus in particular on how Plato, through the voice of Socrates, disproves the commonly held belief that the unjust man is happier and more successful than the just man, proposes a course of education that will produce leaders of great philosophical insight, contrasts the ephemeral nature of worldly pursuits with the lasting value of contemplation, and redefines the nature of religion, society, and the arts.

Republic is perhaps most famous for its haunting allegory of the cave; however, it is not the only Platonic dialogue to make use of a well-told myth for the sake of illustration and illumination. Indeed, nearly all of Plato's middle dialogues contain memorable allegories that point to some aspect of the journey toward truth. It is the burden of chapters three and four to survey the wisdom contained in these richly imaginative myths and discover how they work together to provide a multifaceted picture of the internal struggle that impels some toward the beast below and others toward the heavens above.

With chapter five, I move past Plato's middle dialogues to consider the crowning achievement of his later years, a dialogue titled *Laws* that, like most of his other later dialogues, does not use Socrates as its mouthpiece. In this partial reworking of *Republic*, we encounter again the central issues of education, virtue, and the arts that continued to trouble, challenge, and fascinate Plato to the end of his life.

In chapter six, I take a slight step backward to consider a Platonic dialogue that stands firmly in between *Republic* and *Laws*, a dialogue that, though much shorter than the other two, deserves a chapter to itself—not only because of its inherent brilliance but also because it was the only dialogue of Plato to be widely available throughout most of the Middle Ages. I speak, of course, of *Timaeus*, a Platonic work that is less a dialogue than an extended myth, an account of creation that bears striking similarities to Genesis 1 and that, of all Plato's dialogues, contains the most powerful foreshadowings of Christianity.

I have titled this book *From Plato to Christ*, and, in keeping with that title, I consider in part two Plato's influence on later Christian authors. To set the stage, I offer in chapter seven a Christian reading of Plato's myths that seeks to assess, from the point of view of the Christian faith, how close the pre-Christian Plato came to glimpsing higher biblical truths. I argue that there are a number of key elements of Plato's philosophical and spiritual vision that can not only be reconciled with those of Christ but can actually increase and empower the spiritual life of the Christian humanist who desires to drink from those two streams (the Greco-Roman and Judeo-Christian) that flow from Athens and Jerusalem and meet together in Rome.

In chapter eight I begin my analysis of Plato's influence on Christian writers with a reading of a strange and wonderful book by an early church father that makes a spirited and courageous—if at times heterodox—attempt to filter the vision of Plato through a Christian lens. His name is Origen, and I argue that his book *On First Principles* successfully balances a firm belief in the essential doctrines of Christianity with a free and contagious spirit of inquiry that calls back from his grave the author of *Republic*.

After this long effusion on Origen, I offer a series of shorter chapters that trace Plato's influence through the early church, the Middle Ages, the Renaissance, the Enlightenment, the Romantic age, and the twentieth century. In chapters nine and ten, I survey the influence of Plato on three key figures in Eastern Orthodoxy (Gregory of Nazianzus, Gregory of Nyssa, and Gregory Palamas) and Western Catholicism (Augustine, Boethius, and Dante). All six of these writers found ways to strengthen their own Christian faith and vision by meditating on the truths revealed in Plato.

Chapter eleven begins with a close look at the work of a chief architect of the Reformation and Renaissance, Erasmus, who chose not to follow Luther into Protestantism but who found ways to carry the legacy of Plato into the areas of spiritual growth and political justice. From Erasmus, I move to the father of Enlightenment and modern philosophy, Descartes, whose Platonic methods helped keep him, I argue, closer to Christianity than the philosophers who followed in his wake. Finally, I consider how the great Romantic poet and critic Samuel Taylor Coleridge wrestled with Plato in his influential theories of the imagination.

In chapter twelve, I turn to the greatest Christian apologist of the twentieth century, C. S. Lewis, to assess how his radically creative yet fully orthodox views on the nature of choice, sin, and heaven represent a perfect fusion of Platonic thought and Christian doctrine.

The book concludes with a bibliographical essay of books by and about Plato that have influenced my own thoughts and that should prove accessible to a general readership.

A NOTE ON TRANSLATION

FOR THE SAKE OF CONSISTENCY, all passages from the dialogues of Plato are quoted from the translations of the great Victorian
classicist Benjamin Jowett (1817–1893). Still accurate and highly
readable, Jowett's translations capture the beauty and complexity of
Plato's syntax, reminding us that the philosopher who kicked the poets
out of his ideal republic was himself one of the finest prose poets of
all time.

I have also chosen to limit myself to Jowett because of the accessibility of his translations to the average reader. As well as being available
in a number of different inexpensive editions from such publishers as
Modern Library (*Selected Dialogues of Plato*), Anchor (*The Republic
and Other Works*), and Dover (*Six Great Dialogues*), the complete
translations of Jowett can be read for free online either at Project
Gutenberg[1] or at The Internet Classics Archive.[2] Finally, those who
own a Kindle can download the complete Jowett Plato for a nominal fee.

As for the referencing of my quotes, rather than using page numbers
from a specific edition, I use the standard Stephanus numbers. These
numbers are taken from the page and section numbers of the 1578

---

[1] www.gutenberg.org
[2] classics.mit.edu

edition of Plato's complete works by Stephanus (Henri Estienne). As nearly all editions of Plato today, regardless of the publisher or translator, include the Stephanus numbers in the margin or (less helpfully) at the top of each page, these numbers will allow readers to locate the passage I am quoting no matter what edition they have in their library.

Finally, although all my quotes are taken from Jowett, in my bibliographical essay, I share with the reader a number of more recent translations and editions that I have found to be helpful.

PART I

PLATO'S PRE-CHRISTIAN VISION

SOCRATES, THE SOPHISTS,
AND THE PRESOCRATICS

LET ME BEGIN with what may seem a strange admission. Though I love Plato above all philosophers, if all we had of Plato were his early Socratic dialogues (for example, *Ion*, *Laches*, *Lysis*, *Charmides*, *Hippias Major*, *Hippias Minor*, and *Euthydemus*), I would hardly rank him in the top echelon of philosophers. Still, these dialogues, with their abrupt endings and seeming inability to provide answers, stand as necessary stepping stones to the great dialogues of Plato's middle period (*Republic*, *Phaedo*, *Symposium*, *Phaedrus*, *Gorgias*, *Meno*, and *Protagoras*). They are stepping stones in at least three ways: (1) they seem to present the thought and approach of the historical Socrates rather than that of his precocious pupil, Plato; (2) they build a methodological (dialectic-driven) and theoretical (definition-based) framework on which Plato's mature philosophy rests; and (3) they strip away the many, the partial, and the false to make room for the one, the full, and the true.

TRUTH AS REVELATION

If I were to buy an old house that had fallen into a woeful state of disrepair, my attempts at restoration would have to be carried out by means of a two-step process. Before covering the chipped and faded walls with new, vibrant paint, I would have to expend considerable time and energy stripping off the old paint and filling in the holes with putty. Likewise, before laying down expensive Carrara marble, I would first have to do the backbreaking work of ripping up the torn and stained carpets and removing the moldy pads and rusty tack boards. Neither the stripping nor the ripping makes for glamorous work, but the work must be done if the house is to reach its pinnacle of beauty.

With the skill of a master painter and the precision of a master stonemason, Plato built a glorious palace of philosophy, but he could only do so because his teacher, Socrates, had done the hard work of preparing the walls and floors. Philosophy, as Plato practiced it, meant a search after Wisdom: not after those thousand-and-one little systems that compete for supremacy in the marketplace of ideas, nor those relativistic, man-made opinions that masquerade as divinely revealed standards, but that one and eternal Truth that transcends our ever-shifting world, that abides and endures.

Unfortunately, such a search, difficult at any time and place, was rendered even more difficult by the sophists, teachers for hire who, by instructing the sons of the wealthy in the methods of logic, rhetoric, and oratory, guaranteed them success in the economic and political life of the polis (city-state) of Athens. Unlike Socrates, who believed in divine standards of behavior and belief, the sophists as a group considered ethical actions and philosophical truths to be relative: something that shifted from polis to polis.

Socrates set as his limited, humble philosophical goal, not the reaching of that capital-*T* Truth to which Plato dedicated his life, but the clearing away of all those sophistical, small-*t* truths that make it impossible for students or their teachers to catch even a faint glimpse of Truth. In this world of shifting shadows in which we live, it is nearly impossible to peer through all the many veils of untruth to catch sight of that faint glimpse—impossible, that is, unless we can first find a way to dispel the shadows.

I often assure my students that if they will just concentrate harder and focus their minds more firmly that the meaning of what they are reading will emerge and become clear to them. What I am telling them, in effect, is that the knowledge they are seeking is already there, hidden and embedded in the work they are studying. If they can only strip away what is preventing them from seeing it, the knowledge will be released, and they will reap the fruits of their labor.

If they seem skeptical, I back up my assurance with a well-known anecdote from the Renaissance that is most likely apocryphal but that nevertheless conveys a great truth. When asked, the story goes, how he could create a sculpture as perfect as his *David*, Michelangelo replied that when he first stood before the single piece of (flawed) marble that would yield his masterpiece, he saw David, simple and whole, in the midst of the stone. After that moment of vision, he needed only to chip away all the marble that was not David.

Like the statue of Israel's messianic king, Truth is not so much something that we build up to as something we dig down to. The philosopher who would seek after truth must be a miner, one who burrows down through layers of error and illusion to uncover the truth that lies at the heart of the mine. Or, to switch the metaphor without switching its meaning, he must be like a mountaineer who climbs through layers of mist and cloud to reach the seemingly inaccessible peak of Mount Everest. Or, to switch it once again, like the high priest of Israel pushing his way past a series of increasingly thick veils until he reaches the ark of the covenant that lies at the center of the holy of holies. The journey to the bottom, the top, or the center is finally the same journey, for its telos (its goal and its purpose) is the same: to reach the First Principle, the Essential Origin, the Transcendent Truth.

The original title of the last book of the Bible is Apocalypse, a Greek word that means, literally, "uncovering." Translated into Latin, the word becomes "revelation" (re-veiling, which is to say, unveiling). It may at first seem odd that the most obscure and cryptic book of the Bible should bear a title that means "uncovering." Wouldn't "covering" more accurately describe the effects of reading John's great prophecy? But the book is aptly named. The reason Revelation seems so strange to us is that we are not used to gazing directly on eternity. Through the power of revelation, John rips away the veils of time and space, allowing us to peer into the divine, supratemporal workings of history.

Unless the philosopher be trained in the almost mystical art of uncovering, of stripping away the veils until truth is revealed in all its glory and splendor, he cannot hope to approach the deeper recesses of wisdom.

IN SEARCH OF DEFINITIONS

It was, I believe, Plato's lifelong mission to lift our vision from the small-*t* truths of our shadowy world to the capital-*T* Truth that dwells beyond, on the other side of the door. But what part exactly did Socrates play in this process? Although, it is not possible to disentangle with complete accuracy the thought of Socrates from the thought of Plato, I would argue, on the basis of the differences between Plato's early and middle dialogues, that Socrates prepared the way for Plato by doing the "grunt" work of clearing away the accretion of false idols and notions that prevent us from apprehending Truth. Socrates achieved this clearing-cleansing by means of a vigorous question-and-answer dialectic. But what did he use as the jumping-off point *for* his dialectic? Or, to borrow an image from Archimedes, what was the fulcrum that allowed Socrates to move the world of philosophy?

Even a cursory reading of the early dialogues will make the answer to that question immediately apparent. Socrates's fulcrum was the humble but persistent search for the definition of such key virtues as courage (*Laches*), friendship (*Lysis*), self-control (*Charmides*), and goodness/beauty (*Hippias Major*). By asking, and asking, and asking again what courage *is*—not just a particular form or example of courage but courage *itself*—Socrates set philosophy on the road to Truth. In time, Plato would follow the definition trail, and it would lead him upward to the Forms. Socrates's goal, I would argue, was more limited and preparatory. Rather than construct a metaphysical system, or locate the absolute origins of all things, Socrates pushed his interlocutors, especially those of a sophistical bent, to question any definition that could not account for a host of conflicting particulars.

By doing so, Socrates sought to stem the relativism that he perceived in the thought and arguments of the sophists.

It is surely significant that in most of the early dialogues, Socrates is portrayed in dialogue, not with his friends and disciples—as he is in most of the middle dialogues—but either with the sophists or with those who are sympathetic to them and their teachings. Further, though Socrates conducts himself in a friendly, genial fashion, a strong subtext of competition with the sophists and their disciples ever simmers beneath the surface, even if it is often, and entertainingly, diffused through the exchange of barbed witticisms.

Granted, Plato may have presented his teacher in conflict with sophistry as a way of defending him from the charge of being a sophist himself—a charge that was leveled against him in Aristophanes's anti-sophist comedy, *Clouds*, and that led to his trial and execution in 399 BC—but the portrait makes good historical sense. Both Socrates and the sophists practiced philosophical debate, and both used question and answer, but they differed in the way they used the dialectic and in their ultimate goal. And that dual difference not only gives the early dialogues much of their interest and tension but also explains why Socrates, and not the sophists, deserves to be honored as the father of philosophy.

In the defense he gave at his trial (immortalized in Plato's *Apology*), Socrates questions, tests, and examines one of his accusers (Meletus) to determine who it is that benefits the youth of Athens. The Greek word for such a process of cross-examination is *elenchus*, and it was used by the sophists as well as by Socrates. In Socrates's hands, elenchus proved invaluable as a system for wiping the slate clean, for eliminating wrong knowledge and erasing wrong definitions. For the sophists, on the other hand, it was more often a tool for tripping up one's opponent and wearing down his stamina. Indeed, in the hands of a wily and aggressive sophist, elenchus often gave way to eristic. Taken from Eris, the Greek goddess of discord whose golden apple set the gods against each other and ignited the Trojan War, eristic connotes a more polemical, disputatious kind of debate that makes heavy use of verbal tricks and rhetorical badgering. Socrates rarely engages in full-blown eristic, though, like the sophists, he does make frequent use of questionable logic—particularly false analogies and the either/ or fallacy—to push the dialectic in the direction he wishes it to go.

Admittedly, when Socrates uses poor logic or pushes an argument so far that it threatens to topple into illogic, he does come quite close to being guilty of one of the charges brought against him at his trial: of making the weaker argument the stronger. Still, in such instances, intention and motive are everything. In contrast to most of the sophists with whom he debates, when Socrates takes an illogical or even an eristic turn, he does so not because he cares only about winning the argument or because he is hungry for power or money, but because such missteps are often necessary in the search for truth. Though the end—the reaching of a true definition, or at least the clearing away of false ones—does not justify a conscious distortion of logic or a flagrant manipulation of one's opponent, it does provide a proper impetus and reward for philosophy.

By the end of *Hippias Major*, Socrates has come close to bullying his interlocutor into admitting that good persons commit crimes deliberately while bad ones do so involuntarily. However, when Hippias refuses to agree with this conclusion, Socrates ends the dialogue with these genial words: "Nor can I agree with myself, Hippias; and yet that seems to be the conclusion which, as far as we can see at present, must follow from our argument. As I was saying before, I am all abroad, and being in perplexity am always changing my opinion. Now, that I or any ordinary man should wander in perplexity is not surprising; but if you wise men also wander, and we cannot come to you and rest from our wandering, the matter begins to be serious both to us and to you" (376b-c). Socrates may play rough, but his ultimate goal is always the same: to faithfully follow the argument wherever it leads.

C. S. Lewis, arguably the greatest Christian apologist of the twentieth century, made honest and effective use of the Socratic dialectic/ elenchus to ferret out and defend doctrinal truths and theological first principles in such works as *Mere Christianity*, *The Problem of Pain*, and

Miracles. During his college years, however, when he was a confirmed atheist, he more often used the tools of philosophy as a way to show off or to gain prestige or simply to pass the time. One of the key turning points on his long road to faith occurred when Lewis overheard one of his Christian friends and one of his students discussing Plato. As he listened, he realized, in a flash of illumination, that they were discussing philosophy as if it really mattered, as if what they read could cause them to change their beliefs and even their behaviors. For the first time in his life, the sophistical Lewis encountered, face-to-face and in the flesh, a nobler, ultimately more satisfying reason for studying and engaging in philosophical debate.[1]

Socrates, in Plato's early dialogues, is spurred on by a desire to formulate definitions that can delve the true, essential meanings of spiritual, intellectual, ethical, and political virtues, not merely as a linguistic end in itself but as a spur to understanding and embodying those virtues. The goal is a high one, and it laid the groundwork for Plato's grand metaphysics, and yet, there is something vaguely unsatisfying about the early dialogues. Though they are dramatically robust, and though they make important strides toward truth, they are flawed both by their strained logic and by the frustrating fact that Socrates never arrives at the definition he sets out in search of. As a result, one comes away from them interested and even edified, but neither awed nor inspired.

Indeed, my contention that Socrates played the more "negative" role of demolishing false systems and definitions while Plato played the more "positive" role of constructing true systems and definitions rests primarily on the failure of the early dialogues to achieve the kind of philosophical clarity that one encounters in the middle dialogues. As I shall argue in the next chapter, one can even identify the exact moment in the *Republic* when Socrates presses past the kind of impasse that would have ended an early dialogue to propound new definitions and systems that can account for the true and transcendent

---

[1]C. S. Lewis, *Surprised by Joy: The Shape of My Early Life*, in *The Inspirational Writings of C. S. Lewis* (New York: Inspiration Press, 1991), 123.

nature of justice. Although, again, the evidence is not sufficient to afford conclusive proof, I would argue that it is in that transitional moment that we can discern the shift from teacher to pupil, from Socrates to Plato.

Most of the early dialogues begin with a chance meeting between Socrates and a group of young men who respect, even if they disagree with, him and who are eager to engage him in conversation. The meetings are generally linked to topical events like the Peloponnesian War—often as a way of exonerating Socrates from the later extreme behavior of his young followers (especially the far-right Critias and the far-left Alcibiades)—but they quickly devolve into a debate over the definition of words. Though Socrates's opponents will, at times, gain the upper hand, especially when they resort to eristic, Socrates always finds a way to get back on top and control the parameters of the debate. One by one, he eradicates false definitions that either fail to account for all the particulars or that contradict themselves. He does so insistently, relentlessly, until all the definitions put forth by society or the sophists—they inevitably turn out to be the same—have been exposed as inadequate, and then—and then—the dialogue ends!

Though skilled at exploding false definitions, Socrates never seems willing or able to give a full definition of his own. On the one hand, this failure is linked to the famous (or infamous) claim that he makes in his apology, that his wisdom resides not in his knowledge but in the fact that he, unlike the sophists, knows that he does not know: "He, O men, is the wisest, who, like Socrates, knows that his wisdom is in truth worth nothing" (*Apology* 23b). On the other hand, it suggests that Socrates had a firm understanding of his vital but limited role as a philosophical gadfly (to borrow the seriocomic image he uses of himself and his teaching methods in *Apology* 30d-31b). Most of the early dialogues end in an impasse—the Greek word is *aporia*, or waylessness— but it is a creative impasse that spurs the reader forward on his own search for truth.

Ironically, Jacques Derrida and many of his deconstructionist heirs have taken to themselves the word *aporia* to embody their belief that absolute truths and transcendent principles do not exist—and that even if they did, they could not be reached, known, or communicated by human beings.[2] I call this ironic, because deconstructionism stands in relation to our (post)modern world very much as sophistry did to the culture of ancient Athens. Though much variety exists among modern deconstructionists and ancient sophists, both groups ultimately taught that the pursuit for absolutes circles back on itself, yielding a set of theological or philosophical or ethical or aesthetic principles that shift, often radically, from polis to polis and culture to culture. Aporia ends the debate by exposing as naïve the search for meaning in the creeds we recite or the books we read or the commandments we follow.

Not so the aporias of Socrates, which are more like the paradoxes of Jesus: they can, and will if we let them, trouble us into wisdom. Far from rendering the quest for truth a dead end, they stand guard at the doorway of philosophy, keeping away those who are not willing to have their beliefs and behaviors altered by that quest. Rather than leave us stranded in a relativistic universe, they point forward toward real standards of right and wrong, good and evil, virtue and vice. And, beyond that, toward the unity of truth and the unity of virtue—toward eternal, unchanging touchstones of thought and action that remain constant, no matter the polis.

When, in his Apology, Socrates questions Meletus as to which Athenians improve the youth, he pushes him into an aporia. By the time Socrates is done with him, Meletus has made the ridiculous claim that all the politicians and citizens of Athens, *except Socrates*, have a salutary effect on the young men of the city. Once the absurdity of this conclusion has had time to settle in the minds of the jury, Socrates unwinds the aporia by arguing that there are, in fact, very few people who make the young better while most do them harm, or at least no

---

[2]See Jacques Derrida, "Structure, Sign and Play in the Discourse of the Human Sciences," in *Critical Theory Since Plato*, rev. ed., ed. by Hazard Adams (New York: HBJ, 1992), 1117-26. See also Roland Barthes, "The Structuralist Activity," in *Critical Theory Since Plato*, 1128-33.

good (*Apology* 24c-25b). Socrates may play games with his opponents, but only as a way of exposing relativism and, by so doing, point back toward a center of meaning and truth.

THE PRESOCRATIC RIDDLE

Though I think it perfectly justifiable to call Socrates the father of philosophy, it must be understood that philosophy did not spring fully armed out of the mind of Socrates as Athena did out of the head of Zeus. The ideas and methods that would culminate with Socrates took a full century and a half (roughly 600–450 BC) to percolate through the ancient world. During the five or six generations before the golden age of Athens, a group of innovative thinkers from across the Mediterranean—most notably, Anaxagoras, Anaximander, Anaximenes, Democritus, Empedocles, Heraclitus, Parmenides, Pythagoras, and Thales—sowed the seeds of scientific and philo-sophical thought. We call them the Presocratics, not only because they precede Socrates chronologically, but also because they laid down a framework that would be both developed and critiqued by Socrates, Plato, and Aristotle.

Although one can profitably define Plato as a philosopher who chose to follow the mystical, numbers-driven, reincarnation-affirming theories of Pythagoras over the materialistic, methodological natu-ralism of Thales, Anaximander, and Anaximenes (known collectively as the Milesians), I will here position Plato between the pluralism of Heraclitus and the monism of Parmenides. For it was Plato, rather than Empedocles, Anaxagoras, or Democritus, who came up with the most brilliant and enduring answer to the philosophical riddle of his day: Is the nature of reality plural or singular, changing or fixed, per-petual flux or unmoving perfection?

According to Heraclitus, we live in a world of ceaseless change. Nothing does or can remain the same. Indeed, the only constant in the universe is change itself. Far from existing in a state of static perfection, our universe is the battleground for a perpetual war among the four elements (earth, water, air, and fire) and their qualitative pairs (hot and cold, dry and wet). Though this elemental strife was constant and fierce, Heraclitus viewed it as a positive and creative one. In fact, to help illustrate this cosmic paradox, Heraclitus used the twin images of the bow and the lyre to express how harmony can arise out of opposing, seemingly destructive forces. Just as an arch is held together by the very forces that would tear it apart, so Heraclitus saw the strife among the elements as an ultimately stabilizing one.[3]

Heraclitus's vision, strange as it may sound, accords well with the world we perceive around us. The same cannot be said for that of Parmenides, who held, counterintuitively, that the universe is fixed and static and reality is one and unchanging. In the language of philosophy, Heraclitus's position is referred to as pluralism, for it holds that the cosmos is composed of many different substances that are in motion. Parmenides, on the other hand, was a monist: the universe, he believed, is composed of a single uniform substance that does not move or change.

To make matters worse for commonsense thinkers like Heraclitus, Parmenides held that true knowledge rests on nature (*physis* in Greek) and is apprehended by speculative reason, while mere opinion rests on custom (*nomos*) and is perceived by the senses. Of course, Parmenides here uses the word *nature* not to refer to the material stuff we see around us with our physical eye but the ultimate nature of things that we can only perceive with our mind's eye. To trust our senses, and the philosophical, theological, and scientific systems that rest on the foundation of the senses, is to trust folly. It is the things that we cannot see that are the most real, for they are eternal and unchanging.[4]

Among those who sought to solve the Presocratic riddle, Empedocles was perhaps the most bold and creative. Though he did not invent the theory of the four elements, Empedocles transformed it into a fully-worked-out system that influenced scientists and inspired poets for two millennia. Building on the work of the Milesians,

---

[3]Reginald E. Allen, ed., *Greek Philosophy: Thales to Aristotle* (New York: Free Press, 1966), 41-43.
[4]Allen, *Greek Philosophy*, 44-47.

Empedocles conjured a vast cosmic stage on which the ceaseless dance of the elements unfolds in all its power and glory. Like the endless systole/diastole of some giant heart, the elements move and flow and beat in a rhythm that makes life and growth possible. In the first movement of the dance, the force of strife tears apart earth, water, air, and fire; in the second, those same elements are welded back together by the force of love. The process is, as Heraclitus knew, one of continual motion and change, but the result is, as Parmenides theorized, one of stasis and perfection.[5]

In the very different cosmic scheme of Anaxagoras, the universe was composed, not of four distinct elements in a dance of love and strife, but of a chaos of tiny particles (or seeds) that are ordered by the universal mind (or *nous*). Anaxagoras, it seems, taught that these material seeds have always existed—that is to say, he agreed with Parmenides that matter is eternal and indestructible—but that their arrangement, à la Heraclitus, is in constant flux.[6]

Somewhere between Empedocles and Anaxagoras lies Democritus, who proposed a system similar to that of seeds plus *nous*, but who emptied *nous* of all purpose, intelligence, and consciousness. According to his scheme of things, all that exists in the universe are atoms and the void. By *atom*, Greek for "that which cannot be divided," Democritus meant the smallest, most fundamental building block of matter; by *void*, he meant an empty space of nonbeing that Parmenides refused to allow into his monistic paradigm, where all is One and all is Being.[7]

PLATO'S SOLUTION

Empedocles, Anaxagoras, and Democritus all struggled valiantly to reconcile the two poles of the Presocratic riddle. But it would be Plato himself who would provide the West with its most glorious reconciliation of monism and pluralism—a reconciliation that set Western

---

[5] Allen, *Greek Philosophy*, 50-51.
[6] Allen, *Greek Philosophy*, 52-54.
[7] Allen, *Greek Philosophy*, 54-56.

philosophy on a truly noble path. Though Plato's solution would fuel some of the Gnostic heresies of the early church, it would also help orthodox Christian theologians to understand the true nature of earth and heaven, of time and eternity, and of spiritual growth. Indeed, his solution reads like a pre-Christian commentary on 2 Corinthians 4:18: "For the things which are seen are temporal; but the things which are not seen are eternal."

With great insight and ingenuity, Plato posited that *both* Parmenides and Heraclitus were correct. The seeming impasse between their teachings resulted from the fact that their monistic and pluralistic visions referred to two different worlds. Our physical, natural, material world, the world in which we live out our lives and that we perceive through our senses, is a world of constant change, flux, and decay. As our world ever strives for, but is ever unable to reach, perfection, Plato called it the World of Becoming. The ever-shifting nature of our flawed and broken world precludes our forming true knowledge about it; of it and its endless fluctuations we can only formulate opinions (*doxa* in Greek).

But there is another, higher world, Plato believed, where all exists in a state of eternal and changeless perfection. Knowledge of that invisible, nonphysical World of Being can only be gained through reason and contemplation. Plato explains the dichotomy succinctly in book six of the *Republic*: "And the soul is like the eye: when resting upon that on which truth and *being* shine, the soul perceives and understands and is radiant with intelligence; but when turned towards the twilight of *becoming* and perishing, then she has opinion only, and goes blinking about, and is first of one opinion and then of another, and seems to have no intelligence?" (508d; emphasis added).

Though the four elements dominate the physical dance of the World of Becoming, the true first principle (*archē*) can only be found in the World of Being. In our world, there is an endless variety not only of physical objects (chairs, desks) but also of abstract nouns (beauty, truth); these Plato referred to as "the many." Only in the fixed, unchanging world above do we encounter the One or the Essence, the

Originals (Chair, Desk, Beauty, and Truth) of which our chairs, desks, beauties, and truths are but pale, shadowy imitations. Plato referred to these originals as the Forms (or Ideas) and insisted that knowledge of them was not available to the senses. This too Plato expresses succinctly in *Republic* 6: "There is a many beautiful and a many good, and so of other things which we describe and define; to all of them 'many' is applied. . . . And there is an absolute beauty and an absolute good, and of other things to which the term 'many' is applied there is an absolute; for they may be brought under a single idea, which is called the essence of each. . . . The many, as we say, are seen but not known, and the ideas are known but not seen" (507b).

Parmenides was *right* to establish a dichotomy between reason/ *physis*/knowledge on the one hand and senses/*nomos*/*doxa* on the other. What he did not realize was that the pluralistic world of our senses actually exists, though it is finally superseded by the monistic world that is only available to our reason. Thus, whereas Parmenides called for us to reject totally the data received by our senses, Plato called for us to lift our vision above the (real) shadows of our world to gaze on the absolute, naked truth of the Forms.

The divided line. To help explain, and incarnate, the two-tiered nature of the universe and guide his pupils on the journey upward, Plato goes on in *Republic* 6 (509d-511e) to construct a simple yet profound model of a divided line. The lower half of the line represents the World of Becoming. It is illumined by the sun and apprehended by the five senses, but it can only yield, at best, mere opinion. The upper half represents the World of Being. It is illumined by the Good—for Plato, the ultimate Form, which gives form and light to all the other Forms— and apprehended by reason; it alone yields true knowledge.

The lower half is further subdivided into physical objects and the shadows of those objects. Though the entire lower half is cut off from the kind of real insight that can be gained only by contemplation of the invisible Forms, the upper portion of the lower half nevertheless yields a kind of knowledge that can function as a first step toward higher truth. Thus, while the World of Becoming can afford only *doxa*, those who study objects themselves rather than the imitations *of* those objects are participating in a higher order of thinking. Sadly, for those who, like myself, have devoted themselves to studying the kinds of truth and beauty found in the imitative arts (fiction, poetry, drama, painting, and sculpture), Plato consigns all such manifestations of the creative mind to the bottom of the line; for they, like images in a mirror or reflections in water, are insubstantial and turn one away from reality toward illusion.

As Plato explains in *Republic* 10 (595a-597e), just as earthly chairs, desks, beauties, and truths are but shadows of the real Chair, Desk, Beauty, and Truth that dwell in the World of Being, so a painting of a chair or a sculpture of a desk or a poem about beauty or a drama about truth are themselves shadows of an earthly chair, desk, beauty, or truth. As such, artistic representations are imitations of imitations, twice removed from the Forms and thus doubly distant from the kind of Truth that we were created to contemplate. In our post-Romantic world, we tend to put a high premium on imagination. Plato, in sharp contrast, considered imagination to be the lowest order of thinking and the riskiest method for interacting with Beauty and Truth. It inevitably leads us astray from that which is really real and truly true.

In terms of our World of Becoming, the natural sciences are superior to the arts for they fix our senses on real objects that have real substance—even if those substances are finally shadows of the eternal Forms. By closely studying and analyzing our physical world, as the Milesians had so admirably done, one could progress from imagination (or conjecture) to belief. Still, until we spring across the central division into the upper half of the line, we cannot hope—as the Milesians wrongly hoped—to encounter first principles. Although the sun has the power to reveal to us the full nature of our physical, visible world, it cannot illumine those greater truths that transcend the capacity of our senses. To perceive the Truth that resides in the invisible (or intelligible) world, our mind's eye must be illumined by the Good. Only then will we be able to move from imagination and belief to understanding and reason.

As Plato subdivides the bottom portion of the line, so he subdivides the upper portion as well. In the lower part of the upper half, he places the kind of thinking carried out by mathematicians like Pythagoras. Pythagoras's study of triangles does not concern itself with the physical triangles that architects use to build temples or teachers draw in the sand to instruct their students. On the contrary, his concern is with the perfect Triangle that cannot be seen or tasted or touched or heard or smelled. Unlike the natural sciences, which work upward (inductively) from empirical observation, geometry works downward (deductively) from abstract principles (or givens) that define the eternal harmonies and balances of the cosmos.[8]

Still, Plato explains, though geometry works from givens, thus drawing it upward toward the Forms, it does not seek to reach those givens and contemplate them as ends in themselves. For that task, we must move from the mathematician to the philosopher—to the one who, like Socrates, uses the dialectic to ascend the ladder of truth toward what Plato himself called the Beatific Vision (*Republic* 7; 517d).

The allegory of the cave. Though I have tried my best to describe Plato's divided line in clear, accessible terms, I confess that the abstract nature of the line makes it difficult to grasp and absorb. Of course, such difficulties are not unique to Plato. The principles and proofs of such brilliant philosophers as Aristotle, Aquinas, and Kant are equally, if not more, difficult to bend the mind around. Thankfully, Plato does not leave us stranded in the dark pit of philosophical abstraction but throws us a ladder by which we can mount to the light of understanding. How does Plato accomplish this bold feat? By shamelessly and unapologetically ignoring—indeed, contradicting—his warnings against the dangers of the poetic imagination. For the ladder that Plato throws us in *Republic* 7 (514a-517a) is a metaphorical one. With the

---

[8]"The Pythagoreans, as they are called, devoted themselves to mathematics; they were the first to advance this study, and having been brought up in it they thought its precepts were the principles of all things. Since of these principles numbers are by nature the first, and in numbers they seemed to see many resemblances to the things that exist and come into being— more than in fire and earth and water." Aristotle, *Metaphysics* 985b; quoted in Allen, *Greek Philosophy*, 38.

poetic skill of a Homer or a Sophocles, Plato constructs a vivid allegory/myth—an unforgettable narrative that embodies and incarnates the philosophical principles laid out in his divided line. Once we read and experience Plato's allegory of the cave, the nature of the divided line is made luminously clear, not only to our minds, but to our hearts and souls as well. With the mesmeric power of a showman-storyteller, Socrates/Plato exclaims:

> And now let me show in a figure how far our nature is enlightened or un-enlightened:—Behold! human beings living in an underground den, which has a mouth open towards the light and reaching all along the den; here they have been from their childhood, and have their legs and necks chained so that they cannot move, and can only see before them, being prevented by the chains from turning round their heads. Above and behind them a fire is blazing at a distance, and between the fire and the prisoners there is a raised way; and you will see, if you look, a low wall built along the way, like the screen which marionette players have in front of them, over which they show the puppets. (514a-b)

The puppets, Socrates goes on to explain, are made in the shapes of humans and animals, trees and stones, and they move round and round in an endless, revolving succession. The fire casts the shadows of the puppets on the cave wall, and the prisoners, who have never known another world, take the shadows for reality. Indeed, most of them spend their lives studying the shadows so that they can predict when and in what order they will next appear. They even hold contests and award prizes, with the winners applauding themselves for their skills of observation and analysis.

Now imagine, Plato continues, what would happen if one of the prisoners should break his chains and turn to face the fire. At first he would be blinded by the direct light of the fire, but if he persisted in his attempts to see the truth of his situation, he would eventually be able to study the puppets themselves, whose shadows had once made up his entire reality. Imagine then that the escaped prisoner should struggle his way out of the cave into the upper air. As with the glaring light of the fire, the even more brilliant light of the sun would temporarily blind him from seeing the objects of the outer world. Eventually, his eyes would adjust, but, for the first few days, he would only be comfortable looking at the reflections of trees and stones in rivers and ponds. With renewed persistence, however, a day would come when he would be able to lift his gaze from pale images in water to gaze, first, on trees and stones, and then on the stars and the sky. "Last of all he will be able to see the sun, and not mere reflections of him in the water, but he will see him in his own proper place, and not in another; and he will contemplate him as he is" (516b).

The epic journey of the escaped prisoner is meant by Plato to parallel the journey of the philosopher who ascends through the four sections of the divided line. The shadows on the cave wall are like the arts: imitations of imitations, twice removed from the real men and animals and trees and stones that dwell in the real world above. Though we, like the prisoners, think that these shadows are reality, and accordingly devote our energies to studying them, they have but the slimmest connection to true reality. When the prisoner turns his gaze from the shadows to the puppets, he moves from the arts to the natural sciences—from reflections to actual physical objects that bear at least some relationship to the real objects of which they are imitations. A study of the puppets will afford him a sounder type of knowledge, though the presence of illusion will still be strong, and he will still be trapped in the subterranean realm of *doxa*.

Once he leaves the cave, however, he crosses the great divide from the World of Becoming to the World of Being. In the allegory, the fire in the cave represents the sun of our world, while the sun outside the cave represents the Good that illumines all things in the invisible, intellectual world. Only there, outside the cave, which corresponds to the perfect, unchanging world above the moon, will the prisoner see things as they really are. And yet even here, there are, as in the divided line, two distinct stages. The reflections in rivers and ponds are like the givens that mathematicians work with in their geometric proofs, while the actual trees, stones, and sky represent the Forms on which the philosopher fixes his gaze. Only by moving steadily from one stage to the next, from shadows to puppets to reflections to objects, can the initiate hope to lift his gaze from the cave wall to the sun.

And then, having touched the heart of the eternal, he must return to the cave to bring the light to those who lie chained below. True, when he returns, he will find himself blinded by darkness, confused by shadows, and ill-equipped to participate in futile guessing games; nevertheless, he must descend. Chances are the prisoners will kill him, as they did Plato's beloved master, but then the calling of the philosopher is a high one—one that does not shy away from danger or count too highly the demands and blandishments of fame, fortune, and the flesh. Plato concludes his allegory by admitting that we "must not wonder that those who attain to this beatific vision are unwilling to descend to human affairs" (517d). Still, such considerations do not absolve the philosopher of his "evangelical" duty to descend and share the light and truth with others.

If I may conclude my survey of Plato and the Presocratics with some personal speculation, I would suggest that if Plato were asked to rank the various thinkers discussed in this chapter, he would do so in this manner:

1. Sophists: worshippers of shadows

2. Heraclitus and the Milesians: students of puppets

3. The Eleatics and Pythagoras the mathematician: lovers of real reflections

4. Pythagoras the religious leader and Socrates: seekers after the sun

If we, like Plato, would reach the true *archē*, we must forsake sophistical illusions, struggle past the four elements, and ascend beyond deductive premises to touch the Form of the Forms.

REPUBLIC

MANY OF THE MOST beloved works in literature (for example, *Odyssey, Aeneid, Divine Comedy, Canterbury Tales, Don Quixote, Pilgrim's Progress, Huckleberry Finn*) take place, as it were, on the road. It may be no coincidence then that Plato's greatest and most enduring work, *Republic*, begins with Socrates walking down the road from Athens to Piraeus. As often happens in the early dialogues, Socrates is essentially kidnapped and then convinced to engage in dialogue with his kidnappers. He is happy to comply and, as is his manner, quickly coopts the conversation; however, before doing so, Socrates asks the following question of his elderly host:

> There is nothing which for my part I like better, Cephalus, than conversing with aged men; for I regard them as travellers who have gone a journey which I too may have to go, and of whom I ought to enquire, whether the way is smooth and easy, or rugged and difficult. And this is a question which I should like to ask of you who have arrived at that time which the poets call the "threshold of old age"—Is life harder towards the end, or what report do you give of it? (328e)

It is a beautiful thing, and an increasingly rare one, to see so learned a man as Socrates treat an elder with such respect. But then true wisdom always respects age, for the aged are those who have traveled farther down the road than we, and who thus possess greater experience. They are also, though our modern culture prefers to ignore such obvious truths, closer than we are to the grave, a proximity to death that makes most, though not all, men more humble and reflective.

As someone who has neared the end of his road, Cephalus has come to learn that it is not so much the ailments and indignities of old age that make the closing years of one's life difficult as it is the state of one's soul. No, Cephalus assures Socrates, the regrets and complaints that so often accompany old age "are to be attributed to the same cause, which is not old age, but men's characters and tempers; for he who is of a calm and happy nature will hardly feel the pressure of age, but to him who is of an opposite disposition youth and age are equally a burden" (329d). The advice, as advice, is sound, and we would do well to heed it today, but it also performs a vital function within the context of *Republic*: it immediately trains the reader to look at the inside as well as the outside, the soul as well as the body. Indeed, it privileges the former over the latter as the true source of joy or sorrow, virtue or vice, justice or injustice.

And the same goes for wealth: though poverty is difficult even for a good man, "a bad rich man [can never] have peace with himself" (330a). Socrates presses Cephalus further on the issue of wealth, only to provoke mention of a second essential theme in *Republic*: "When a man thinks himself to be near death," Cephalus tells Socrates, "fears and cares enter into his mind which he never had before; the tales of a world below and the punishment which is exacted there of deeds done here were once a laughing matter to him, but now he is tormented with the thought that they may be true" (330d). In the next chapter, I will discuss Plato's decision to end *Republic* with an allegory (the myth of Er) about the afterlife and the final rewards of virtuous or vicious behavior. For now, let it suffice to say that Cephalus's mention of the fear of judgment casts over *Republic* an air of seriousness—justice is not only an issue of the state but also of the individual soul and its ultimate destiny. Plato engages and entertains us, as he does his interlocutors, but he never lets us forget that the stakes are high.

As if sensing that Cephalus's very Greek admonition to look to the end—the medievals called such a moment a *memento mori* (remember that you must die)—has sobered up his conversation partners, Socrates seizes the opportunity to steer the dialogue to the subject that he wants to discuss: the nature of justice. And so, though Cephalus has said nothing about justice, Socrates plunges in headfirst and asks Cephalus whether it is always just to pay one's debts and tell the truth: both of which topics Cephalus *has* mentioned but not in terms of their relation to justice. When Cephalus hesitates, Socrates quickly fashions a hypothetical situation in which it would not be just to pay a debt: If a man who had just gone mad asked you to return to him the weapons he had let you borrow when he was in his right mind, would it be just to give him back what rightly belongs to him?

Polemarchus, Cephalus's son, leaps into the fray to answer Socrates, while his father, proving that age has brought with it wisdom and good sense, seizes his own opportunity to leave the room and let the younger folks wrestle with Socrates over the nature of justice.

And so the debate begins.

INTIMATIONS OF NIETZSCHE

As so often happens in the early dialogues, book one of *Republic* invites us to eavesdrop on the entertaining, if somewhat frustrating Socratic dance of aporia: Socrates asks for a definition of justice, one of the interlocutors gives one, Socrates turns the definition on its head, and we are left with an impasse. The first definition, put forward by Polemarchus, is that justice means doing good to one's friends and evil to one's enemies (332d). At first it seems like a good definition, until Socrates subjects it to the reductio ad absurdum: if justice means doing good to your friends, then it would be just to steal something if the stealing benefited a friend; if you mistake your enemy for your friend and do him good, then you are actually helping an enemy and thus not being just; if by hurting an enemy we make him less just, then we are saying that a just act can bring about injustice. And so it goes until Polemarchus bows his head in defeat, even promising

Socrates that he will now assist him in combating this false definition of justice.

With a burst of enthusiasm, Socrates invites someone to offer a second definition—and that's when the dialogue takes an ominous turn. Incensed by the way Socrates has just handled Polemarchus, an angry young hothead named Thrasymachus accuses Socrates of being a fool (336b-c). He has no patience for Socrates's protestations that his wisdom resides in the fact that he knows that he does not know. All Thrasymachus sees is a busybody who cuts down the definitions of others without offering one of his own. To be fair to Thrasymachus, many of my own students have been equally irritated by Socrates's refusal to venture his own definition and his sneaky way of arguing people into corners while slipping out himself. Many have even, if I have judged rightly the look in their eyes, felt the urge to swat the annoying gadfly.

But Thrasymachus's anger and frustration go deeper, revealing a far darker underside of resistance to the Socratic (and Platonic) ethos and method. To Thrasymachus's Machiavellian mind, Socrates is more than a buffoon and a quibbler: he is a weak idealist who insists on looking at the world through rose-colored glasses, woefully out of touch with the pragmatic and political realities of Athens. No, Thrasymachus asserts, justice has nothing to do with good and evil, virtue and vice. Justice is nothing more than the will of the stronger: might makes right, and it always has (399a). At first, it seems that Socrates will as easily demolish the definition of Thrasymachus as he did that of Polemarchus. Skillfully wielding his dialectical sword, Socrates gets Thrasymachus to admit that doctors do what is best for their patients and not themselves, and that they put most of their focus on helping the weak. Then Socrates moves in for the kill, concluding that just rulers, like the most skilled doctors, do what is in the best interest of their subjects (342e).

Thrasymachus, however, is not to be caught so easily! Socrates, in his naive folly, seems to think that shepherds do what is best for the sheep, when in fact they fatten their sheep for their own financial gain.

Holding up his analogy as superior to that of Socrates, Thrasymachus then concludes with his own assessment of the true nature of rulers, of justice and of injustice:

> So entirely astray are you [Socrates] in your ideas about the just and unjust as not even to know that justice and the just are in reality another's good . . . for the unjust is lord over the truly simple and just: he is the stronger, and his subjects do what is for his interest, and minister to his happiness, which is very far from being their own. (343c)

And the most successful unjust man, Thrasymachus adds triumphantly, is the tyrant:

> By fraud and force [the tyrant] takes away the property of others, not little by little but wholesale; comprehending in one, things sacred as well as profane, private and public; for which acts of wrong, if he were detected perpetrating any one of them singly, he would be punished and incur great disgrace—they who do such wrong in particular cases are called robbers of temples, and man-stealers and burglars and swindlers and thieves. But when a man besides taking away the money of the citizens has made slaves of them, then, instead of these names of reproach, he is termed happy and blessed, not only by the citizens but by all who hear of his having achieved the consummation of injustice. (344a-b)

"Kill one man," wrote Jean Rostand in *The Substance of Man* (1939), "and you are a murderer. Kill millions of men, and you are a conqueror."[1] In this broken world of ours, the smalltime crook is thrown in jail while the large-scale malefactor is hailed as a brilliant general or an innovative leader or a national hero. How is Socrates, how is anyone, to answer Thrasymachus's realpolitik vision of the world?

Even more urgently, how do we answer what Thrasymachus says next: "For mankind censure injustice, fearing that they may be the victims of it and not because they shrink from committing it" (344c). Some 2,300 years later, Nietzsche, in the spirit of Thrasymachus, would argue that all religion is a slave ethic—that religion, with its Platonic standards of justice, virtue, ethics, and morality, is merely something

---

[1]Jean Rostand, *Pensées d'un biologiste* (Paris: Stock, 1939).

invented by poor and weak people to keep the rich and mighty in check. To fight this ethic, Nietzsche called for an *übermensch* ("overman" or "superman"), a charismatic leader who would have the courage to rise above petty bourgeois notions of good and evil and assert his own indomitable will to power. Nietzsche, like Thrasymachus before him, believed that men followed standards of justice, not because they really believed such standards existed but because they were too weak not to and because they felt that paying lip service to morality was a small price to pay if it succeeded in placing chains on the hands of those in power.[2]

That, at least, is how Nietzsche's slave ethic works when the rulers are too timid to resist the will of the poor and the weak. When the ruler finds courage and shatters the schoolboy ethics of the masses, a change in the moral structure of culture can be achieved. That is why for Thrasymachus and Nietzsche justice, in the long run, is not something given by God and inscribed on our conscience but whatever the ruler says it is. It is not just the history books that the victors write, but the law codes as well. Indeed, according to French historian Michel Foucault, another heir of Thrasymachus, Truth and Justice are not Platonic absolutes but ideological structures of power established by political regimes as a way of controlling how people act, communicate, and think.[3]

In a very real sense, *Republic* exists—and thank God it does exist—as a vehicle for disproving Thrasymachus's position. Indeed, the very possibility of civilization, I would argue, rests on whether Plato can answer the Thrasymachuses of the world. And not just answer them as Socrates does in the early dialogues, by pushing the issue to an impasse, but by coming up with a viable countervision to the Machiavellian expediency, the ends-justifies-the-means ethos, that Thrasymachus articulates and embodies.[4]

---

[2]For Nietzsche's slave ethic, see essay one of *The Genealogy of Morals* (1887); for the need to rise above bourgeois ethics, see part five of *Beyond Good and Evil* (1886); for the *übermensch*, see the first part of *Thus Spake Zarathustra* (1883–1892).

[3]See Michel Foucault, "Truth and Power," in *Critical Theory Since Plato*, Revised Edition, edited by Hazard Adams (New York: HBJ, 1992), 1135-45.

[4]See chapters 17-18 and 25 of Machiavelli's *The Prince* (1516).

As if conscious of the multistep process that he must take to answer
Thrasymachus's critique of justice, Plato ends book one not with a full
refutation and the positing of a proper definition of justice, but with
an aporia. Socrates, with his usual sleight of hand, pushes Thrasymachus to admit that justice creates unity while injustice creates disunity. Having established that, he then shows that the kind of unjust
rulers whom Thrasymachus extols as being the most powerful and
fortunate will destroy themselves through fostering civil war. And that
civil war will manifest itself not only in the state he rules but in his own
chaotic (because unjust) soul (352a). Rather than acknowledge that
Socrates has refuted him, Thrasymachus refuses to speak any further,
leaving Socrates to admit that his victory is only partial. Perhaps he
has exposed a weakness at the core of injustice, but he has failed to
define justice or even show that such a thing as justice actually exists
in the state and in the soul.

The student becomes the teacher. Were _Republic_ an early dialogue,
that would be the end of the matter, but Plato is ready to flex his
muscles—and, I would argue, it is here (and other similar moments in
the middle dialogues) that he steps out of the shadow of his master and
moves from the earnest but negative deconstruction of false definitions and systems of Socrates to the positive construction of his own
definitions and systems. Once Thrasymachus stops speaking, Glaucon,
a devout pupil of Socrates, begs his master not to stop with so flimsy
a refutation of Thrasymachus, but to go on to sing the praises of justice
as no one has done before. In fact, so insistent is Glaucon that Socrates
must mount this full and necessary defense of justice that he takes it
upon himself to play the role of devil's advocate. Though he in no way
agrees with Thrasymachus, he volunteers to articulate the position of
Thrasymachus in its most extreme form so as to provoke Socrates to
address the issue head on, with no evasions or rhetorical tricks.

Thus Glaucon pleads with all the ardor of his youth:

> I want to hear justice praised in respect of itself; then I shall be satisfied,
> and you are the person from whom I think that I am most likely to hear
> this; and therefore I will praise the unjust life to the utmost of my power,

and my manner of speaking will indicate the manner in which I desire to hear you too praising justice and censuring injustice. (358d)

To this most challenging proposal Socrates agrees, thus setting in motion not, as Plato's critics have argued for centuries, the establishment of a totalitarian state, but the defense of justice as a living and universal standard that we are behooved to follow and that will make us better people with healthy and balanced souls if we follow it.[5]

Foreshadowing Hobbes and Locke as Thrasymachus does Nietzsche, Glaucon argues, in the mode of devil's advocate, that because people lack the power to protect themselves from the predation of the strong, they willingly bind themselves by a social contract in which they promise not to commit injustice to others.[6] But they make this promise, not because they truly believe that justice exists, but as a way to prevent others from practicing injustice against them. Justice, according to the "practical" view, which should not be confused with Aristotle's later positing of virtue as the mean between the extremes, is not a universal standard but

> a mean or compromise, between the best of all, which is to do injustice and not be punished, and the worst of all, which is to suffer injustice without the power of retaliation; and justice, being at a middle point between the two, is tolerated not as a good, but as the lesser evil, and honoured by reason of the inability of men to do injustice. For no man who is worthy to be called a man would ever submit to such an agreement if he were able to resist; he would be mad if he did. Such is the received account, Socrates, of the nature and origin of justice. (359a-b)

Thus Glaucon takes Thrasymachus's slave ethic and places it in a wider social and political context. No one, it seems, acts justly as an end in itself: because it is, somehow, the right thing to do. On the contrary, those who act justly only do so because they lack the power to act unjustly; if they had the power, they would not be so foolish as

---

[5]The strongest modern critique of Plato's supposed totalitarianism was leveled by Karl Popper in volume one of his *The Open Society and Its Enemies* (1971).

[6]See part one of Thomas Hobbes's *Leviathan* (1651) and chapter two of John Locke's *Second Treatise of Government* (1690).

to sign the social contract. Or, to quote a line from William Blake, whose *Marriage of Heaven and Hell* anticipated Nietzsche's slave ethic by a full century, "Those who restrain desire do so because theirs is weak enough to be restrained."[7]

So argues Glaucon, and then goes on to embody and personalize his position by spinning for us the tale of the Ring of Gyges—of how a shepherd found a ring that, when he put it on his finger, rendered him invisible. What did Gyges do with his ring? Did he use it to serve the poor and protect the weak? He did not. He did what all of us would do, whether we pride ourselves on being just or unjust. He used it to seduce the queen, kill the king, and take the throne for himself. No, Glaucon concludes, the tale of Gyges stands as "a great proof that a man is just, not willingly or because he thinks that justice is any good to him individually, but of necessity, for wherever any one thinks that he can safely be unjust, there he is unjust" (360d).

The point seems unassailable, but Glaucon is not yet done; he will not let Socrates, or us, off that easily. Having finished his tale and made his argument, he next paints for Socrates two contrasting portraits, one of the perfectly unjust man and the other of the perfectly just man, and asks him—simply, directly, pragmatically—which one of them has the more enviable life. True to his promise to state Thrasymachus's case in its most extreme form, Glaucon pulls no punches in presenting his hypothetical unjust man as one whose cleverness allows him, "while doing the most unjust acts, to [acquire] the greatest reputation for justice" (361b). The hypothetical just man, on the other hand, he presents as one who has everything taken away from him but his justice. The former, Glaucon informs us, will go from success to success, but what will happen to the "just man who is thought unjust"? He "will be scourged, racked, bound—will have his eyes burnt out; and, at last, after suffering every kind of evil, he will be impaled" (361d, 362a).

Glaucon's portrait of the perfectly just man sounds eerily like a prophecy about Christ, and indeed, in chapter seven I will discuss the

---

[7]*Blake's Poetry and Designs*, ed. Mary Lynn Johnson and John E. Grant (New York: Norton, 1979), 87.

many ways in which Plato's dialogues seem to prepare the way for the fuller revelation of Christ and the New Testament. Here, however, Plato seems to have in mind Socrates himself, who, though he did not suffer a painful or humiliating death, as Jesus did on the cross, was condemned and executed as an enemy of the state—his lifelong commitment to the pursuit of justice twisted by his fellow citizens into a charge of injustice. In that sense, Plato must mount a defense not only of justice as an innate and absolute virtue but also of the ultimately fatal choice made by his beloved master to devote himself fully to the pursuit of that virtue.

But how is he to accomplish such a task? How, asks Socrates, is he to succeed in defining justice and injustice when all previous writers have failed? "No one has ever adequately described either in verse or prose the true essential nature of either of them abiding in the soul, and invisible to any human or divine eye; or shown that of all the things of a man's soul which he has within him, justice is the greatest good, and injustice the greatest evil" (366e). The reason, of course, is that no one can *see* what justice and injustice do to the soul—for the site of their working lies within the human person and is therefore invisible. But what if we were to magnify and render concrete the soul? What if we were to examine the workings of the individual soul as if it were a mighty state, a place where both justice and injustice can thrive and have visible effects and consequences? Perhaps if we were to construct, not in real life but hypothetically, a perfectly just state, then we could locate, in that state, the essence of justice. And if we could do that on the macrocosmic level of the state, then would it not be easy to work our way back to the microcosmic level of the individual soul?

So Plato reasons, and so the city-building begins.

Noble Lies and True Definitions

Readers of *Republic* often forget that the complex state that Socrates constructs over the course of the dialogue is not his first choice. Before piecing together his ideal republic, with its (to us) totalitarian class structure and educational system, Socrates presents as the best kind of society an Edenic, pastoral village where citizens live moderate lives, practicing their trade in peaceful coexistence with their neighbors, eating neither meat nor fancy spices, and neither importing nor coveting luxuries from distant lands. Such is the city Socrates suggests, but Glaucon will have none of it. To his mind, Socrates has just described a city for pigs, not for human beings. The wise master replies,

> Now I understand: the question which you would have me consider is, not only how a State, but how a luxurious State is created; and possibly there is no harm in this, for in such a State we shall be more likely to see how justice and injustice originate. In my opinion the true and healthy constitution of the State is the one which I have described. But if you wish also to see a State at fever heat, I have no objection. For I suspect that many will not be satisfied with the simpler way of life. They will be for adding sofas, and tables, and other furniture; also dainties, and perfumes, and incense, and courtesans, and cakes, all these not of one sort only, but in every variety; we must go beyond the necessaries of which I was at first speaking, such as houses, and clothes, and shoes: the arts of the painter and the embroiderer will have to be set in motion, and gold and ivory and all sorts of materials must be procured. (372e-373a)

Thus, with some reluctance, Socrates is prodded into constructing a complex, multitiered city, the kind that needs merchants, armies, and a bureaucratic structure to provide its citizens with gold and pearls, poetry, dance, and the visual arts, silk shawls and peacock fans, exotic perfumes, and ivory-inlaid serving tables.

Empires, after all, cannot exist without trading routes guarded by navies, adventurers willing to risk life and limb for personal glory, fierce competition in every sector, and an abundance of cheap labor. Yes, Socrates concedes sadly, it takes just such things to build and maintain a luxurious state, but then perhaps such a state will serve better the ultimate purpose of locating justice. For to take such a city, in which injustice is so endemic, and construct it in such a way as to make it just—what better method could there be for identifying and defining the essential qualities of justice?

But what manner of people will have the wherewithal to guard such a state, and what virtues will they need to possess if they are to fulfill their role as guardians? Certainly they must have a spirited, even savage nature if they are to defeat the enemies of the city, but then they must also be gentle and loving if they are to be a blessing and not a curse to their fellow citizens. But that leads to a problem: "He will not be a good guardian who is wanting in either of these two qualities; and yet the combination of them appears to be impossible; and hence we must infer that to be a good guardian is impossible" (375d). Were this an early dialogue, Socrates would have allowed this seemingly insurmountable impasse to stop his search for the perfect guardian, and thus for justice. In fact, Plato seems conscious of this, for he has Socrates say to himself, "Here feeling perplexed I began to think over what had preceded" (375d).

Once again, and for the rest of this dialogue and the succeeding dialogues of Plato's middle and late period, I would argue, the mature Plato steps in, and negative Socratic aporia gives way to positive Platonic definition. Plato is on a quest for justice, and he will not allow his journey to be impeded by seeming contradictions. To the casual observer it may seem that a person cannot be both fierce and gentle, but the one with the keener eye will see that nature does provide examples of creatures that possess both of these qualities: "Well-bred dogs are perfectly gentle to their familiars and acquaintances, and the reverse to strangers" (375e). The same, then, can be true for the guardians of the republic—as long as they possess the wisdom to distinguish friend from enemy. Note that the same argument that is used as a reductio ad absurdum in the more Socratic book one (that justice can't mean doing good to one's friends and bad to one's enemies, since we often confuse the one for the other) is used in the more Platonic book two to draw us closer to an understanding of what justice truly is. The real problem is not that discerning friend from enemy, good from evil, justice from injustice is impossible, but that special care has to be taken to train guardians to be able to distinguish the one from the other.

Educating in justice. This leads Plato to perhaps the most contro-versial aspect of *Republic*: the institution of a censorship-based educational system for the purpose of training the guardians of the state in proper discernment. The early dialogues of Socrates, most of which are devoted to defining a key virtue, all end with an impasse. But then the dramatic dates for most of the dialogues are set during the final stages of the Peloponnesian War (431–404 BC), a period when Athens increasingly ignored fixed standards of justice to indulge in political and military expediency. The final upshot of this abandonment of ab-solutes was the execution of Socrates. Plato, for whom the memory of such things never faded, surely factored these memories into the edu-cational plan for his ideal republic—a plan whose main goal is not so much to produce philosophers as it is to ensure safety and justice for the state as a whole.

Thus, in the voice of Socrates, Plato goes on to explain in books two and three that if we wish our guardians (and philosophers and teachers and politicians) to be able to distinguish the true from the false, we must not expose them, during the impressionable age of youth, to poetry like *Iliad* and *Odyssey*, which presents the gods as petty, changeable, lustful, proud, and unjust. Furthermore, we must not allow them to read descriptions of the underworld (*Odyssey* 11, for example) that present the afterlife as universally gloomy and miserable without proper rewards and punishments for the just and the unjust. Worst of all, we must not let them read literature that teaches "that wicked men are often happy, and the good miserable; and that injustice is profitable when undetected, but that justice is a man's own loss and another's gain—these things we shall forbid them to utter, and command them to sing and say the opposite" (392b).

For the sake of his guardians, Plato proscribes not only the content of their education but also the mode in which it is to be presented. In general, imitative arts like drama—where the poet does not speak in his own voice but mimics the voice of another—is to be avoided, es-pecially in cases where the guardians are, by watching the drama, en-couraged to imitate a cowardly or base character. In a similar way, mixed styles of music or art should be avoided lest they encourage guardians to be double-minded (397d-e). Whereas modern conservatives will often argue that certain kinds of music should be censored on account of profanity and violent or sexual lyrics, Plato was more concerned with the actual rhythms and musical modes employed— whether they inspired in their listeners courage or softness, virtue or indolence, freedom or decadence.

Far from dismissing the arts as irrelevant fluff, Plato takes them very seriously. For Plato, improper and excessive complexity in music breeds licentiousness in the soul in the same way that improper and excessive complexity in gymnastics breeds ill health in the body (404e). A lack of harmony in the former leads to the rise of law courts, while a lack of harmony in the latter leads to the rise of hospitals (405a): together, these two forces tear away at the healthy fabric of the body politic.

Committed to not allowing such disharmony, excess, and contradiction to get a foothold in his leaders, and thus his state, Plato takes great care to monitor what his young guardians see, hear, read, and experience. The most valuable teachers, musicians, and coaches in his republic are those who use a proper regimen of music and gymnastics to achieve balance in the souls and bodies of their students. Most valuable of all are those who can do both at once: "He who mingles music with gymnastic in the fairest proportions, and best attempers them to the soul, may be rightly called the true musician and harmonist in a far higher sense than the tuner of the strings" (412a). Only by such a dual process of learning will the guardians grow up to be both spirited and gentle, to have a body finely trained and ready for combat matched with a soul that is at peace with itself and others.

"Very well, Socrates," the modern critic might say, "it is a good thing to train the body along with the mind, but if we prevent the young from having direct contact with the darker, seamier, less virtuous side of life, will they not grow up to be naïve and ill-equipped to function in a world marked by evil and treachery?" Just so, families today that choose to educate their children in the controlled environment of their home are often criticized for sheltering their children and preventing them from being socialized. Plato's response to this kind of critique is, I believe, instructive: "Vice cannot know virtue too, but a virtuous nature, educated by time, will acquire a knowledge both of virtue and vice: the virtuous, and not the vicious, man has wisdom" (409d-e). It is the bank teller who knows intimately the look and feel and smell of true money who will recognize immediately a counterfeit dollar, no matter the type of counterfeiting process that was used. In contrast, the counterfeiter who spends a year studying three different forgery processes will not be nearly as successful as the bank teller at recognizing a fake bill that was made using a fourth process unrelated to the other three.

In *Mere Christianity*, C. S. Lewis, expanding on Plato's distinction, reminds us that the people who understand sin the best are not the sinners who give in to it immediately, but the saints who spend their lives resisting it. In the same way, we know the strength of our enemy, not by immediately surrendering to him, but by resisting his advance, even if it leads to our defeat. Many moderns believe that the more we give in to sexual temptation, the better we will understand the nature of lust. The truth, Lewis counters, is exactly the opposite: "You understand sleep when you are awake, not while you are sleeping. . . . You can understand the nature of drunkenness when you are sober, not when you are drunk. Good people know about both good and evil; bad people do not know about either."[8]

Natural callings. Having slowly won over his readers to the need for censorship in the education of his guardians, Plato boldly climaxes book three with an even more audacious plan. In order to convince the three classes of his ideal republic—the guardians/rulers, the auxiliaries/soldiers, and the artisans/farmers—that they will be most content if they fulfill their role in society without resistance, Plato invents a noble lie about their origins under the earth. The three classes "are to be told that their youth was a dream, and the education and training

---

[8]C. S. Lewis, *Mere Christianity* (New York: Macmillan, 1960), 87.

which they received from us [in leadership, war, or craftsmanship], an appearance only; in reality during all that time they were being formed and fed in the womb of the earth, where they themselves and their arms and appurtenances were manufactured; when they were completed, the earth, their mother, sent them up" (414d-e). Further, they shall be told that although they are all brothers of the same mother, "God has framed you differently. Some of you have the power of command, and in the composition of these he has mingled gold, wherefore also they have the greatest honour; others he has made of silver, to be auxiliaries; others again who are to be husbandmen and craftsmen he has composed of brass and iron" (415a).

Though this noble lie may seem at first to advocate an inflexible caste system based on birth and bloodline, Plato does make it clear that occasionally brass or iron parents will give birth to a gold child or silver parents give birth to a child of brass. Further, to critics of aristocracy who would accuse Plato's noble lie of fostering a two-class system of haves and have-nots, Plato also makes it clear that his guardians and auxiliaries, who have gold and silver, as it were, running through their veins, will be strictly forbidden from possessing either gold or silver.

In fact, when Adeimantus, who like Glaucon looks to Socrates as his master, complains that he is treating his rulers as though they were mercenaries and that no one will want the job of ruler, Socrates reminds him that the purpose of the noble lie, and of the entire educational and social structure of his republic, is not to make one class more happy than the other, but to do what is best for the city as a whole. Far from building a city of powerful haves and dispossessed have-nots, Socrates does all he can to prevent his republic from becoming like all the other cities of the world—cities that, though they claim to be one, are actually "divided into two, one the city of the poor, the other of the rich [and] these are at war with one another" (423a).

In Socrates's republic there is harmony, and behind and within that harmony lurks that elusive virtue of justice that Socrates and his friends have been seeking ever since the wise old Cephalus absented himself from the conversation. Justice is realized, Socrates explains, when each individual practices "one thing only, the thing to which his nature [is] best adapted" (433a). When the guardians rule, and the auxiliaries fight, and the craftsmen work, then justice reigns throughout the city. When, conversely, people rebel against their calling and their nature—when the rulers seek to accumulate wealth for themselves rather than rule in the interest of the citizens; when the soldiers abandon the battlefield or fight for personal glory alone; when the farmers grow lazy or profligate and shirk their duty to grow food and cultivate the land—then injustice is fostered within the city, and the body politic grows sick.

Justice, then, is the virtue that guides the interaction of the three classes, but what of the classes themselves? Are they not defined individually by their own unique virtue? As it turns out, in constructing his ideal republic, Plato succeeds in locating and defining not only the virtue of justice but the other three virtues that make up the four classical (or cardinal) virtues of the ancient world: wisdom (or prudence), courage (or fortitude), and self-control (or temperance). The virtues that Socrates fails to define in the early dialogues Plato now defines, embodying each one in the three classes of the republic. If they move their way successfully through their rigorous education, the guardians will acquire the virtue of wisdom, which rests on the ability to discern between virtue and vice, good and evil, knowledge and ignorance, reality and illusion.

As for the soldiers, they, when they are worthy of their class, embody courage, which Plato defines as a "universal saving power of true opinion in conformity with law about real and false dangers" (430b). That is to say, courage is both able to distinguish between what is to be feared and what is not to be feared and to persevere through both. Courage holds fast to its convictions as a good piece of cloth holds its dye (429d-e); it endures and stays true. Temperance, on the other hand, which the craftsmen and farmers should demonstrate, but which they generally do not unless they are guided properly by the wisdom of the guardians and the courage of the auxiliaries, is defined by Socrates as "the ordering or controlling of certain pleasures and desires" (430e), a proper ordering that empowers a man to be master of himself. Like justice, Socrates adds, temperance is a virtue that should ideally pervade the city. In fact, he further and more precisely defines the communal virtue of temperance as "the agreement of the naturally superior and inferior, as to the right to rule of either" (432a).

That, at least, is how the virtues manifest themselves within a well-ordered polis—but what of the individual soul? Do the same three classes-virtues-forces that wrestle with each other in the struggle for communal justice have counterparts within the soul? If we recall that the very reason Plato set out to build his ideal republic was in order to construct a macrocosm that would shed light on the microcosm, then we will realize that the answer must be yes.

THE TRIPARTITE SOUL

Picture a teenaged Catholic girl who gives up chocolate for Lent. She comes home late one night to find on the dining room table a tray full of fudge that her mother has just made. Immediately, an inner voice cries out to her to break her fast and sample a piece of the fudge; in response, a second voice cries out that she must stay true to her vow and not touch it. For several minutes, the two voices wrestle within her soul, each competing for mastery. Tired from her long day and overwhelmed by the smell of the fudge, she is just about to give in to the first voice, when a third speaks up in defense of the second. The two voices combined succeed in beating down the first, and the girl leaves the room without sampling the sweets that have tempted her so sorely.

In book four of *Republic*, Socrates analyzes just this kind of *psychomachia* (soul-war), identifying the elements that are common to all such internal struggles (439c-442d). First there is the initial urge that bids us indulge (in gluttony, in envy, in anger, in lust, in greed, in pride, in sloth), and then there is the second urge that pleads with us to abstain. The first urge Socrates identifies with appetite (or passion); the second with reason. In the case of the girl, the urge to eat the fudge rises up from the appetitive part of her soul, a part that Socrates says is essentially irrational. The counter-urge, to remain true to her Lenten vow, finds its source in the rational part of her soul, which urges us to reflect on our actions and chose the reasonable course. But what of the third voice? In *Republic*, Socrates explains that this third voice comes from the spirited part of our soul, and that it most often manifests itself in a kind of anger or indignation that rushes to the defense of our besieged reason and enables it to overcome the repeated assaults of appetite: "so may there not be in the individual soul a third element which is passion or spirit, and when not corrupted by bad education is the natural auxiliary of reason?" (441a).

Socrates clearly means for these three distinctive parts of the soul (the appetitive, the rational, and the spirited) to mirror the three classes of his republic (craftsmen, guardians, and auxiliaries). When well-trained soldiers come to the defense of properly educated rulers, the often irrational masses can be kept in check and made to follow the virtue of temperance. That is to say, when each class performs its proper function (Plato's definition of justice), peace and harmony reign. If, however, the soldiers abdicate their responsibility to aid the rulers, or, worse, allow their spirited nature to be swayed by the base demands of the masses, then the rulers will not be able to resist the onslaught. The result, whether in city or soul, will be chaos, injustice, and civil war.

Musing on the fierceness of these internal struggles, Plato concludes that justice is concerned

> not with the outward man, but with the inward, which is the true self and concernment of man: for the just man does not permit the several elements within him to interfere with one another, or any of them to do the work of others,—he sets in order his own inner life, and is his own master and his own law, and at peace with himself; and when he has bound together the three principles within him, which may be compared to the higher, lower, and middle notes of the scale, and the intermediate intervals—when he has bound all these together, and is no longer many, but has become one entirely temperate and perfectly adjusted nature, then he proceeds to act, if he has to act, whether in a matter of property, or in the treatment of the

body, or in some affair of politics or private business; always thinking and calling that which preserves and co-operates with this harmonious condition, just and good action, and the knowledge which presides over it, wisdom, and that which at any time impairs this condition, he will call unjust action, and the opinion which presides over it ignorance. (443d-e)

It has been said that a person's character is best defined by the way he acts when no one is looking. To that I would add that a person whose character is such that he acts virtuously when he is alone is someone who has *integrity*: a beautiful word that comes from a Latin root that means wholeness or completion. Virtue, character, integrity: all these things connote an internal harmony, one in which the competing voices within the soul are kept in a proper balance.

Platonic justice, as we have seen, is defined by just this kind of singleness, this ordering of desires that emanate from the appetitive, rational, and spirited parts of our soul. When it exists within a soul or state, wisdom and temperance are preserved and life, joy, and honor thrive. In contrast to this ideal state, Plato defines injustice, and its effects, as

a strife which arises among the three principles—a meddlesomeness, and interference, and rising up of a part of the soul against the whole, an assertion of unlawful authority, which is made by a rebellious subject against a true prince, of whom he is the natural vassal,—what is all this confusion and delusion but injustice, and intemperance and cowardice and ignorance, and every form of vice? (444b)

Note that when such a state of anarchy seizes control of a city or a soul, the virtues of justice, temperance, courage, and wisdom are replaced by their opposing vices. Then does life become, in the words of Thomas Hobbes (*Leviathan* I.13), "solitary, poor, nasty, brutish, and short."

The corruption of the prince. In book one, Thrasymachus extols the unjust man as being wiser and more fortunate than his counterpart. In book two, Glaucon, playing devil's advocate, illustrates Thrasymachus's argument by offering two hypothetical portraits of a perfectly unjust man who wins a reputation for justice and a perfectly just man who is executed as a villain. Here, finally, Socrates succeeds in giving the lie to Thrasymachus and Glaucon. Having defined the true nature of justice and injustice and identified those things that proceed from them, Socrates again asks the question that inspired him to construct his ideal city: "Which is the more profitable, to be just and act justly and practise virtue, whether seen or unseen of gods and men, or to be unjust and act unjustly, if only unpunished and unreformed?" (445a). In response, Glaucon, all his reservations exploded, exclaims,

> In my judgment, Socrates, the question has now become ridiculous. We know that, when the bodily constitution is gone, life is no longer endurable, though pampered with all kinds of meats and drinks, and having all wealth and all power; and shall we be told that when the very essence of the vital principle is undermined and corrupted, life is still worth having to a man, if only he be allowed to do whatever he likes with the single exception that he is not to acquire justice and virtue, or to escape from injustice and vice; assuming them both to be such as we have described? (445a-b)

It would appear that using Gyges's ring to seduce the queen, kill the king, and take his throne is not the best policy after all. True, the practice of injustice may enable you to become a tyrant, but what good is it to make slaves of those under you if you yourself become a slave of your own sick and corrupted soul?

Indeed, in book eight, Plato shows how radical democracy eventually breeds tyranny. On the political level, excessive freedom encourages citizens to overindulge their appetites. In time, such citizens become incapable of moral self-regulation; all discipline is lost and all resources squandered. In the end, they are compelled to put a tyrant over themselves so that they will be assured (so they think) of a steady stream of pleasures and delights. In the same way, the son of a radical democrat will eventually morph into the worst of tyrants. The insidious process that leads inexorably to the corruption of his tripartite soul begins when the prince's self-indulgent lifestyle causes him to reject his earlier training and surrender to "insolence and anarchy and waste and impudence" (560e)—a surrender that pits the worse part of his soul against the better.

This internal imbalance leads to chaos in his daily life: "He lives from day to day indulging the appetite of the hour; and sometimes he is lapped in drink and strains of the flute; then he becomes a water-drinker, and tries to get thin; then he takes a turn at gymnastics. . . . His life has neither law nor order; and this distracted existence he terms joy and bliss and freedom" (561c-d).

And so it goes, until the prince loses all control of the rational part of his soul. Worse yet, the spirited part, which should come to the defense of the rational, is exhausted in a disordered life that swings violently from joyless hedonism to amoral asceticism. It is at this point, when the rational and spirited parts cease to function as they should, that appetite turns perverse:

> Then the wild beast within us, gorged with meat or drink, starts up and having shaken off sleep, goes forth to satisfy his desires; and there is no conceivable folly or crime—not excepting incest or any other unnatural union, or parricide, or the eating of forbidden food—which at such a time, when he has parted company with all shame and sense, a man may not be ready to commit. (571c-d)

Needless to say, such a person experiences even more misery within his twisted soul than the misery he causes to those without. In the end, he becomes his own worst enemy, his own executioner. This is hardly a picture of the happy and successful unjust leader that Thrasymachus and Glaucon present in the opening books.

The sin-sick soul. Though it is here, in *Republic*, that Plato makes his strongest case against injustice, in *Gorgias* he faces a slightly gentler version of Thrasymachus, another proto-Nietzschean named Callicles who dismisses justice as a social convention invented by the weak and who calls for an *übermensch* who will not be afraid to seek out all his desires. "How, Socrates," he asks,

> can a man be happy who is the servant of anything? On the contrary, I plainly assert, that he who would truly live ought to allow his desires to wax to the uttermost, and not to chastise them; but when they have grown to their greatest he should have courage and intelligence to minister to them and to satisfy all his longings. And this I affirm to be natural justice and

nobility. To this however the many cannot attain; and they blame the strong man because they are ashamed of their own weakness, which they desire to conceal, and hence they say that intemperance is base. As I have remarked already, they enslave the nobler natures, and being unable to satisfy their pleasures, they praise temperance and justice out of their own cowardice. (491e-492b)

As he does in *Republic*, Plato here articulates fully Nietzsche's slave ethic over two thousand years before the German philosopher. The existence of the natural law, which Aristotle and Aquinas defended with equal logic and vigor, is not a thing that was believed in in the "old days" and then rejected in the "modern world." Natural law has always had its defenders and its detractors; if Europe had to wait for Nietzsche to construct a powerful refutation of the existence of essential, God-made rules of virtue and morality, it is only because Plato and Aristotle so thoroughly bested Nietzsche's ancient heirs that it took them two millennia to regroup.

Plato, whose mature voice sounds through *Gorgias* as clearly as it does though *Republic*, rebuts Callicles, as he does Thrasymachus, by exposing the sickness of soul that attends the doer of injustice. Indeed, as Socrates explains earlier in the dialogue to a young man named Polus who refuses to accept Socrates's assertion that it is better to suffer wrong than to do wrong, the more successful the unjust man is in his injustice, the sicker his soul becomes. And the sicker his soul, the more miserable he grows: "more miserable," Socrates adds, "if he be not punished and does not meet with retribution, and less miserable if he be punished and meets with retribution at the hands of gods and men" (472e). How sadly ironic: the only thing that can cure the tyrant's misery (to be caught and punished) is the very thing he will not accept, and which his unjustly won throne gives him the power not to accept. The absolute tyrant, argues Socrates, is most like "a person who is afflicted with the worst of diseases and yet contrives not to pay the penalty to the physician for his sins against his constitution, and will not be cured, because, like a child, he is afraid of the pain of being burned or cut" (479a-b).

PHILOSOPHER-KINGS

Although Socrates argues passionately for his just city and its just guardians, his interlocutors nevertheless express doubt as to whether such an ideal republic can ever be realized. In response, Socrates freely admits that the city he has thus far described is only a model or ideal pattern. It should no more be dismissed because it cannot be realized than Michelangelo's *David* should be dismissed because no living man can be found who possesses, in the flesh, the physical perfection depicted in the sculpture. Still, Socrates continues, if they would like to know how such a city might conceivably come into existence, then he will share with them how something approximating it might be achieved.

And then Socrates reveals what he has been carefully concealing up until now, the outrageous idea that he fears will cause his friends to ridicule him. He shares with them what change would have to occur before his ideal republic could hope to be born:

> Until philosophers are kings, or the kings and princes of this world have the spirit and power of philosophy, and political greatness and wisdom meet in one, and those commoner natures who pursue either to the exclusion of the other are compelled to stand aside, cities will never have rest from their evils,—nor the human race, as I believe,—and then only will this our State have a possibility of life and behold the light of day. (473d-e)

Earlier in *Republic* 5, Socrates shares his utopian scheme of eliminating marriage among his guardians and replacing it with a community of wives in which reproduction is based on eugenics and no one knows who their biological offspring are.[9] Though Socrates is aware that his "family planning" scheme will scandalize his interlocutors, he actually expects that they will be *more* scandalized by his call for philosopher-kings to rule his republic.

---

[9]Though many modern readers will approve of Socrates's argument that male and female guardians should be given the same education and training (451d-452a), most (I hope) will be opposed on ethical grounds to his argument that, for the sake of equality and eugenic purity, "the wives of our guardians are to be common, and their children are to be common, and no parent is to know his own child, nor any child his parent" (457d).

And perhaps he is right. Throughout history, philosophers have been dismissed as impractical dreamers who spend most of their day with their heads firmly fixed in the clouds. What do such people know of the "real world" of manipulation and greed and the bottom line? How can they possibly function as leaders when they are cut off from the ever-changing idols of the marketplace, the swirl of technological progress, the ebb and flow of cultural reform, and the ceaseless getting and spending of the masses? Plato's answer: the reason philosophers need to be kings is precisely because they are not caught up with the ephemeral illusions of the world.

As discussed in the previous chapter, the true philosopher is the one who has escaped from the cave and its feverish game of counting shadows. He is the one who has ascended the divided line from mere opinion to true knowledge. He is the one who is not mesmerized, as the crowd is, by imitations of imitations. The philosopher alone sees the Forms, and therefore he alone can rule properly and justly. How can a guardian institute true justice in his state unless he knows what true justice is? Justice and the other virtues cannot be judged against the whims of the crowd, for those whims are in a constant state of flux. To institute justice one must have a fixed standard to measure it against, but the only place where those standards exist is in the World of Being—and only the philosopher has glimpsed that perfect, unchanging world.

The king who is not also a philosopher—who has not, by means of the education system laid out in *Republic*, moved from the bottom to the top of the line or the inside to the outside of the cave—must trust to his senses alone in making his decisions. And that is a problem, Plato warns us, for those "who see the many beautiful, and who yet neither see absolute beauty, nor can follow any guide who points the way thither; who see the many just, and not absolute justice, and the like,—such persons may be said to have opinion but not knowledge" (479e). Today, we tend to choose our leaders on the basis of their charisma, their ability to think on their feet, and their skill for getting things done. Plato would encourage us to look for different qualities:

a passion to see and know and experience the Good, the True, and the Beautiful; an ability to think through problems slowly and logically; a settled conviction to perform only those actions that square with justice and the moral law. Today we seek leaders who can think for themselves; Plato sought rulers who could think right thoughts.

After all, argues Plato, would you hire an architect to build your building who was unable to read the blueprint? Would you buy a painting of a beautiful woman from an artist whose eyesight was so weak he could not see the model clearly? Only philosophers, Socrates insists, "are able to grasp the eternal and unchangeable" (484b), and that is why only philosophers can govern in accordance with divine standards of justice. What would happen if a group of rowdy, ignorant sailors dismissed their true captain as a useless "star-gazer" (489a) and took over the ship? Would they not crash against the rocks for lack of a skilled pilot?

Or what if they threw the captain overboard and chose their own pilot, not one who truly knows and understands how to navigate a ship by the fixed stars, but one who merely panders to their lusts? If they were to do so, the pseudopilot they chose would be a great deal like the sophists whom Plato criticizes in his dialogues. Though the masses often attacked the sophists—as they did Socrates, whom they falsely accused of being one—the fact is that the teachings of the sophists merely ape the misdirected and inordinate desires of the crowd. The sophists, explains Socrates,

> teach nothing but the opinion of the many, that is to say, the opinions of their assemblies; and this is their wisdom. I might compare them to a man who should study the tempers and desires of a mighty strong beast who is fed by him. . . . When, by continually attending upon him, he has become perfect in all this, he calls his knowledge wisdom, and makes of it a system or art, which he proceeds to teach, although he has no real notion of what he means by the principles or passions of which he is speaking, but calls this honourable and that dishonourable, or good or evil, or just or unjust, all in accordance with the tastes and tempers of the great brute. Good he pronounces to be that in which the beast delights and evil to be that which he dislikes. (493a-c)

Ignorant of the Forms, the sophists can only practice a kind of situational ethics that takes its cue from the lusts and whims of the crowd.

Indeed, what sets the true philosopher apart is that, unlike the sophist, he does not take cues from the crowd. Through the study of philosophy and the dialectical method, he is freed from the delusions that overwhelm us when we trust only to our senses: "Dialectic, and dialectic alone, goes directly to the first principles and is the only science which does away with hypotheses in order to make her ground secure" (533c). The philosopher alone sees things as they really are: sees their *archē*, rather than their imitation, and thus knows their telos, their purposeful end, rather than their mechanical function. Only such a person can rule a state wisely and well, and that is why Socrates insists that philosophers must not only be offered the helm of the ship of state but must be compelled to accept the offer. Just so, the prisoner who escapes from the cave must be forced to return into its dark inner recesses to lead other prisoners out into the light of freedom, truth, and reality.

THE MYTHS: PART I

EDUCATION COMES FROM a Latin root that means "to draw out."
Though I am not opposed to the traditional lecture format, I have
always believed strongly that my role as an educator involves not only
pouring wisdom into my students' minds but drawing it out as well.
Students, like all people, know far more than they think they know.
There is much wisdom buried deep in the subterranean recesses of our
souls—if only we can access it. Or, to put it another way, it is not solely
by means of our five senses that we gain access to knowledge; true
knowledge may reach us as well from outside our spatiotemporal
world (via revelation) and from within our heart-soul-mind (via intuition and recollection).

Despite the prodigious powers of his finely honed, systematic brain,
Plato knew that logic, empiricism, and reason have their limits. Neither
the negative dialectic of Socrates nor the more positive one of Plato
can, by itself, lead the philosopher up the ascending path toward the
Truth. Even the sophisticated dialectic of *Republic* cannot reach those
heights unaided. Inevitably, a moment comes when the search for definition must give way to an intuitive, revelatory leap into the unknown.
In the great middle dialogues of Plato, that leap comes in the form of
a myth (or allegory) that offers insight into our origins (*archē*), our end
(*telos*), or both.

In our post-Enlightenment world, we tend to make a sharp and nonnegotiable division between fact and fiction, history and myth, logical proof and "fanciful" allegory. Plato's mind did not accept such strict divisions. Indeed, just before recounting the grand story-allegory-myth with which he ends *Gorgias*, Socrates states, "Listen, then, as story-tellers say, to a very pretty tale, which I dare say that you may be disposed to regard as a fable only, but which, as I believe, is a true tale, for I mean to speak the truth" (523).

In *The Problem of Pain*, the Platonic-minded C. S. Lewis spins what he calls "a 'myth' in the Socratic sense, a not unlikely tale" to help explain the origin and nature of human suffering. In order to define more precisely what he means by "a 'myth' in the Socratic sense," Lewis adds the following note: "i.e., an account of what may have been the historical fact. Not to be confused with 'myth' in Dr. Niebuhr's sense (i.e., a symbolical representation of non-historical truth)."[1] For Lewis, as for Plato, "myth" is not a synonym for "untrue." To the contrary, it often offers the only direct road to truths that cannot be contained within the narrow confines of logical method, empirical observation, and scientific experimentation.

Though Plato's middle dialogues take up a variety of different questions and themes, they all—from *Gorgias*, *Protagoras*, and *Phaedo*, to *Meno*, *Republic*, and *Symposium*, to *Phaedrus*, *Timaeus*, and *Critias*—revolve around a climactic moment when Plato weaves a memorable story about creation or the destiny of the soul or the upward pilgrimage of the philosopher. The allegory of the cave (*Republic* 7; 514a-517a), which not only illustrates and humanizes Plato's divided line but also functions as its ultimate source of truth, is the best known of the myths, but it is only one of many—including the myth of Er with which *Republic* ends. If we choose to overlook or, worse, patronize Plato's myths, we will not be able to understand and analyze the rudiments of his philosophy. On the contrary, if we want to journey *with* Plato, if we want to *know* truth and not merely know *about* it, then we can only do so by means of the myths.

---

[1] C. S. Lewis, *The Problem of Pain* (New York: Macmillan, 1962), 77.

The student or professor who works his way doggedly through the intricacies of the dialogues and then refuses to soar on the wings of the myths is like someone who carries out an abstract study of the opposite sex but balks at the idea of falling in love. Or again, like a boy who spends months studying the Wild West, and then hides in the closet when a real cowboy shows up at his door. If we moderns can't handle the myths, it is not because they are too fanciful, but because they are too real.

THE PREEXISTENCE OF THE SOUL

In the previous chapter, I identified the exact moment in *Republic* 2 when Socratic aporia gives way to the Platonic quest for a fuller definition that can illuminate the true nature of virtue. A similar moment occurs in *Meno*, though this time the moment marks a transition, not from Socratic impasse to Platonic search, but from the realistic, pragmatic, semi-sophistical approach of Socrates to the idealistic, mystical, ultimately Pythagorean vision of Plato. As myths go, the one Plato tells in *Meno* is decidedly brief and to the point, but that is precisely why it provides a good entry point for exploring Plato's allegories. Further, the *Meno* myth provides the very raison d'être for all teachers who believe that their students know more than they think they know and who view their pedagogical task as a dual process of pouring in and drawing out.

Rather than begin with an elaborate framing device, as he does in most of his dialogues, Plato begins the *Meno* by throwing us head first into a conversation already in progress. "Can you tell me, Socrates [asks Meno], whether virtue is acquired by teaching or by practice; or if neither by teaching nor practice, then whether it comes to man by nature, or in what other way?" (70a). The reason for the abrupt opening is likely due to the fact that, in the earlier *Protagoras*, Socrates had vigorously debated the same question (i.e., "Can virtue be taught?"), only to end with a sort of semi-impasse.

Although Protagoras the sophist proves, arguably, to be Socrates's wisest and most successful sparring partner, the shrewd—at times outrageously and inexcusably wily—Socrates eventually maneuvers his opponent into a dialectical corner. Whereas Protagoras holds that the virtues are as distinct as features on a face, Socrates presses him to admit that all the virtues are really one—and that the oneness that unifies them all is knowledge. Whether it manifests itself in terms of justice or temperance or courage, virtue is essentially a type of knowledge. In contrast to his pupil Aristotle, Plato, and perhaps Socrates as well, seems to have believed that no one can knowingly do evil, that evil is not a misuse of free will but a byproduct of ignorance.

And yet, ironically, in the finale of *Protagoras*, Plato's contention that virtue is knowledge forces him to rethink his earlier contention that virtue cannot be taught. Despite the fact that Socrates maintains, throughout *Protagoras*, that no one can teach virtue—that is why great statesmen like Themistocles and Pericles were unable to pass down their civic virtue and skill to their sons—his victorious assertion that knowledge is the key factor that unites all the virtues brings with it an unintended consequence. In a wonderful moment of Socratic humility, the philosopher shares with his interlocutor what their argument would say to them if it could speak:

> Protagoras and Socrates, you are strange beings; there are you, Socrates, who were saying that virtue cannot be taught, contradicting yourself now by your attempt to prove that all things are knowledge, including justice, and temperance, and courage,—which tends to show that virtue can certainly be taught; for if virtue were other than knowledge, as Protagoras attempted to prove, then clearly virtue cannot be taught; but if virtue is entirely knowledge, as you are seeking to show, then I cannot but suppose that virtue is capable of being taught. (361b-c)

Those critics, both ancient and modern, who have accused Socrates of elitism would do well to read this passage again. Socrates and Plato were as much teachers as they were philosophers. If they didn't care for the masses, then it was for the same reason they didn't care for the sophists: because they believed that the sophists lacked ears to hear and a heart that yearned for wisdom.

That Socrates shows himself willing to follow his dialectical argument wherever it leads, even if it turns against him, is proof of his own willingness to see, to hear, and to yearn. Indeed, it is this very willingness that sets Socrates (and Plato) apart from the sophists, most of whom were more likely to alter the truth to suit their own agendas than vice versa. Sadly, to the great frustration of the reader who longs to know whether virtue can be taught, Socrates no sooner makes his admission than the dialogue grinds to an abrupt halt. The debate ends, the party breaks up, and the question on the table is never answered— not, at least, until *Meno*, which begins as abruptly as *Protagoras* ends.

At first, Socrates addresses Meno's opening question with the same fast-and-loose evasive maneuvers that he uses in his face-off with Protagoras. Every time Meno tries to define the word *virtue*—since Socrates won't address the question until the terms are properly defined—Socrates deconstructs his definition, either for being too limited in its applicability or for treating a part as if it were the whole. Finally, exasperated and in despair, Meno tells Socrates that he is not a man but a "flat torpedo fish [or stingray], who torpifies those who come near him and touch him, as you have now torpified me" (80b). In response, Socrates falls back on his classic claim not to know the very things he presses others to explain to him:

> As to my being a torpedo, if the torpedo is torpid as well as the cause of torpidity in others, then indeed I am a torpedo, but not otherwise; for I perplex others, not because I am clear, but because I am utterly perplexed myself. And now I know not what virtue is, and you seem to be in the same case, although you did once perhaps know before you touched me. (80c-d)

And that, it seems, will be that: another impasse, another false start on the road to truth. Meno himself senses the coming stalemate and asks Socrates a simple but vital question: "If you find what you want, how will you ever know that this is the thing which you did not know?" (80d). Socrates acknowledges the importance of the question and the seeming futility of seeking after something you wouldn't recognize even if you found it. And then . . .

Socratic aporia gives way to Platonic leap, and philosophy blossoms into metaphysics.

A GREAT AND MYSTERIOUS TRUTH

"I have heard," says Socrates in a hushed whisper, "from certain wise men and women who spoke of things divine that . . ." (81a). "What?" begs Meno, filling in the pause in Socrates's words. "What have you heard?" Not from the sophists or from the (non-Pythagorean) Presocratic philosophers, but from priests and priestesses and divinely inspired poets, Socrates—or Plato, whose voice, I would argue, takes over from this point on—has learned a great and mysterious truth: "that the soul of man is immortal, and at one time has an end, which is termed dying, and at another time is born again, but is never destroyed" (81b). Here, in a nutshell, Plato expresses a belief that is central to many of his greatest myths: reincarnation. Whereas the earlier, more Socratic myths of the afterlife that grace the closing sections of *Apology*, *Gorgias*, and *Phaedo* do not make reference to souls returning again to the earth, those that appear in the later, more Platonic dialogues (*Meno*, *Republic*, *Phaedrus*, and *Timaeus*) rely heavily on the metaphysical implications of the transmigration of souls.

In chapter seven, I will discuss some of those implications. For now, it must be understood that the central myth of the *Meno* lies midway between those of *Apology-Gorgias-Phaedo* and those of *Republic-Phaedrus-Timaeus*. Rather than meditate on the mechanics of reincarnation, the *Meno* myth focuses on the pedagogical ramifications that ensue if we accept that, before entering our body, our soul existed in heaven in a noncorporeal state. If that is the case, it means that each of our souls has, at some point in the past, dwelled in the World of Being and thus communed with those very essences of Goodness, Truth, and Beauty that the Platonic philosopher who escapes from the cave yearns to glimpse.

And if *that* is the case, then the process of learning higher truths becomes as much one of study as of recollection. As Socrates explains,

The soul, then, as being immortal, and having been born again many times, and having seen all things that exist, whether in this world or in the world below, has knowledge of them all; and it is no wonder that she [the soul] should be able to call to remembrance all that she ever knew about virtue, and about everything; for as all nature is akin, and the soul has learned all things; there is no difficulty in her eliciting or as men say learning, out of a single recollection all the rest, if a man is strenuous and does not faint; for all enquiry and all learning is but recollection. (81c-d)

The true Platonic teacher uses the dialectic not so much to expose false definitions as to provoke the student into recollecting his own past memories of the World of Being. Indeed, the Socrates of the *Meno* goes on to "prove" Plato's hypothesis by "teaching" a slave boy higher theories of math by drawing out of his soul, rather than putting into his mind, the rudiments of geometry that the slave boy once knew, directly and intuitively, in his preexistent state.

In the early nineteenth century, William Wordsworth would take up Plato's myth of recollection and the preexistence as, in part, a critique of the tabula rasa myth of John Locke. In response to the Enlightenment philosopher's argument that we are born as blank slates bereft of any and all innate knowledge,[2] the Romantic poet suggests, in his "Ode: Intimations of Immortality from Recollections of Early Childhood," that

> Not in entire forgetfulness,
> And not in utter nakedness,
> But trailing clouds of glory do we come
> From God, who is our home. (lines 62-65)[3]

For Wordsworth, the possibility that our soul might have had an earlier existence in heaven helped him resolve a personal struggle: why it was that when he was young all of nature seemed bathed in celestial light, but when he got older that glory mostly faded away. The child's

---

[2]See book 1, chapters 1–2 and book 2, chapter 2 of Locke's *An Essay on Human Understanding* (1689). Locke actually uses the phrase "white paper" instead of blank slate.
[3]William Wordsworth, "Ode: Intimations of Immortality from Recollections of Early Childhood," in *English Romantic Poetry and Prose*, ed. Russell Noyes (New York: Oxford University Press, 1956), 328.

intuitive perceptions of greater spiritual realities, Wordsworth pro-claims, is not the product of a childish, "savage" delusion that has not yet evolved, but of a true link between heaven and earth that has not yet been eviscerated by the soul-destroying forces of worldliness.

To be clear, this is not to say that Wordsworth, whose Christian faith matured as he aged, meant to advocate reincarnation in his poem. To the contrary, neither Wordsworth's critique of Locke nor the peda-gogical dimensions of the *Meno* myth compels us to believe that our souls will return again in different bodies. All that is necessary to support Wordsworth's trailing-clouds-of-glory theory or Plato's learning-through-recollection theory is a belief in the preexistence of the soul: a doctrine that, though heterodox, is not utterly inconsistent with orthodox Christianity.

Think of what it would mean if our soul entered this world already in possession of deep spiritual and philosophical understanding. All parents can attest to the fact that their child's unique personality mani-fested itself almost from birth. None of us is a complete tabula rasa, but a carefully fashioned being hard-wired with yearnings for God, for love, and for purpose. If part of that hardwiring includes direct, un-mediated knowledge of God and heaven, then the whole educational enterprise, as Plato knew, takes on a different dimension.

Attentive teachers notice that some of their students "get" things more quickly: not because they are necessarily smarter in the way that the modern educational world measures intelligence, but because they grasp what you are saying even before they can explain it on a test or describe it in a paper. Although the experience of déjà vu could be used as proof for reincarnation—that we lived on earth before in dif-ferent bodies—it can just as easily be used to support a belief that our souls enter our bodies stored with prior (innate) knowledge of Goodness, Truth, and Beauty.

After all, isn't the greatest joy of learning that of recognition? Is it not that frozen instant when a connection is suddenly forged between previously unrelated categories of knowledge? What is generally re-ferred to as the "aha (or eureka) moment" cannot be measured or calculated in logical, mathematical terms. The essence of the theory of relativity came to Einstein at the dawn of the twentieth century in a light-bulb flash of insight; in the late nineteenth century, the periodic table of elements came to Mendeleyev in a dream. Newton's universal laws of gravitation came to him in a similar moment in 1666 when the apple fell on his head, and he intuited, as by revelation, that the relationship between the top of the tree and the ground was parallel to that between the moon and the earth.[4]

Plato's answer, then, to the question of whether virtue can be taught is yes, but not in the way that we normally define teaching. Our soul is born not only with innate, inchoate knowledge of eternal things but also with a moral dimension that needs to be prodded into shape. Prophets and holy men, C. S. Lewis argues in *Mere Christianity* 3.3, do not so much teach us morality as remind us of it.[5] Morality, like justice in *Republic*, is less a set of memorized law codes than a proper balance and harmony of the soul. The true teacher of virtue helps bring the student into alignment with those higher notions of Goodness (morality), Truth (philosophy), and Beauty (aesthetics) that are already imprinted in the soul. In the Pythagorean system that so strongly influenced Plato, the sign that the alignment has been achieved comes in a joyous, mystical moment when the initiate hears the celestial music of the spheres and can then proceed upward to participate in it. In the myths of Plato that moment comes, for good or ill, at judgment day.

JUDGMENT DAY

In what I would call the proto-Platonic myth that comes at the end of *Apology*, Socrates speaks only of the good side of death, of the marvelous journey from injustice, error, and decay to a better world where all is true and pure, and fellowship and conversation thrive (40e-41c).

---

[4]These three eureka moments in science, together with a dozen others, are helpfully documented by Bruno Lemaitre at this site: http://brunolemaitre.ch/history-of-science/discoveries-in-science
[5]C. S. Lewis, *Mere Christianity* (New York: Macmillan, 1960), 78.

In the full-blown Platonic myth that comes at the end of *Gorgias*, the picture conjured is far more sobering: not pie in the sky by and by, but a final judgment that yields joy and blessing for some but terror and despair for others.

Gorgias, like Protagoras, is a sophist, and though Socrates treats the former with more respect, both teachers for hire are critiqued for being amoral peddlers of a virtue and knowledge that they do not understand. In the case of *Gorgias*, which focuses specifically on the dangers of rhetoric, Socrates finds in the oratory of the sophists the same ignorance masquerading as knowledge as he claims (in *Apology*; 21a-22e) to have found in the politicians, poets, and craftsmen of Athens: "Does [the successful rhetorician] really know anything of what is good and evil, base or honourable, just or unjust in [his audience]; or has he only a way with the ignorant of persuading them that he not knowing is to be esteemed to know more about these things than someone else who knows?" (459d). In fact, Socrates boldly and unapologetically states his firm belief that rhetoric "is not an art at all, but the habit of a bold and ready wit, which knows how to manage mankind: this habit I sum up under the word 'flattery'" (463a-b).

Near the end of *Meno*, Socrates's disparagement of the ability of Athenian statesmen to teach virtue to their children leads Anytus (who would later be one of the accusers at his trial) to prophesy Socrates's coming conviction by the citizens of Athens (94e-95a). At a similar point in *Gorgias*, Socrates's even stronger disparagement of rhetoric's ability to instill justice in his fellow citizens—coupled with his somewhat prideful claim to be a more effective teacher of virtue—leads Callicles to make a similar prediction (521b-c). Both predictions seem to be Plato's way of foreshadowing the trial of his beloved teacher; however, in *Gorgias*, Plato goes further than this, putting in Socrates's own mouth an even clearer prediction both of his trial and of his defense.

After subtly warning Socrates that he may someday be dragged before the Athenian assembly, Callicles questions Socrates as to how a man like him could defend himself before the jury if he refused to resort to the persuasive power of rhetoric. Socrates replies,

> Yes, Callicles, if he have that defence, which as you have often acknowledged he should have—if he be his own defence, and have never said or done anything wrong, either in respect of gods or men; and this has been repeatedly acknowledged by us to be the best sort of defence. And if any one could convict me of inability to defend myself or others after this sort, I should blush for shame, whether I was convicted before many, or before a few, or by myself alone; and if I died from want of ability to do so, that would indeed grieve me. But if I died because I have no powers of flattery or rhetoric, I am very sure that you would not find me repining at death. For no man who is not an utter fool and coward is afraid of death itself, but he is afraid of doing wrong. (522d-e)

The sentiment is nearly identical to that expressed near the end of *Apology*: a determination to choose righteousness over self-preservation and not to allow a foolish fear of death to impel him to compromise his teachings or his manner of life (39a-b). Truth and the testimony of his actions will defend him, not rhetorical devices and displays of emotion.

In *Apology*, Socrates backs up his convictions by first arguing that death is not a bad thing—for it is either an eternal sleep or a journey to a better place—and then weaving in a myth of a chatty Elysian Fields (40c-41c). In *Gorgias*, he backs up his convictions by means of a different, more sobering argument: not that death is an absolute good but that it is *only* a good for the soul that has chosen virtue over vice. Thus, directly after speaking the passage quoted above, Socrates adds these two sentences: "For to go to the world below having one's soul full of injustice is the last and worst of all evils. And in proof of what I say, if you have no objection, I should like to tell you a story" (522e). And with that, the myth of *Gorgias* unfolds in all its beauty and terror.

According to a law established by Cronus (the father of Zeus), Socrates explains, "He who has lived all his life in justice and holiness shall go, when he is dead, to the Islands of the Blessed, and dwell there in perfect happiness out of the reach of evil; [while] he who has lived unjustly and impiously shall go to the house of vengeance and punishment, which is called Tartarus" (523b). Whereas in the days of Cronus we were judged while on our deathbed, in the days of Zeus, the time and place for judgment was shifted to the moment *after* death. When we were judged before, says Socrates, rich tyrants would obscure the wickedness of their deeds by dressing in fine clothes and wrapping themselves in luxury and pride of race. Now, however, souls are stripped of their bodies and judged in a state of utter nakedness. "At fifty," George Orwell once quipped, "every man has the face he deserves."[6] Anticipating Orwell's deeply moral-psychological-theological insight, one that is reflected most powerfully in the naked state of the sinners in Dante's inferno, Plato suggests that once our soul is separated from our body, it will stand forever fixed in the virtues or vices that have shaped and molded it.

Like the horrific marks and stains that appear on the picture of Dorian Gray, each evil action committed by a living man imprints itself deeply on his soul. Perhaps, muses Socrates, Rhadamanthus, the judge of Asia, might come upon the soul of a tyrant that is

> marked with the whip, and is full of the prints and scars of perjuries and crimes with which each action has stained him, and he is all crooked with falsehood and imposture, and has no straightness, because he has lived without truth. Him Rhadamanthus beholds, full of all deformity and disproportion, which is caused by licence and luxury and insolence and incontinence, and despatches him ignominiously to his prison, and there he undergoes the punishment which he deserves. (525a)

Not all the polished rhetoric in the world can hide the true state of the tyrant's soul or prevent it from being cast headlong into Tartarus. Evil will out, and the soul cannot escape from what it is—or, better, what it has become.

Well, actually, the situation is not quite so dire. In order to complicate his myth, and the philosophy that it both illustrates and

---

[6]www.orwellfoundation.com/the-orwell-foundation/orwell/library/d-j-taylor-orwells-face/.

authorizes, Socrates further explains that the marks left on the souls of sinners are of two distinct kinds: those that are curable and those that are not. As with the later Catholic distinction between venial sins (which only merit temporal punishment) and mortal sins (which, as they violate the Ten Commandments and are committed with full knowledge and deliberate consent, can lead to damnation),[7] the *Gorgias* myth holds out the hope of remediation and rehabilitation for those whose deeds, and marks, are of the curable kind (525b; the same hope is held out in the Phaedo myth, 113d-e).

But of course it is far better to come before the eternal judges with the clean soul of a philosopher, of one who has ever sought virtue and turned away from the path of vice. That is why Socrates has made it his lifelong goal to "consider how I shall present my soul whole and undefiled before the judge in that day. Renouncing the honours at which the world aims, I desire only to know the truth, and to live as well as I can, and, when I die, to die as well as I can" (526d-e). Indeed, at the very end of the dialogue, Socrates rests his twin paradoxical beliefs that it is better to suffer wrong than to do wrong and that a rhetoric that would rescue us from a punishment that would benefit our soul is to be rejected, not on the dialectical arguments that he devotes most of *Gorgias* to developing, but on the myth of judgment he has just presented. For it is the allegorical tale and not the logical argument that ultimately teaches us that "the best way of life is to practise justice and every virtue in life and death" (527e).

---

[7]For the distinction between mortal and venial sins, see part three, section one, chapter one, article eight, subsection four of the *Catechism of the Catholic Church*, 2nd ed., which can be accessed for free online at www.usccb.org/sites/default/files/flipbook/catechism/.

THE MYTHS: PART II

SOCRATES'S CALL in *Gorgias* is to reject rhetorical flattery, and the perks that go with it, in favor of a life of virtue that finds its justification in an allegorical tale of final judgment. Just so, Socrates's more complex call in *Republic* to live the life of the just philosopher, even if that life gives one a reputation for injustice, finds *its* justification in a more complex, and more aesthetically rich, myth of judgment that factors into its narrative the mature Platonic belief in reincarnation. Like the *Gorgias* myth, *Republic*'s myth of Er (614b-621d) is introduced with a dual assertion that (1) what happens to us after death is what *really* matters (614a), and (2) the story we are about to hear is not a pipe dream but a true account of the reality that awaits us (614b).

As he builds up to telling the myth that climaxes his greatest dialogue, Plato, via Socrates, asserts that, in matter of fact, the just generally do reap rewards on this earth—just so, Jesus promises (Mark 10:29-30) that those who abandon all to follow him will reap earthly benefits (along with persecution), *in addition to* gaining eternal life. Still, directly after promising rewards in this life to the just man, Socrates adds that "all these [earthly rewards] are as nothing, either in number or greatness in comparison with those other recompenses which await both just and unjust after death. And you ought to hear them, and then both just and unjust will have received from us a full payment of the debt which the argument owes to them" (614a). Indeed, it is imperative that we hear them, for the logical argument that is not accompanied by the allegory is incomplete and, to borrow a line from George Herbert, in the ear, not conscience, rings.

And so Socrates plunges into his tale, but not before making something clear: "I will tell you a tale; not one of the tales which Odysseus tells to the hero Alcinous, yet this too is a tale of a hero, Er the son of Armenius, a Pamphylian by birth" (614b). By carefully distinguishing his myth of Er from the tales that Odysseus tells to the king of Phaeacia over the course of *Odyssey* 9–12 (particularly his descent into the underworld in book eleven), Socrates means to say that his account of the afterlife will be a true and reliable one. Earlier in *Republic* 3 (386a-387c), Socrates had strongly criticized the view of hades propagated in the epics of Homer as false tales that built up in young men a wrongful dread of the underworld as a gloomy and miserable place. At that point in the dialogue, Socrates simply asserted that Homer's depiction of hades was untrue; here, in his concluding myth, Plato presents his readers with a countervision of the postmortem reality that we shall all, one day, encounter.

Like Orpheus, Hercules, Theseus, and Odysseus (and Aeneas and Dante after them), Er is allowed by the gods to visit hades and return to tell the tale. Interestingly, however, rather than frame his myth in terms of an epic descent into the underworld, Socrates tells it in a way that sounds eerily like the life-after-life (or near-death) experiences recounted by modern people who have been pronounced clinically dead and then miraculously returned to life bubbling over with amazing tales of a journey back and forth through a tunnel into the light of heaven.[1]

The first part of the tale Plato relates bears much similarity to the *Gorgias* myth. Once again, we see souls judged and then sent to bliss

---

[1]See, for example, Raymond Moody's *Life After Life* (1975), Dinesh D'Souza's *Life After Death: The Evidence* (2007), Roy Abraham Varghese's *There is Life After Death* (2010), and Don Piper's *90 Minutes in Heaven* (2004).

or woe. This time, however, the geography of the underworld—likely filtered through the *Phaedo* myth (107c-115a), which meticulously maps out the winding tunnels and branching rivers of hades (111c-113d)—is more precise in its physical details:

> [Er] came to a mysterious place at which there were two openings in the earth; they were near together, and over against them were two other openings in the heaven above. In the intermediate space there were judges seated, who commanded the just, after they had given judgment on them and had bound their sentences in front of them, to ascend by the heavenly way on the right hand; and in like manner the unjust were bidden by them to descend by the lower way on the left hand; these also bore the symbols of their deeds, but fastened on their backs. (614c-d)

As if anticipating the Cartesian coordinate system, Plato has the souls of the just go into the "positive" quadrant (up and to the right) and the wicked into the "negative" (down and to the left). Like those in the *Gorgias* myth, the souls of the just and wicked are marked, though here the wicked bear their evil deeds fastened to their backs as Jacob Marley is doomed to drag behind him the iron money boxes that symbolize his life of avarice.[2]

Continuing in the mode of the *Gorgias* myth, Plato assigns punishments and blessings to the souls, though here again the myth of Er is more exact (and exacting) in its details. Thus, we learn that each soul receives its penalties or rewards in accordance with a tenfold ratio. For each vice committed, a penalty is meted out once each century; for every virtue, a similar program of rewards is assigned. Impiety to the gods and to one's parents yields even worse punishments as does suicide (615a-c).

When the thousand years are over, the sinners exit the cave mouth and their punishments cease—unless, that is, they were guilty of tyranny in their previous life. If that is the case, what greets them is something truly Dantean in its horror:

---

[2]Charles Dickens, *A Christmas Carol*, in *The Christmas Books*, (London: Penguin Classics, 1985), 1:61.

They [Ardiaeus and his fellow tyrants] were just, as they fancied, about to return into the upper world, but the mouth, instead of admitting them, gave a roar, whenever any of these incurable sinners or some one who had not been sufficiently punished tried to ascend; and then wild men of fiery aspect, who were standing by and heard the sound, seized and carried them off; and Ardiaeus and others they bound head and foot and hand, and threw them down and flayed them with scourges, and dragged them along the road at the side, carding them on thorns like wool, and declaring to the passers-by what were their crimes, and that they were being taken away to be cast into hell [Tartarus in Greek]. (615e-616a)

Even a skeptical reader who denies the immortality of the soul cannot help but shiver in fear at Plato's description of roaring hell mouths and fiery demons that chain and flay evil souls. Meanwhile, Christians who read this passage would do well to remember that the supposedly "meek and mild" Jesus spoke more about the horrors of hell than any other figure in the Bible (see, for example, Mt 5:29; 10:28; 13:42, 49-50; 24:51; 25:30, 41).

As if realizing that his listeners/readers will be in need of narrative relief after hearing/reading about the horrific fate of sinners, Socrates/Plato lifts our eyes and hearts from the depths of Tartarus to the heights of Pythagoras's ordered cosmos. In sharp contrast to the grim fate of the tyrants, Socrates explains, the souls of the just and of those who have paid fully for their crimes are vouchsafed a vision of the heavenly spheres. As the souls watch in awe, the spheres rotate in perfect concentric circles around the earth. Atop each sphere sits a siren who sings eternally a single note; together the blended notes of the sirens produce that celestial chorus that Pythagoras called the music of the spheres—the hearing of which, as I noted earlier, releases the soul of the initiate to ascend heavenward and join in the cosmic symphony (616c-617b).

For Plato, the turning of the spheres is linked to the force of Necessity, which is itself linked to the three Fates who spin out our lives, our destinies, and our deaths. It is the Fates who lay before the souls a myriad of lots and of lives from which they must choose (617c-e). Based on the number of their lot, they each choose for themselves the life of a man, a woman, or an animal. Once the soul chooses, it is reborn into its new life and returns again to the earth. I think it no coincidence that Plato moves from the first half of his myth (which, *Gorgias*-like, suggests a single judgment) to the second (which centers on the transmigration of souls) via a Pythagorean vision of the universe— for it was from the Presocratic Pythagoras that Plato adopted the philosophical teaching and allegorical image of reincarnation.

The long and complicated dialectic that wends its way through the ten books of *Republic* is, at its core, concerned with what justice and injustice do to our souls and how the choices we make shape us into certain types of people. We watch, in awe, as the souls proceed forward one by one to choose their new lives, and we realize that what Plato is allowing us to witness is that terrifying moment of crisis toward which all our education and philosophical training leads. As the souls are warned before they choose:

> Hear the word of Lachesis, the daughter of Necessity. Mortal souls, behold a new cycle of life and mortality. Your genius will not be allotted to you, but you choose your genius; and let him who draws the first lot have the first choice, and the life which he chooses shall be his destiny. Virtue is free, and as a man honours or dishonours her he will have more or less of her; the responsibility is with the chooser—God is justified. (617d-e)

Once we choose our life, we will be bound to it by necessity, but the choosing is ours, and ours alone, to make. If we choose poorly, we have only ourselves to blame.

As if to make clear that this aspect of the myth of Er is meant both to illustrate and give credence to the ideal system of education laid out in *Republic*, Socrates breaks the narrative flow of his story to address Glaucon directly:

> And here, my dear Glaucon, is the supreme peril of our human state; and therefore the utmost care should be taken. Let each one of us leave every other kind of knowledge and seek and follow one thing only, if per-adventure he may be able to learn and may find some one who will make him able to learn and discern between good and evil, and so to choose always and everywhere the better life as he has opportunity. (618c)

The life of the philosopher will not only guarantee us a good life now but will also prepare us to choose wisely when the time comes to select what our next life will be. It is the philosopher who will see that a life which promises power may bring ruin in the end, while the life of a poor man can be lived in such a way as to bring peace, joy, and contentment.

Furthermore, lest we think the system of lots unfair—since some are allowed first pick of lives while others must wait until most have been chosen—the voice of the prophet of the underworld makes it clear that the lottery is truly a fair one: "Even for the last comer, if he chooses wisely and will live diligently, there is appointed a happy and not undesirable existence. Let not him who chooses first be careless, and let not the last despair" (619b). As if to drive home the point, Socrates tells us what happens to the man who draws the first lot. He

> came forward and in a moment chose the greatest tyranny; his mind having been darkened by folly and sensuality, he had not thought out the whole matter before he chose, and did not at first sight perceive that he was fated, among other evils, to devour his own children. But when he had time to reflect, and saw what was in the lot, he began to beat his breast and lament over his choice, forgetting the proclamation of the prophet; for, instead of throwing the blame of his misfortune on himself, he accused chance and the gods, and everything rather than himself. (619b-c)

Just so, as the sinners in Dante's inferno cross over the river Acheron into hell (*Inferno* 3:103-105), they blame God and their parents and the land that gave them birth—everything, that is, except themselves. The soul steeped in injustice is as blind to the nature of goodness as it is to the depths of its own folly and depravity.

But hope remains. Unlike the fool who draws the first lot, the one who draws the last uses his wisdom and good sense to make a proper choice from the lives that remain:

> There came also the soul of Odysseus having yet to make a choice, and his lot happened to be the last of them all. Now the recollection of former toils had disenchanted him of ambition, and he went about for a considerable time in search of the life of a private man who had no cares; he had some

difficulty in finding this, which was lying about and had been neglected by everybody else; and when he saw it, he said that he would have done the same had his lot been first instead of last, and that he was delighted to have it. (620c-d)

Though Plato makes it clear at the outset that his myth of Er will be a true tale, not a false one like those told by Odysseus, he here gives to Homer's ideal man the honor of embodying the very kind of wisdom that he advocates throughout *Republic*. Odysseus, who plays a prominent role in both *Iliad* and *Odyssey*, is perhaps Homer's greatest creation. While Odysseus journeys through the underworld (*Odyssey* 11), the poet Homer even allows him to receive a prophecy of his final voyage and his peaceful death. But it is the philosopher Plato who alone possesses the wisdom and insight to recount for us the true end of Homer's hero.

Once the soul has chosen its new life, it is forced to drink from Lethe, the river of forgetfulness. Washed clean of the memory of its past incarnation, it is then ready to begin its new life on the earth. Thus Plato ends his great myth, a myth that, Socrates tells Glaucon, "will save us if we are obedient to the word spoken; and we shall pass safely over the river of Forgetfulness and our soul will not be defiled" (621c).

The Journey of the Philosopher

To read Plato is to plunge headfirst into a world of imagination, a magic land full of scintillating possibilities, at least for those who have eyes to see. Plato may have expelled the poets from his republic, but, as I hope this chapter has shown, he himself was the greatest of all poets. When reason and logic and the dialectic failed him, he fashioned himself wings out of the feathers of myth and the wax of allegory, and soared, like Daedalus and Icarus, toward Goodness, Truth, and Beauty.

Thus far, we have seen Plato use myths to explore the nature of the afterlife: not as an end in itself or to fulfill idle curiosity, but as a spur for seeking truth and enacting virtue. Plato's interest in the life to come, however, was not confined to divine judgment; he was interested as well in the greater spiritual journey of which life, death, and rebirth are but the stage on which the drama unfolds. In the central myth of *Phaedrus* (245c-257b), Plato joins together a meditation on reincarnation and the preexistence of the soul with an inspirational call to journey upward. And he does so not by working through a syllogism but by constructing a breathtakingly beautiful myth that illuminates the final cause, as opposed to efficient cause, for why it is that when we fall in love and gaze deep into the eyes of our beloved our whole body shivers and our skin turns to goose flesh.

In the days of its preexistence, explains Socrates in a myth whose primary purpose is to celebrate love, our soul had wings and freely soared through the heavens. During one of its celestial flights, it flew so high that it broke through the boundaries of our tiny universe of time and space and entered in to that higher realm of Being in which all is perfection and all is whole: free from change and death and decay. And there, in that kingdom of absolutes, it was whirled, like the Tennyson of "In Memoriam A. H. H.,"

> About empyreal heights of thought,
> And came upon that which is, and caught
> The deep pulsations of the world. (95.38-40)[3]

For a thousand years, it followed in the procession of the gods as they made their majestic circuit around the outside rim of our cosmic sphere. Most wonderful of all, it communed directly with the glorious Forms of Beauty and Truth. It gazed on the face of the immortal, the indestructible, the uncreated, and it understood. For it not only saw, it knew (247c-e).

In a haunting, unforgettable image that parallels the tripartite soul of *Republic* (reason-spirit-appetite), Plato pictures our winged soul as a charioteer (reason) whose chariot is pulled by two very different horses: one noble and self-controlled (spirit); the other violent and lustful (appetite). As long as the charioteer keeps the two horses working in unison, his flight upward continues unimpeded, but a time

---

[3]*Tennyson's Poetry*, ed. Robert W. Hill Jr. (New York: Norton, 1971), 170.

eventually comes when the fiery horse so pulls at the reins and champs at the bit that the charioteer is thrown off course. When that happens, base and mundane impulses from the earth pull down on the soul and tear its wings, causing it to fall headlong into our earthly World of Becoming. There, for a cycle of ten thousand years, the soul moves from one body of flesh to another until, by means of a long, weary climb toward the glory it once knew, the soul once more sprouts wings and freely soars through the heavens (248a-e).

But this is not the whole story. For there are moments during our bittersweet, ten-millennia sojourn when the captive, domesticated soul catches, in the face of his beloved, a brief but real glimpse of that glorious World of Being he once knew. There, lurking beneath the physical beauty of the one whom we love, our soul perceives a visionary flash of that ideal Beauty with which it once communed. Indeed, just as it sometimes happens while listening to an orchestra that during a lengthened pause in the music a deeper harmony seems to swell up in our ears and draw us almost from our seat, so as we stare transfixed at our beloved, a veil seems to lift, revealing a deeper, more essential beauty untouched by time or change. And when that happens, the soul begins to stir, and its limp, bedraggled wings begin to fan out, and its torn and molting feathers begin, once more, to grow.

As Plato describes it, when the soul gazes upon the beloved,

> there is a sort of reaction, and the shudder passes into an unusual heat and perspiration; for, as he receives the effluence of beauty through the eyes, the wing moistens and he warms. And as he warms, the parts out of which the wing grew, and which had been hitherto closed and rigid, and had prevented the wing from shooting forth, are melted, and as nourishment streams upon him, the lower end of the wing begins to swell and grow from the root upwards; and the growth extends under the whole soul—for once the whole was winged. During this process the whole soul is all in a state of ebullition and effervescence,—which may be compared to the irritation and uneasiness in the gums at the time of cutting teeth,—bubbles up, and has a feeling of uneasiness and tickling. (251b-c)

Hardly a scientific explanation for goose flesh, yet so much more satisfying, so much more real than any talk of hair follicles and swollen papillae. No, I do not believe that my soul has physical wings, but then neither did Plato. And yet, when, in the presence of beauty, tears form in my eyes and my skin tightens and warms, I could almost swear that a mass of snow-white feathers were pricking me from within. For you see, though our souls are noncorporeal, they have presence and weight. They expand and contract in sympathy with our spiritual journey toward or away from Goodness, Truth, and Beauty: now swelling and glowing with light as we ascend toward the life and the glory for which we were created, now shrinking and wasting away as we fall further and further into the lust and the sloth and the blank indifference of the animal and even vegetable world.

I have met (have we not all met) people in that latter, almost soulless category; their eyes seem empty and dull, their fire almost extinguished. But I have also met those in the former category; their eyes burn with a passion for Life and Beauty and Truth. Their sights are set on things above, on the Father of lights in whom there is no shadow of turning (Jas 1:17). Though they may not be philosophers in the technical, academic sense of the word, they are truly so in the etymological sense: lovers of wisdom. They pursue truth with all the ardor of a lover, and since, as Plato well knew, the highest Truth ever dwells in the company of Goodness and Beauty and Joy, they yearn too after these things. They shun whatever in them would weigh them down, whatever would mire their souls in the instinctual, barely conscious life of the beast. Mere subsistence is abhorrent to them; they must strive and grow and develop. What they seek, finally, is freedom, freedom to resist the animal part of their nature, to redeem the human part, and to release the divine.

And with this articulation of the highest goal of man, we are led back to the myth of the winged soul. According to Plato, though the soul typically must wait ten thousand years before returning to the World of Being, if it is incarnated three times in the body of a philosopher its spiritual gestation period will be reduced to a mere three thousand years (249a). Thus it is that throughout the dialogues, especially *Republic*, Plato exhorts us time and again to honor philosophy as the highest of callings. Indeed, Plato devotes considerable effort to mapping out in great detail the stages through which the would-be philosopher must pass on his quest for wisdom—maps it out in the dialogues, that is, and then brings it to life in the myths.

The education of the lover. Though Plato's musings on the education of the philosopher surface in a number of his myths—in the allegory of the cave in particular—the two that offer the fullest account are found in *Symposium* (which, like the myth of *Phaedrus*, celebrates love) and *Phaedo* (which prefaces its closing myth of judgment with an earlier myth of the soul's postmortem journey). In both of the myths, Plato addresses the soul's desire to transcend the physical to become, as it were, an initiate in the mysteries of philosophy. The mysteries spoken of in *Symposium*, like those in *Phaedrus*, are not those of philosophy, but of love; and yet, whether wittingly or unwittingly, Plato, by treating these twin mysteries of philosophy and love as essentially equivalent, broadens the scope of the philosopher to include all those who seek after higher things, after that Love and Beauty and Goodness and Truth that only descend from above. Indeed, in the *Phaedrus*, Plato states that "the soul which has seen most of truth [in its empyreal flight through the World of Being] shall come to the birth as a philosopher, or artist, or some musical and loving nature" (248d). The desire, it seems, to ascend to the Beatific Vision is not rigidly limited to the modern conception of the philosopher but defines rather a type of life that longs and yearns for union with that greater love that medieval theologians and poets believed moved the planets.[4]

Of all Plato's dialogues, *Symposium* is surely the most dramatic and entertaining, and yet, in the midst of the laughter and fun, there rises up a vision of the journey of the philosopher that rivals the allegory of the cave in the awe that it provokes in its readers. The word *symposium*, in Greek, means "drinking party," and the dialogue offers us the rare

---

[4]See, for example, the famous closing line of Dante's *Divine Comedy*.

opportunity to eavesdrop on just such a party that could conceivably have occurred during the golden age of Athens. The guests include Socrates, the brilliant and bawdy comic playwright Aristophanes, the popular but scandalous statesman Alcibiades (who crashes the party), a popular tragedian, a somewhat pompous doctor, and Phaedrus, who, as in the dialogue named after him, is the one who suggests that each guest should offer up a rhetorical praise of love. As in *Canterbury Tales*, the different stories told by the different guests range from comic to serious, sensual to mystical, but none of them seems able to touch on the essential mystery that lies at the core of love.

In *Phaedrus*, after the title character and then Socrates recite a rhetorically effective criticism of love, Socrates's *daimon*—his oracle or inner voice that he explains, in *Apology* (40a), never tells him what to do but only stops him from doing what he should not—scolds him for his impiety to the god Eros, son of Aphrodite, and better known by his Roman name, Cupid (242c-d). Saved from impiety by his oracle, Socrates goes on to sing the great myth of the charioteer/winged soul as a way of revealing the true glory of love. In *Symposium*, the role of the *daimon* is taken by Socrates's recollection of a woman named Diotima who, many years earlier, had initiated him—philosophically rather than physically—into the mysteries of love (201d). In recreating for his fellow revelers the truths that Diotima, midwife-like, had birthed in him, Socrates lays out an at once amorous and philosophic educational program that takes the initiate up a rising path that is as thrilling and eye-opening as the path taken by the cave dweller who moves in stages from contemplating the shadows of shadows to gazing directly on the sun (210a-212a).

According to Diotima/Socrates, the long process that leads finally to a mystical union with that God who is Love, Beauty, and Truth begins, rather mundanely, with the love of physical beauty as it is manifested in one particular person. But the initiate does not stop here. Love of a single beloved must expand, in time, to include love for all forms of physical beauty. Once this level has been achieved, the philosopher-lover must learn "that the beauty of the mind is more honourable than the beauty of the outward form" (210b), a glorious achievement that will, in turn, allow him to find true beauty, not only within other people, but also within activities, institutions, and the moral and natural sciences.

If he makes it this far up the rungs of the ladder, Plato promises, then

> he who has been instructed thus far in the things of love, and who has learned to see the beautiful in due order and succession, when he comes toward the end will suddenly perceive a nature of wondrous beauty (and this, Socrates, is the final cause of all our former toils) . . . a beauty absolute, separate, simple, and everlasting, which without diminution and without increase, or any change, is imparted to the ever-growing and perishing beauties of all other things. (210e-211b)

He will see, that is, not only the Forms, but the Form of the Forms. He will see Beauty as it is in itself, a beauty that does not change or grow dim or die. Seeing that Beauty will mark the end of his journey (his *telos*), but the Beauty itself will be revealed to him as the *archē*, the origin or final cause of all his yearning.

As if contemplating that Beauty alongside the philosopher-lover of his myth, Plato, in a great swell of passion, celebrates the ineffable bliss of the initiate who reaches his goal:

> But what if man had eyes to see the true beauty—the divine beauty, I mean, pure and clear and unalloyed, not clogged with the pollutions of mortality and all the colours and vanities of human life—thither looking, and holding converse with the true beauty simple and divine? Remember how in that communion only, beholding beauty with the eye of the mind, he will be enabled to bring forth, not images of beauty, but realities (for he has hold not of an image but of a reality), and bringing forth and nourishing true virtue to become the friend of God and be immortal, if mortal man may. Would that be an ignoble life? (211e-212a)

A noble calling indeed, this life of the philosopher-lover who attains the Beatific Vision: a vision that draws the initiate away from the physical toward the spiritual, away from images toward reality, away from ugliness, ignorance, and decay toward beauty, truth, and the eternal.

And something more. Not only does the initiate come to perceive things he was formerly blind to; he succeeds in mastering a whole new way of perceiving.

Remembering the beginning. That leads us to the *Phaedo*, where Plato makes a vital distinction, as he does in the divided line of *Republic*, between mere opinions (imagination and belief), which are arrived at through information supplied by the bodily senses, and true knowledge (understanding and reason), which can only come via direct spiritual apprehension. In the Platonic economy, as in that of Parmenides, the senses finally deceive, for their raw data comes solely from objects that change and decay. To gain wisdom, therefore, the soul—which is "in the very likeness of the divine, and immortal, and intelligible, and uniform, and indissoluble, and unchangeable"—must ignore all stimuli that originate from the body—which is "in the very likeness of the human, and mortal, and unintelligible, and multiform, and dissoluble, and changeable"—and turn its focus toward those objects and beings that are as divine and immortal as itself (80b).

Of course, as we learned above in the myth of the winged soul, there was a time when our souls did actually commune with the divine Forms; that is why Plato is able to assert in the *Phaedo* what he also asserts in the *Meno*: that all true philosophical teaching is actually a kind of remembering, a recollection of what we formerly knew before our souls "fell" into these bodies of clay. Thus, as in the *Symposium*, we see that in moving forward toward our final spiritual goal (*telos*), we are simultaneously moving backward toward our equally spiritual beginning (*archē*).

The practice, then, of philosophy includes not only the performance of the right kind of actions but also the thinking of the right kind of thoughts. The gradual freeing of oneself from the control of the flesh is more than just an ascetic form of discipline; it is a way of cleansing what William Blake called "the doors of perception."[5] To study only those physical objects that tickle our senses, to learn only from their

---

[5]*Blake's Poetry and Designs*, ed. Mary Lynn Johnson and John E. Grant (New York: Norton, 1979), 93.

shifting, finally illusory forms, is to limit our vision, to ensure that it will never rise beyond this earth.

Thus it is that if we train and free our perceptions to soar above this worldly dance of shadows, then, when the time comes for our soul to leave its corporeal shell, it will follow its liberated perceptions forward (and backward) to the World of Being. But the soul,

> which has been polluted, and is impure at the time of her departure, and is the companion and servant of the body always, and is in love with and fascinated by the body and by the desires and pleasures of the body, until she is led to believe that the truth only exists in a bodily form, which a man may touch and see and taste and use for the purposes of his lusts—the soul, I mean, accustomed to hate and fear and avoid the intellectual principle, which to the bodily eye is dark and invisible, and can be attained only by philosophy—do you suppose that such a soul as this will depart pure and unalloyed? (81b)

Plato's answer of course is no. Such a soul, like the winged soul of *Phaedrus* whose feathers are twisted and torn by the recalcitrance of the fiery horse and the heavy pull of the earth, will be dragged downward.

Yes, dragged downward as in *Phaedrus*, but not immediately into another body. In what I have always considered to be a particularly fine specimen of philosophical-etiological mythmaking, Plato, in his *Phaedo* myth, makes a fascinating suggestion as to what happens to these heavy souls that are pulled earthward by the force of the corporeal and mundane:

> And this [the corporeal], may be conceived to be that heavy, weighty, earthy element of sight by which such a soul is depressed and dragged down again into the visible world, because she [the soul] is afraid of the invisible and of the world below—prowling about tombs and sepulchres, in the neighborhood of which, as they tell us, are seen certain ghostly apparitions of souls which have not departed pure, but are cloyed with sight and therefore visible. (81c-d)

Plato's point here is a strong one. Why would a soul that has never desired to lift its vision toward higher things, that has lived its life bathed in a continual flood of physical sensations, possess any desire

to ascend to the invisible world above? Surely it will cling on tenaciously to the only reality it has ever known or seen. And since that
reality is, by nature, "heavy, weighty, [and] earthy," the soul cannot
help but be dragged downward.

But Plato's allegory does not stop here. Of these "heavy" souls, Plato
goes on to say, "They continue to wander until the desire which haunts
them is satisfied and they are imprisoned in another body" (81e). And
that body, Plato argues, will be one in keeping with the nature of the
soul. If the soul is gluttonous and selfish, it will take on the shape of a
donkey; if lawless and violent, it will return in the form of a hawk or a
wolf. And so on.

How different is the fate of him who follows the philosophical road
of freedom:

> The lovers of knowledge are conscious that their souls, when philosophy
> receives them, are simply fastened and glued to their bodies: the soul is only
> able to view existence through the bars of a prison, and not in her own
> nature; she is wallowing in the mire of all ignorance; and philosophy, seeing
> the terrible nature of her confinement, and that the captive through desire
> is led to conspire in her own captivity . . . shows her that this is visible and
> tangible, but that what she sees in her own nature is intellectual and in-
> visible. (82e-83b)

Again, we have here the Platonic insistence that the philosopher not
only acts but also sees differently from the average man. Freedom is,
in part, the gift of a perceptual change that liberates the soul from its
reliance on and its enslavement to the bodily senses. That is to say, the
will of the philosopher—his choices, his motivations, his desires—is
not controlled by the endless fluctuation of physical sensations that so
defines our life on earth.

"Each pleasure and pain," asserts Plato, "is a sort of nail which nails
and rivets the soul to the body, and engrosses her and makes her believe that to be true which the body affirms to be true" (83d). This
statement should not be confused with Stoicism. Plato is not speaking
here of a monastic withdrawal from life, but of a need on the part of
the philosopher to gain a heightened perspective on his own existence

as a physical/spiritual being. He must not allow himself to become a slave of his bodily impulses, but must, instead, enslave his impulses to the control of his soul. Only then will his soul be able to rise above sense-based opinion, which ultimately deceives, to that higher knowledge that cannot be seen, but only known. Whatever shifts the focus of the philosopher from the corporeal to the spiritual, whatever guides and inspires him to privilege thought over sensation, knowledge over opinion, understanding over imagination, reason over belief is considered good and useful in training the soul to free itself from its chains and ascend the rising path.

This is the program Plato lays out, logically and systematically, in his *Republic*, and then incarnates, imaginatively and aesthetically, in his myths. The former speaks to the mind, but it is the latter that has kept Plato's program alive in the hearts and souls of countless generations.

LAWS

IN BOOK FIVE of *Republic*, Socrates makes it clear that the city he is building is an imaginary one, meant to serve as a model for an ideally just state rather than as a blueprint for a real one:

> We are enquiring into the nature of absolute justice and into the character of the perfectly just, and into injustice and the perfectly unjust, that we might have an ideal. We were to look at these in order that we might judge of our own happiness and unhappiness according to the standard which they exhibited and the degree in which we resembled them, but not with any view of showing that they could exist in fact. (472c-d)

The same, however, cannot be said for the greatest of Plato's later dialogues, *Laws*. In this dialogue, the only one, apart from *Republic*, to be long enough to break into separate books, Plato constructs a second city that one might imagine living in. As the title of the dialogue suggests, Plato grounds his second attempt at city-building not on a corps of specially educated philosopher-kings but on a system of laws: not *rex lex* (where the king is the law) but *lex rex* (where the law is the king).

This shift from the ideal to the real, the theoretical to the practical, was likely motivated by Plato's failed attempt to mold an actual philosopher-king out of the spoiled and self-indulgent son of the tyrant of Syracuse: an experiment that would fail again in the days of the early Roman Empire, when the Stoic philosopher Seneca, who tutored Nero, would prove equally unable to stem the excesses of the narcissistic emperor.[1] In the case of Plato, the recalcitrant student was named Dionysus II, son of Dionysus I, a ruthless politician who seized control of Syracuse, Sicily, about 400 BC but who matured into a patron of the arts and competed himself in Athens in the categories of poetry and tragedy. Impressed by the culture of Athens, Dionysus I personally invited Plato to sail to Sicily. The philosopher did so in 388, but Plato—who, like Socrates, was more Spartan than Athenian when it came to the pleasures of the flesh—never cared for the hedonistic ways of the Sicilians, complaining that they were a people who overate twice a day and never slept alone (326c).

But his visit to Sicily did not prove a total failure, for, during his time there, Plato became close friends with the brother-in-law of Dionysus I, Dion, an intelligent young man of high moral character who heartily agreed with Plato's political theories. Accordingly, when Dionysus I died in 367 and was succeeded by his son Dionysus II, Dion, who was likely familiar with the theories laid forth in *Republic*, urged Plato to return to Syracuse and help train the young Dionysus II in the ways of philosophic rule. Plato was reluctant at first, for he did not believe Sicilian hedonism could breed philosopher-kings; however, in honor of the hospitality that Dion had shown him during his earlier visit (329b), Plato, in true Homeric fashion, agreed to give the venture a try. Though Dionysus II seemed at first to be a willing student, his advisors convinced him that if he allowed himself to be molded by Plato, Dion would have won a victory over him. Giving in to his impulsive side, Dionysus II banished Dion but, for appearance's sake, kept Plato on for some time longer. Plato, realizing that Dionysus II was not willing to be taught, eventually returned home to Athens, only to sail back to Sicily for a third time in 361 in hope of reconciling Dionysus II and Dion. He was again unsuccessful, and in 357, Dion, taking matters into

---

[1]Episode three of the four-part PBS documentary series *Empires: The Roman Empire in the First Century* (2001) does a particularly fine job showing the tragic relationship between Seneca and Nero, which ended with Seneca taking part in a failed assassination plot against Nero that led to his forced suicide.

his own hands, attacked Sicily and seized control of the city. Alas, Dion, though a true student of Plato's theories, proved unable to reform the Syracusan constitution and was murdered in 354.

After the death of Dion, his followers wrote to Plato for advice and received in reply a lengthy letter in which Plato retells in his own words and from his own perspective the entire Sicilian affair, beginning in 388. This letter represents the seventh of thirteen letters purportedly written by Plato. Though the majority of the letters have been dismissed as spurious, most scholars accept the authenticity of *Letter 7*, which is as long as the other twelve letters combined and which provides us with a wealth of autobiographical information. It is from this letter that we learn of Plato's dislike of Sicilian hedonism and his determination to honor his guest-host relationship with Dion. From it we gain as well an incisive psychological portrait of Dionysus II as an egocentric young man who desires to be associated with the wisdom of Plato while refusing to alter his behavior in any way (330b). Dionysus II's "handling" of Plato even leads the philosopher to anticipate Jesus' sage advice that we not cast our pearls before swine lest they trample them underfoot and then turn and rend us to pieces (Mt 7:6). Learning from his failure with Dionysus II, Plato comes to the full realization that Socrates was right when he argued, in his *Apology*, that an honest man cannot be a politician and live: if a wise man "thinks anything amiss with [his] government he will speak out, provided that his words are not going to be wasted or to bring him to his death" (331d).[2]

But the failure in Sicily taught Plato something of even greater importance, something he tried, unsuccessfully, to pass on to the friends of Dion but succeeded in embodying in his *Laws*. Plato attempts to teach the recipients of *Letter 7* the only lasting means for bringing good government to a state: "Sicily, like other states, should be subject

---

[2]As Benjamin Jowett did not translate *Letter 7*, my quotations from this letter are taken from the Penguin Classics edition of *Phaedrus and the Seventh and Eighth Letters*, trans. Walter Hamilton (London: Penguin, 1973). Hamilton's brief but incisive introduction to Letters 7 and 8 (pp. 105-8) recounts the full history of Plato's interactions with Dion and Dionysus II.

not to the tyranny of men but to the rule of law" (334d). Indeed, Plato expresses his certainty

> that if Dion had become master of the state the form which his rule would have taken would have been this. First of all, once he had freed his native Syracuse from the yoke of slavery and washed away her stains and dressed her in the garb of liberty, he would have spared no pains to equip her citizens with a fitting system of law based on the best principles. (335e-336a)

Reflecting back not only on Dion's coup d'état but also on the party strife that tore apart Athens between 404 and 399 BC and culminated in the execution of Socrates, Plato further advises that the only way a polis can move from civil war to a just and stable government is if the victors in the war

> restrain themselves and, having established for the common good a system of law as much to the advantage of the vanquished as of themselves, compel their former foes to be law-abiding by shame and fear—fear, because the winners have shown that they have a superiority of force, and shame, because they are clearly better at controlling their desires and more able as well as more willing to subject themselves to the law. (337a)

Moral Virtues and Aesthetic Taste

I must admit that the first time I sat down to read Plato's *Laws* I expected to be bored by a dull and drawn-out legal treatise. I couldn't have been more wrong. Though there is less drama and less character development in *Laws* than there is in the earlier dialogues, and though the charismatic character of Socrates is replaced by an anonymous Athenian who functions as a simple mouthpiece for Plato, the dialogue is nevertheless sharp, provocative, entertaining, and even playful. The same genius that runs through *Republic* is on display here as well, with the added benefit that the strictures laid down by Plato's Athenian are practical in a way they are not in *Republic*. Would-be philosopher-kings, like Dionysus II, might turn from the path of wisdom, but if the laws are grounded in absolute, eternal principles of justice, then the polis will survive. In *Laws*, the realization of utopia rests less on training moral guardians than on isolating fixed moral standards that can then be instilled in the citizens. Indeed, though the censorship that troubles modern readers of *Republic* reappears in *Laws*, this time around the reasons Plato gives for keeping certain subjects and genres away from the young are both subtler and more justified.

The dialogue, set on the island of Crete, begins immediately, with the unnamed Athenian (whom I shall henceforth refer to as Plato) asking his two friends—a Cretan named Cleinias and a Spartan named Megillus—who it was that gave birth to their law codes. Both men insist that their laws were given not by men but by Zeus (in the case of Crete) and Apollo (in the case of Sparta). Rather than dispute the divine origin of their legal systems, Plato, like Socrates, slowly but deliberately steers the conversation toward the subject of virtue. He does this by first arguing that the worst danger to a state is civil war, and then arguing that the only way to win a civil war is to win the myriad civil wars that go on within the soul of each citizen. But to do that a state needs both good education and fixed laws.

And that leads us, as it inevitably does in Plato's dialogues, to the four classical virtues, which Plato here ranks in descending order of importance as wisdom, self-control, justice, and courage (631c-d). Carrying on a thread that runs from the early dialogues through *Republic*, Plato asserts the essential unity of the virtues, reminding his friends that a mercenary may have courage but if he lacks the other three virtues, he will neither be good nor noble. In fact, though Plato, like his master before him, thought more highly of Spartan timocracy than of Athenian democracy—a predilection that certainly played a factor in the execution of Socrates—he pointedly warns his Spartan friend of the limitations and dangers of putting all the focus of a state on the least of the four virtues, courage.

True, the Spartans train their youth to show courage in the face of pain, but what of courage in the face of pleasure (634a-b)? To achieve the second type of courage, a young man needs to cultivate self-control and guard against the lusts of the flesh. Whereas the Plato of *Symposium* allows for homosexual relationships as a stepping stone toward the love of the Good—though he makes it clear that such relationships are best if they are nonphysical—the Plato of *Laws* unambiguously condemns homosexuality as unnatural: "I think that the pleasure is to be deemed natural which arises out of the intercourse between men and women; but that the intercourse of men with men, or of women with women, is contrary to nature, and that the bold attempt was originally due to unbridled lust" (636c). Anticipating the traditional Christian view of homosexuality as a form of misdirected desire, Plato presents the cardinal virtue of temperance as a balancing act between the twin temptations of pain and pleasure. A city that does not train its youth to properly handle both will destroy itself in the end (636d-e).

Still, though Plato calls on us to bridle our misdirected sexual desires, that does not mean he favors a puritanical approach in the negative sense of that word. In book one, and again in later books, Plato mounts a vigorous defense of the Athenian symposium (or drinking party), a practice that the abstemious Spartans both scorned and rejected. Carefully discerning between the morally justifiable drinking of wine and the vice of drunkenness, Plato explains that young men who participate in supervised symposiums are given the opportunity to learn and practice self-control in a safe environment. A young Spartan whose courage slips in battle is liable to end up dead; a young Athenian who overindulges at a symposium can be sobered up and taught to exert more willpower the next time.

In a powerful metaphor, Plato compares each of us to "a puppet of the Gods," and our various emotions and impulses to "cords and strings, which pull us different and opposite ways" (644d-e). Hidden among these various strings is "the sacred and golden cord of reason" (645a). As long as we allow the golden cord to pull us, we will live virtuous lives of self-control, but if we give free rein to the cords of pleasure and pain, we will become objects of shame and derision. Now, since wine intensifies the pull on our strings, it also intensifies the nature of the choice that we must make. We still say today that someone's true character is revealed in their cups (*in vino veritas*); what Plato adds to this proverbial wisdom is the educational value that comes when someone is allowed to shame himself as a way of building up in him a determination not to repeat the disgrace. "There are times and seasons," explains Plato, "at which we are by nature more than commonly valiant and bold; now we ought to train ourselves on these occasions to be as free from impudence and shamelessness as possible, and to be afraid to say or suffer or do anything that is base" (649c-d). The militaristic Spartans found such a testing ground in war; the Athenian Plato found it in the symposium.

It is not enough, Plato makes clear, merely to learn virtue as an abstract concept; children must be taught as well how to respond to it. A true education teaches students not only how to react to pleasure and pain but also the proper feelings—love or hate, joy or sorrow, pride or shame, euphoria or disgust—that should accompany those reactions. In building up and reinforcing those feelings, the arts, properly regulated, play a vital role. "The young of all creatures," Plato wisely points out, "cannot be quiet in their bodies or in their voices" (653e). Such excess energy needs to be channeled through a carefully chosen curriculum of dance and song. Unlike animals, men are sensitive to rhythm and harmony, and it is the duty of educators to teach students, both literally and metaphorically, how to join the chorus.

POETS AND LAWGIVERS

Still, though Plato's *Laws* places firm restrictions on the arts, poets at least are better treated in this dialogue than in *Republic*. Rather than being banished from the polis, poets are given a vital role to play both in the education of the young and in the mounting of public religious festivals. Part of the reason for this is that whereas poets are set in opposition to philosophers in the earlier dialogue, in the later one, they are measured against lawgivers. In the first comparison, poets come across unfavorably as perverters of the truth who turn the focus of citizens from reality to illusion; in the second, they come across more favorably as practitioners, in a lesser mode, of a similar trade or *technē*.

In an imagined dialogue in book seven of *Laws* between lawgivers and tragedians, whom Plato considered the most serious of the poets, the former explain how similar their techniques and ends are to those of the latter:

> Best of strangers . . . we also according to our ability are tragic poets, and our tragedy is the best and noblest; for our whole state is an imitation of the best and noblest life, which we affirm to be indeed the very truth of tragedy. You are poets and we are poets, both makers of the same strains, rivals and antagonists in the noblest of dramas, which true law can alone perfect, as our hope is. (817b-c)

Both lawgiver and tragic poet are makers who seek to imitate that which is best and noblest in man and society. And they are eager to display their imitations before the eye of the public.

But the very similarity of their goals and methods makes them rivals for the hearts and minds of the people. As such, Plato's imaginary lawgivers proceed to warn the tragedians not to meddle in affairs that are too wonderful for them and that may compromise the stability of the state:

> Do not then suppose that we shall all in a moment allow you to erect your stage in the agora, or introduce the fair voices of your actors, speaking above our own, and permit you to harangue our women and children, and the common people, about our institutions, in language other than our own, and very often the opposite of our own. For a state would be mad which gave you this licence, until the magistrates had determined whether your poetry might be recited, and was fit for publication or not. Wherefore, O ye sons and scions of the softer Muses, first of all show your songs to the magistrates, and let them compare them with our own, and if they are the same or better we will give you a chorus; but if not, then, my friends, we cannot. (817c-d)

The "song" of the lawgiver must be given priority over that of the poet, lest the citizens be led astray by pretty speeches that do not square with the laws of the polis. For Plato, freedom of speech must not be permitted to challenge the institutions of the state or erode the principles instilled in the citizens through the educational system.

In an earlier passage in book four of the *Laws*, Plato offers clearer insight into why the *technē* of lawgiving is to be privileged over that of poetry:

> The poet, according to the tradition which has ever prevailed among us, and is accepted of all men, when he sits down on the tripod of the muse, is not in his right mind; like a fountain, he allows to flow out freely whatever comes in, and his art being imitative, he is often compelled to represent men of opposite dispositions, and thus to contradict himself; neither can he tell whether there is more truth in one thing that he has said than in another. This is not the case in a law; the legislator must give not two rules about the same thing, but one only. (719c-d)

The lawgiver is duty bound to obey the truth and nothing but the truth. Not so the poet, whose craft often demands placing exalted speeches of great beauty and power in the mouths of characters who are unjust or vicious. Furthermore, as Plato argues in *Ion*, when a poet is seized by a fit of inspiration, he is so carried away that he cannot prevent the verses from flowing out of him—even if those verses might be injurious to the state and its citizens. In *Republic*, Plato argues that the man controlled by reason is always to be accorded more honor than the one controlled by passion; here, he adds another dimension to the distinction, arguing that harmony within the state rests on allegiance to reason-based laws rather than passion-based poetry. Apart from the moral touchstone of laws properly framed, the poet is liable to go astray aesthetically.

Accordingly, in book nine, Plato returns once again to the distinction between poets and legislators: "Is it not true that of all the writings to be found in cities, those which relate to laws, when you unfold and read them, ought to be by far the noblest and the best? and should not other writings either agree with them, or if they disagree, be deemed ridiculous?" (858e-859a). We must never forget that the horrors of Nazi Germany, Soviet Russia, and Maoist China were caused not so much by the state's insistence that all citizens conform to the law as by the fact that the law they were forced to conform to was not tied to any fixed standard of justice but shifted with every whim of the dictator. Plato here does not insist that poetry (or citizens)

adhere to arbitrary standards hobbled together by leaders who refuse
to hold themselves accountable to any law above their own egos, but
to noble and elegant precepts shaped in the image of the Good, the
True, and the Beautiful.

This pattern is seen not only in the enactment of laws for the whole
of a society but also in the education of the young, who are not only
being trained to join society as adults but also educated to pursue the
noble virtues. With that in mind, one might be taken aback by Plato's
categorical rejection of homeschooling: "Children shall come not only
if their parents please, but if they do not please; there shall be compulsory education, as the saying is, of all and sundry, as far as this is
possible; and the pupils shall be regarded as belonging to the state
rather than to their parents" (804d). But it must be remembered that
Plato favored compulsory public education because it was an education in virtue that improved the morals of citizens. That is why, just
a few pages after mandating compulsory public education, he lays
down a law that would heap disgrace on the head of a private citizen
who passed by an unruly child and did not discipline him (809a).

Although Plato's utopianism might place him in the camp of the
later social engineers of the French, Russian, and Chinese Revolutions,
he can be distinguished from Robespierre, Lenin, and Mao by his refusal to abandon fixed, transcendent ethical, philosophical, and aesthetic standards in order to achieve his vision of an ideal state. To the
contrary, he stays faithful to the deposit of wisdom passed down to
him by the wisest of his forefathers, a faithfulness attested to by the
numerous times throughout *Laws* that Plato calls on citizens to honor
their elders in general and their parents in particular. He even man-
dates that "every one shall reverence his elder in word and deed; he
shall respect any one who is twenty years older than himself, whether
male or female, regarding him or her as his father or mother" (879c).

Confirming Original Sin

Despite the distinction just made between Plato and Robespierre,
Lenin, and Mao, it must be admitted that Plato shares a key principle

in common with these revolutionary social engineers: he identifies the problem with man not as sin but as ignorance. That is why Plato crafts his penal system on the basis of remediation and reform rather than punishment, assigning the death penalty only to prisoners who are deemed incurable and thus in need of being purged from the state. "As to the actions of those who do evil, but whose evil is curable," writes Plato in *Laws* 5, "in the first place, let us remember that the unjust man is not unjust of his own free will. . . . The unrighteous and vicious are always to be pitied in any case; and one can afford to forgive as well as pity him who is curable. . . . But upon him who is incapable of reformation and wholly evil, the vials of our wrath should be poured out" (731c-d).

As I suggested earlier, both Socrates and Plato taught that no one is voluntarily evil. This teaching likely influenced Rousseau's rejection of original sin in favor of an "optimistic" faith in the natural goodness of man,[3] a rejection that itself played a central role in the French, Russian, and Chinese Revolutions, with their goal of perfecting man through the extermination of its "irredeemable" elements and the reeducation of those less enlightened but capable of reform. In that sense, Plato has much to answer for.

Still, though Plato's failure to discern the source of evil as man's misuse of free will arguably opened a Pandora's box, a close reading of scattered passages in *Laws* reveals that he was not wholly unaware of man's inherently sinful nature. In a discussion of voluntary, premeditated crimes, Plato asserts that the

> greatest cause of them is lust, which gets the mastery of the soul maddened by desire; and this is most commonly found to exist where the passion reigns which is strongest and most prevalent among the mass of mankind: I mean where the power of wealth breeds endless desires of never-to-be-satisfied acquisition, originating in natural disposition, and a miserable want of education. (870a)

---

[3]Although Rousseau famously began his *The Social Contract* (1762) by proclaiming that man was born free but was everywhere in chains, it was in his earlier *Discourse on the Origin and Basis of Inequality Among Men* (1754) that he propagated a false image of primitive man as innocent and noble until he was corrupted by social, political, and economic forces.

Note here that Plato places the blame on both "natural disposition" and lack of education: a mixture of the biblical teaching of original sin (or total depravity) and the Rousseauian belief that man is by nature good but corrupted by society. Indeed, Plato's word for "lust" comes quite close to the Bible's identification of *cupiditas* (cupidity, avarice, love of money) as the root of all evil (1 Tim 6:10).

In the ultimately practical and traditional way that he constructs his laws, Plato seems to understand that people are not angels and that legal safeguards are thus necessary to rein in our depravity (853c). Thus, in book four, while conjuring up, as he had in *Gorgias*, the golden age of Cronus (the Greco-Roman equivalent to the Garden of Eden, when man lived in harmony with nature and the gods), Plato comments that Cronus appointed not people but demigods to rule since he knew "that no human nature invested with supreme power is able to order human affairs and not overflow with insolence and wrong" (713c). Later, in book five, the same Plato who denies that we can commit evil voluntarily rages with true Dantean passion against wrongdoers who blame others for their misdeeds:

> When a man thinks that others are to be blamed, and not himself, for the errors which he has committed from time to time, and the many and great evils which befell him in consequence, and is always fancying himself to be exempt and innocent, he is under the idea that he is honouring his soul; whereas the very reverse is the fact, for he is really injuring her. (727b-c)

We are, it seems, inherently prone to self-deception in regard to our propensity to evil, a propensity that quickly rises to the surface when power is placed in our hands. These insights, which accord better with original sin than natural goodness, are heightened by Plato's identification of narcissism as the root cause of sin: "The excessive love of self is in reality the source to each man of all offences; for the lover is blinded about the beloved, so that he judges wrongly of the just, the good, and the honourable, and thinks that he ought always to prefer himself to the truth" (731e-732a). What underlies this passage, as well as those quoted in the previous two paragraphs, is an ethos that judges human behavior not against a shifting, man-made standard but against a fixed, divine one.

Though Plato is one of the founders of Western humanism, he makes it clear in book four that he does not approve of Protagoras's famous claim that "man is the measure of all things,"[4] a claim that became one of the rallying cries of Renaissance humanism. Such a notion, when taken to its extreme and not balanced by reverence for God and the natural law, can lead to social chaos and personal misery:

> What life is agreeable to God, and becoming in his followers? One only, expressed once for all in the old saying that "like agrees with like, with measure measure," but things which have no measure agree neither with themselves nor with the things which have. Now God ought to be to us the measure of all things, and not man, as men commonly say: the words are far more true of him. And he who would be dear to God must, as far as is possible, be like him and such as he is. Wherefore the temperate man is the friend of God, for he is like him; and the intemperate man is unlike him, and different from him, and unjust. (716c-d)

Homer, whose depictions of the Olympian gods as jealous, licentious, and cruel forced Plato (in *Republic*) to reject his beloved *Iliad* and *Odyssey* as unfit reading material for his guardians, could not have made such a statement, since his gods are unable to provide or embody a proper measure for goodness or truth. Apart from the biblical revelation of a holy God, the concept of sin cannot really emerge, for sin is that which violates the nature of a holy God. The great strides that Plato made toward positing a single, good God allowed him, I believe, to make statements like that quoted above.

Indeed, there is a passage in book eight in which Plato seems to grope outward for a Greek equivalent of the Ten Commandments. In the midst of discussing the great difficulty of getting citizens to heed laws regulating proper sexual conduct, Plato exclaims, with some consternation, that convincing citizens to regulate their lusts is a

---

[4]Reginald E. Allen, ed., *Greek Philosophy: Thales to Aristotle* (New York: Free Press, 1966), 18.

> matter of great importance and difficulty, concerning which God should
> legislate, if there were any possibility of obtaining from him an ordinance
> about it. But seeing that divine aid is not to be had, there appears to be a
> need of some bold man who specially honours plainness of speech, and
> will say outright what he thinks best for the city and citizens—ordaining
> what is good and convenient for the whole state amid the corruptions of
> human souls, opposing the mightiest lusts, and having no man his helper
> but himself standing alone and following reason only. (835b-c)

Denied the direct revelation granted to Abraham, Moses, David, and
the prophets, Plato despaired that such a thing was possible in our
broken, shadowy World of Becoming. And yet, Plato implies, if it were
possible to receive such revelation fresh from the hand of God, then
the laws would have a secure basis with the power to compel the obedience of the citizens. In the absence of such a divine word, the next
best strategy is to appoint a lawgiver who, with the measured grace of
a gifted poet, can cut through the roar of the crowd to arrive at legal
standards that square with reason, commonsense, and that Form of
Justice that Plato describes with such beauty and force in *Republic*.

APPEASING THE GODS

The passage just quoted from book eight calls out for a God who can serve
as the final touchstone for the laws. As if answering his own call, Plato
then moves on in book ten to offer one of his most powerfully pre-
Christian discussions of God, the cosmos he created, and our relationship
to him. To my mind, only *Timaeus*, which I shall consider in the next
chapter, reaches greater heights of insight on the nature of the divine.

Interestingly, Plato's jumping-off point for his profound meditation
on God is a restatement of his belief that evil is involuntary:

> No one who in obedience to the laws believed that there were Gods, ever
> intentionally did any unholy act, or uttered any unlawful word; but he who
> did must have supposed one of three things,—either that they did not
> exist,—which is the first possibility, or secondly, that, if they did, they took
> no care of man, or thirdly, that they were easily appeased and turned aside
> from their purpose, by sacrifices and prayers. (885b)

Though Plato seems unable to break away from his (ill-founded) faith that a knowledgeable man will always be a virtuous one, he does recognize that sin ("unholy acts") is linked to some kind of breach in our acceptance and understanding of God. Virtuous behavior rests not only on knowledge but specifically on a proper knowledge of who God is.

Here, Plato equates atheism (the belief that God does not exist) with deism (the belief that even if God exists, he does not involve himself in the everyday workings of the world he created). The God who delivered the law to Moses on the top of Mount Sinai (Ex 20:1-17; Deut 5:1-21)—that very God whom Plato gropes for—is not an absentee landlord, as the deists would have it, but an active, dynamic, personal God who participates in, and even invades, historical time and physical space. For Plato, the existence of such a God not only makes sense philosophically and theologically but is also profoundly practical in the social and political sphere: "It is a matter of no small consequence, in some way or other to prove that there are Gods, and that they are good, and regard justice more than men do. The demonstration of this would be the best and noblest prelude of all our laws" (887b). Notice how subtly Plato weaves together a pragmatic link between civic lawfulness and a respect for God with a more theologically rich definition of God that foreshadows a well-known passage from the New Testament: "But without faith it is impossible to please him: for he that cometh to God must believe that he is, and that he is a rewarder of them that diligently seek him" (Heb 11:6).

As for the third error that Plato exposes—an error more indicative of devotees of superstition than of rationalism and scientism—it must be understood that God is not someone who can be bribed by offerings and other empty rituals that mask an unrepentant heart. Though some might use such a statement to cast aspersions on the God of the Old Testament, who demanded of his people ritual sacrifices to atone for their sins, it must be remembered that the God of Israel expresses even greater anger than Plato toward those who

> draw near me with their mouth,
> and with their lips do honour me,
> but have removed their heart far from me. (Is 29:13)

It is obedience, not sacrifice, that he desires from his people (1 Sam 15:22; see also Ps 51:16-17; Is 1:11-17; Hos 6:6; Mic 6:6-8). Unlike Homer and the tragedians, who suggest again and again in their poetry that the gods can be "bought off" with rich offerings of food, wine, and precious metals—yet another reason why Plato proscribes the poets in *Republic*—both Plato and the Bible make clear that God cannot be fooled by outward displays of piety: "Be not deceived; God is not mocked: for whatsoever a man soweth, that shall he also reap" (Gal 6:7).

Unfortunately, laments Plato, the widely held belief that the gods can be bribed is taught and reinforced by poets and priests alike. And that poses a great danger to the polis, "for when we hear such things said of [the gods] by those who are esteemed to be the best of poets, and orators, and prophets, and priests, and by innumerable others, the thoughts of most of us are not set upon abstaining from unrighteous acts, but upon doing them and atoning for them" (885d-e). Sin now; straighten things out with the Almighty later: that is the message conveyed by those who confuse the belief that the gods can be controlled and manipulated by means of ritual spells and incantations with prayer, which affirms the belief in a sovereign, personal God who desires and heeds the sincere and humble cries of his people. Plato's commitment to ending the corrupting effects of the former lies behind a law he lays down at the end of book ten, forbidding the building and use of public shrines—for such shrines encourage their owners to think that "they can propitiate the God secretly with sacrifices and prayers" (910b).

By the end of *Laws*, Plato comes quite close to a biblical understanding of God as a Being who is intimately involved in the world he made but who cannot be bribed with hollow sacrifices and prayers. And yet, it was in the major dialogue that he wrote before *Laws* that he came closest to delving the fuller nature of the Creator of the cosmos.

TIMAEUS

ALTHOUGH THE VATICAN houses countless art treasures that attest to the church's grand fusion of Greco-Roman humanism and Judeo-Christian revelation, two of those treasures raise that fusion to the heady heights of philosophical, theological, and aesthetic genius. The first are the frescoes that Michelangelo painted on the ceiling of the Sistine Chapel. Along the center of the ceiling, the foundational stories of Genesis 1–9 offer mute witness to the glories of creation and the ravages of the fall, while, surrounding them in a vast circle, the figures of the Hebrew prophets and Greek and Roman sibyls bear testimony to God's coming work of redemption. Though the former seers were inspired by direct contact with the God of the Bible while the latter's cryptic sayings captured only the shadow of the Almighty, both find their ultimate fulfillment in the life, death, and resurrection of Christ.

The second treasure is found not in a church or other sacred site but in the pope's apartments. Here, in the Stanza della Signatura, commonly referred to as the "Raphael Rooms," Raphael created his own monumental frescoes of the marriage between Athens and Jerusalem. On one wall, the viewer is greeted by the *Dispute on the Blessed Sacrament*, a painting that celebrates the triumph of the Mass, the church, and the theological truths embodied in the creed. On the facing wall,

The School of Athens presents us with the great pre-Christian philosophers of Greece and Rome. Connecting them on either side are frescoes that depict the classical and theological virtues and the nine muses who inspire the arts—two things that themselves form a bridge between faith and reason.

At the center of *The School of Athens*, at the top of a short flight of stairs, with noble arches rising above them, stand Plato and Aristotle, the great double doorway through which all of Western philosophy has preceded. Plato, who taught us to train our eyes on the World of Being, points upward with his right index finger. Aristotle, in contrast, who brought philosophy "back to earth," motions downward with the palm of his right hand. In his left, Aristotle holds a book with the word *ethics* inscribed on it, a reference to his *Nicomachean Ethics*, whose pragmatic approach to virtue exerted a profound influence on Aquinas, Dante, and the Catholic Church. Plato's left hand also grasps a book whose inscription identifies it as *Timaeus*. The reason Raphael chose *Timaeus*, rather than *Republic* or *Laws* or *Phaedrus* or *Symposium*, as his representative Platonic dialogue is that for most of the previous millennium, *Timaeus* had been the only extant dialogue available to medieval scholars in the West. Though the ideas and teachings of Plato were conveyed to the Middle Ages through such writers as Aristotle, Cicero, Virgil, Ovid, Augustine, and Boethius, *Timaeus* alone provided philosophers and theologians with a direct link back to Plato.

As unscholarly as it may sound to a post-Enlightenment academy that has sundered reason from revelation, I feel compelled to suggest that it was the intervention of the God of the Bible that arranged that *Timaeus* should be the "chosen" work to represent Plato for the medievals. My reason for making such a bold suggestion is that, of all Plato's dialogues, *Timaeus* comes closest to the Bible in its view of God, creation, and the Beatific Vision. Indeed, though it is highly unlikely that Plato had access to the Hebrew Scriptures, parts of *Timaeus* read like a commentary on Genesis 1. It is because of these remarkable correspondences between *Timaeus* and the Bible, correspondences that were noted again and again by early and medieval Christians, that I have saved my discussion of *Timaeus* to the end—even though it was written between *Republic* and *Laws*.

THE FALL OF ATLANTIS

Not only does *Timaeus* fall, chronologically speaking, between *Republic* and *Laws*, but it also marks a transition from the ideal polis of the former to the more realistic city of the latter, a transition that embodies as well a shift from the fanciful allegories of the middle dialogues to the more sober, lecture-like quality of the late dialogues. It is surely no accident that *Timaeus* begins with a summation of the perfect state discussed in *Republic* and then segues into a myth that purports to be backed by historical truth. I speak of the great myth of Atlantis, an advanced civilization whose fall from virtue led to its destruction by a great wave—a myth that even today, 2,400 years after Plato described it in *Timaeus* (and *Critias*), sends Indiana Jones–like adventurers in search of its final resting place beneath the sea. By placing his lost city of Atlantis in the far distant past, long before the days of the Trojan War, Plato succeeds in making it seem at once more epic than Homer and more real than the city of *Republic*.

In both *Timaeus* and *Critias*, Plato parallels his real myth of Atlantis with an assertion that Athens as well was the site of an ancient civilization. Perhaps reworking Homer's story, recounted in book fifteen of *Iliad*, that Zeus, Poseidon, and Hades divided up the realms of sea, earth, and sky between them, Plato spins a lovely tale of how "in the days of old the gods had the whole earth distributed among them by allotment" (*Critias* 109b). In that blessed dawn, the gods tended to us gently, as good shepherds do their flock, moving our wills directly by guiding our souls in the same way that a pilot, by turning the rudder, guides a ship (109c). Hephaestus and Athena are given Greece as their allotment. There, says Plato with Athenian pride, in a land "naturally adapted for wisdom and virtue . . . they implanted brave children of the soil, and put into their minds the order of government" (109d). Alas, this ancient Edenic state was destroyed by a Noah-like deluge (a similar story is told in *Laws* 3; 677a-b) and later repopulated by people who knew nothing of their glorious past—not, that is, until civilization grew again, affording the necessary leisure for a full "enquiry into antiquity" (110a).

Thus fell the ancient civilization of Athens; however, whereas the fall of this dimly remembered Greek state happened naturally, in accordance with vast climactic cycles, the fall of her rival, Atlantis, was brought about by pride and cupidity. Plato's contrasting of the Athenians and Atlanteans recalls the contrast in Genesis of the line of Seth and the descendants of Cain, those who built the Tower of Babel and, like the Atlanteans, brought down on themselves the wrath of God (Gen 11:1-9). According to *Critias*, the race of Atlantean kings was initiated by a coupling between Poseidon and a mortal woman. Its first king was named Atlas, and he stood as high king over lesser kings—perhaps as Agamemnon holds lordship over the other Mycenaean kings in Homer's epics. As Plato describes it, Atlantis was laid out in a complex series of concentric circles that alternated sea and land. As a naval power, her strength came from the sea (hence the link to Poseidon), and the capital city boasted a highly advanced canal system.

"Such," writes Plato, "was the vast power which [Poseidon] settled in the lost island of Atlantis; and this he afterwards directed against our land" (120d). And with this mention of Atlantis's attack on ancient Athens, Plato moves on to recount the fall of the once mighty city:

> For many generations, as long as the divine nature lasted in them, they were obedient to the laws, and well-affectioned towards the god, whose seed they were; for they possessed true and in every way great spirits, uniting gentleness with wisdom in the various chances of life, and in their intercourse with one another. They despised everything but virtue, caring little for their present state of life, and thinking lightly of the possession of gold and other property, which seemed only a burden to them; neither were they intoxicated by luxury; nor did wealth deprive them of their self-control . . . but when the divine portion began to fade away, and became diluted too often and too much with the mortal admixture, and the human nature got the upper hand, they then, being unable to bear their fortune,

behaved unseemly . . . Zeus, the god of gods, who rules according to law, and is able to see into such things, perceiving that an honourable race was in a woeful plight, and wanting to inflict punishment on them, that they might be chastened and improve, collected all the gods into their most holy habitation, which, being placed in the centre of the world, beholds all created things. (120e-121c)

Here the text of *Critias* breaks off abruptly. Though no one can say for sure why Plato left the dialogue unfinished, I think it reasonable to suggest that just as *Timaeus* serves as a bridge between *Republic* and *Laws*, so *Critias* serves as a kind of causeway between *Timaeus* and *Laws*. Having chosen, in *Critias*, to elaborate on the Atlantis myth from *Timaeus*, Plato reached a point where he felt that his time would be better spent creating a future, virtuous state (*Laws*) than analyzing the fall of a vicious state set in the historic-mythic past of Homeric epic.

Regardless, the passage that concludes *Critias* forges a link between virtuous behavior and a well-run state that looks backward to *Republic* and forward to *Laws*. As long as the divine spark remains within the Atlanteans, they possess the needed virtue to handle their power and prosperity; scornful of greed, they hold their dominion lightly and put wisdom above wealth. But when their link to the divine is severed, they lose their integrity and balance and virtue gives way to vice, tearing apart the soul and opening the way to the destruction of the state. Haughty and avaricious, like the biblical Nimrod (Gen 10:8-9), the Atlanteans are thrown down, and the proud mark they would have left on the world is covered forever by the waters of a deluge.

A Clash Between East and West

Does Plato mean for us to accept Atlantis as historical fact? Probably not, though I think it highly likely that Plato modeled Atlantis on a real civilization whose power was also based on trade and who possessed an intricate system of canals. According to *Timaeus*, the story of Atlantis was passed down to Solon by Egyptian priests, who told him that the city had reached its height nine thousand years earlier

(23e). On the one hand, the use of such a large figure may indicate Plato's desire to assert that the civilization of Atlantis, and therefore Athens, predated those of Egypt and Babylon. On the other, if we interpret nine thousand as an exaggeration of nine hundred and then count backward from the year 600 (about the time Solon seized the reins of power in Athens), then we end up with a date of 1500, just the time when the seafaring, highly advanced Minoan civilization of Crete was at its height of glory, before the cataclysmic eruption of the volcano at Thera—one of the worst natural disasters in recorded history—and the massive tsunamis resulting from it led to its downfall as the major economic, political, and cultural center of the Mediterranean world. It was in the wake of the fall of Crete—whose founding king, Minos, was born of Zeus and a mortal woman named Europa—that the Peloponnesian city-states of the Mycenaean Bronze Age rose to power and, when they reached their heyday, sent their famed expedition against Troy.

Furthermore, if we remember that Theseus, the legendary king of Athens, was reputed to have slain the monstrous Minotaur of Crete, to whom King Minos had been feeding the youths and maidens of Athens, it makes sense that the rivalry Plato posits between Atlantis and Athens is meant to refer, in part, to the legendary rivalry between Crete and Athens. Given that Crete, then and now, possesses a culture distinct from that of the Greek mainland, one that is as much African or near Eastern as it is European, it becomes possible to read the rivalry of Atlantis/Crete and Athens as a cultural war between West and East— one that reflects both the legendary conflict between Greece and Troy and the historical war between Greece and Persia. In that sense, Plato writes in the tradition not only of Homer but also of Herodotus, whose epic history of the Persian Wars is presented in terms of a clash of civilizations between the virtuous, freedom-loving Greeks and the proud, slavish-minded Persians.[1]

---

[1]Herodotus establishes the dichotomy between the sober, individualistic West and the ostentatious, flattering East in the story he tells of the meeting between the Athenian sage Solon and the Lydian tyrant Croesus in book 1, chapters 30–33 of his *Histories* (440 BC).

Of course, it must be admitted that the reason the civilization is called Atlantis is because, so Plato tells us, it rested on a gigantic island out in the Atlantic Ocean, beyond the Strait of Gibraltar (what the ancient Greeks referred to as the Pillars of Hercules). Indeed, we are told that the destruction of Atlantis so muddied the ocean that sailors can no longer navigate the waters outside of the strait (25d). Thus it is that modern explorers have expanded their search for Atlantis to the New World; some have even claimed that a great ridge that runs along the bottom of the Atlantic seaboard was once an ancient land bridge between Europe and the Americas. Still, it is no great matter, mythically speaking, to read the mysterious Atlantic Ocean as a stand-in for the Mediterranean, especially if we recall that the legendary founder of Atlantis was Atlas, and that the Atlas Mountains of North Africa stand face-to-face with Europe's Rock of Gibraltar—yet another image of West (Europe) versus East (Africa/Asia). Let us keep in mind as well that the Sicily of Dionysus II (Plato's failed philosopher-king) was a naval power whose relationship to Italy proper is analogous to the relationship between Crete and mainland Greece.

CREATION AND COSMOS

As a marathon runner might warm himself up on the day before his race with a five-mile jaunt through the countryside, so Plato follows his leisurely telling of a nine-thousand-year-old story with a grand philosophical-theological-cosmological leap back to the very beginning of time. The myth of Atlantis, after all, though it helps us to understand the rise and fall of great civilizations, tells us nothing about how we and our earthly home first sprang into being. True, in the myth of *Protagoras* (320d-322d), Plato tells how all living beings were formed out of earth and fire, and how Epimetheus, the foolish brother of Prometheus, gave away each available *technē* to the animals leaving Prometheus with only two to give to man—the twin gifts of reverence and justice, by which men are enabled to live together in cities and engage in politics—but this tale, lovely as it is, does not reach back far enough to describe the process by which, and the telos for which, we and our universe were created. This greatest of all tales would be left for the creation myth of *Timaeus*—which looks backward to the formation of our souls with the same intensity that the myths of *Republic*, *Gorgias*, and *Phaedo* look forward to the judgment of our souls.

According to the Presocratic physicists, all that we see around us, including ourselves, evolved out of a perpetual war among the four elements; according to the poet Hesiod, it was the struggles between warring gods, rather than warring elements, that set in motion the cosmic story of which we are a part.[2] In *Timaeus*, it is neither mechanical forces nor jealous deities who shaped the backdrop against which we act out our small but meaningful lives. It was God, not an impersonal divine mind or a pantheistic force spread out across the universe, but a personal deity to whom Plato, shockingly, gives the titles of Father (37c) and Creator.

Plato presents his creative, paternal God as a divine craftsman (or Demiurge) who fashioned the world in accordance with a preexisting model. Rather than argue deductively (a priori) from the cause (Demiurge) down to the effect (our actual world), Plato argues inductively (a posteriori) from the observed physical and moral complexity of our world to the only cause capable of producing such intricate order and purpose. To realize just how revolutionary Plato's creation myth is, we must recall that, aside from Genesis ("in the beginning, God"), *Timaeus* is the only ancient book to posit a Creator who *predates* matter. Even in Hesiod's *Theogony*, the gods, including the original gods of Earth and Sky (Gaia and Ouranos), evolve out of primal matter, what the Greeks called chaos.[3] The same goes for Babylonian, Egyptian, and Norse creation myths. Though Plato does not specifically say that his Demiurge created the world out of nothing (*ex nihilo*), the *Timaeus* is the only book to come within a thousand miles of this central biblical claim, one that is most clearly expressed in a verse from the New Testament: "Through faith we understand that the worlds were framed by the word of God, so that things which are seen were not made of

---

[2]Hesiod, *Theogony*, in *Hesiod and Theognis*, trans. Dorothea Wender (London: Penguin, 1973).
[3]Hesiod, *Theogony*, 27.

things which do appear" (Heb 11:3). Aristotle, following Plato, taught that matter and spirit are coeternal, but in this the pupil was less radical than the master. For Plato is the only non-Jewish ancient writer to suggest, if not clearly state, that God is the absolute origin of *all* things, whether physical or spiritual, temporal or eternal.

As noted a moment ago, Plato's *Timaeus* teaches not only that the Demiurge crafted the world but also that he fashioned it in accordance with a preexisting model. Given the goodness of the Creator and the beauty of our world, Plato theorizes that that model (or pattern) must be both perfect and unchanging. Our world, he concludes, "has been framed in the likeness of that which is apprehended by reason and mind and is unchangeable, and must therefore of necessity, if this is admitted, be a copy of something" (29a-b). Remarkably, if Hebrews 11 attests to the doctrine of creation *ex nihilo*, then Hebrews 8 supports Plato's teaching that the things of our world are copies (or imitations) of a higher, more perfect model that cannot be perceived by eyes and ears of flesh. The author of Hebrews makes it clear that the earthly temple in which the priests serve is but a "shadow of heavenly things," a shadow that was built in imitation of the "pattern" (Heb 8:5) shown to Moses on Mount Sinai (see also Heb 9:23-24). According to the epistle, the temple in Jerusalem, with all its dense symbolism, represents an earthly copy of the eternal throne room of God.

But Plato makes a claim in *Timaeus* that is even more striking when viewed in the context of the New Testament. In *Republic*, *Symposium*, and *Phaedrus*, Plato moves beyond identifying a Form behind every object and concept on earth; he yearns, and encourages his philosopher-kings to yearn, to soar past the individual Forms to apprehend the Form of the Forms: the Good. So here, Plato identifies the model against which the Demiurge shaped creation as something more than the algebraic sum of all the Forms. The pattern for creation is nothing less than a visible living being that contains within itself all other living things: "For the original of the universe contains in itself all intelligible beings, just as this world comprehends us and all other visible creatures. For the Deity, intending to make this world like the fairest and

most perfect of intelligible beings, framed one visible animal comprehending within itself all other animals of a kindred nature" (30e).
Plato's claim is an odd one indeed, and yet, we are told in John's Gospel
that "all things were made by him [Christ, the Logos or Word]; and
without him was not any thing made that was made" (Jn 1:3). We are
further told by the apostle Paul that this same Christ "is before all
things, and by him all things consist. And he is the head of the body,
the church: who is the beginning [*archē*], the firstborn from the dead;
that in all things he might have the preeminence" (Col 1:17-18). As the
second person of the Trinity, Christ is not only the Son of the Father
but also the one through whom God's glory is revealed and made
manifest in the physical realm. Jesus' claim (Jn 14:6) that he is the way,
the truth, and the life asserts that the path to God is not through things
but a divine person, that Truth is not an "it" but a "he," and that true
life is not accumulated one breath at a time but is attained through
participation in the divine nature. Of these powerful Christian
teachings we catch an intriguing glimpse in Plato's wonderful suggestion that our world and our persons were modeled after "one visible
animal comprehending within itself all other animals of a
kindred nature."

But what exactly, the reader may ask, do I mean by this claim that
Plato caught a glimpse of Christian truths to come? To be clear, what
I am *not* saying is that John or Paul or the author of Hebrews was influenced by Plato to write the things that they wrote. I believe that the
biblical authors wrote what they wrote because the truth was revealed
to them by God. Now, the actual words that they used (*archē*, *logos*)
may reflect an indirect Platonic influence—for when most Christians
say that Paul was inspired by God, they do not mean he was a secretary
taking dictation from God but that he was guided by the Spirit to write
true things without having his personality overridden or obliterated
in the process—but the truths embodied in the Greek words used by
the biblical authors came directly from the God who created the universe. When I highlight a connection between, say, *Timaeus* and
Hebrews, I am not suggesting that the former influenced the latter but

that the similarity between the two suggests, to those who accept the direct inspiration of the Bible, that Plato, working through general rather than special revelation, came close to discovering truths that would not be revealed in full until four hundred years after his death.

It was, I believe, God's plan, and God's grace, to use the writings of Plato to prepare the Greco-Roman world for that greater revelation to come, so that when it came, they would *recognize* it as the fulfillment of what they had already learned from Plato. Such is the thesis of the sermon that Paul preached to the Stoic and Epicurean philosophers at the Areopagus in Athens: "Whom therefore ye ignorantly worship, him declare I unto you" (Acts 17:23).

Acts of love. With those caveats in mind, let us return to another passage in the creation myth of *Timaeus* that not only is unique in the ancient world but also foreshadows the later revelation of Christ and the New Testament:

> Let me tell you then why the creator made this world of generation. He was good, and the good can never have any jealousy of anything. And being free from jealousy, he desired that all things should be as like himself as they could be. This is in the truest sense the origin of creation and of the world, as we shall do well in believing on the testimony of wise men: God desired that all things should be good and nothing bad, so far as this was attainable. (29d-30a)

Though *Timaeus* is the only Platonic dialogue that presents God in such personal terms, and though even the God of *Timaeus* seems almost impersonal when compared to the God of the Bible, the fact remains that Plato presents us here with a God who does more than exist and set the cosmos in motion. The decidedly nondeistic God depicted in the above passage is one who is good himself and who has the will and the means to spread that goodness, a God who plans and then puts those plans into being. Most wonderful of all, he is a God who, like the God of the Bible, does not envy his creation, but desires to bless it.

Granted, there are some today who would dispute the claim that the God of the Old Testament is a God who does not envy or play favorites.

Indeed, it has become fashionable in the popular mind to dismiss Yahweh as a selfish, parochial, tribal deity who cares only about Israel. But this claim is belied by the commission that God gives to Abraham:

> Now the LORD had said unto Abram, Get thee out of thy country, and from thy kindred, and from thy father's house, unto a land that I will shew thee: And I will make of thee a great nation, and I will bless thee, and make thy name great; and thou shalt be a blessing: And I will bless them that bless thee, and curse him that curseth thee: and in thee shall all families of the earth be blessed. (Gen 12:1-3)

From the very beginning, God makes it clear that he intends not only to bless Israel but also to use Israel as a conduit through which he will bless all nations. This vital aspect of God's calling—that he will bless Israel *so that* she may bless "all families of the earth"—is also included in the commissioning of Abraham's son Isaac (Gen 26:4) and his grandson Jacob (Gen 28:14). Furthermore, when Peter (Acts 3:25) and Paul (Gal 3:8) proclaim the universal nature of the gospel, they present that universality as a fulfillment of God's original promise to Abraham to bless all nations through him. I mention this not only to counter the supposed tribal deity of the Old Testament but also to reiterate the point made above—that the links between Plato and the New Testament are not the result of Peter, John, or Paul quoting Plato, but of Plato having glimpsed a prophetic truth about the nature of God.

God's love for all is shown in his desire to bless all nations, but it is first shown in the act of creation. In Christianity, the act of creation is an act of love, for, in creating the world, God, who is complete and perfect in himself, chose to move out of himself. Unlike the petty, selfish, narcissistic gods of Homer and Hesiod, whom Plato rejects so strongly in *Republic* and *Laws*, the God of the Bible (and of *Timaeus*) yearns to shower goodness on his world and his creatures. In that sense, the incarnation is the greatest of all acts of love, for, through it, God moved out of Plato's World of Being to become a flesh-and-blood man in Plato's World of Becoming. That degree of divine love is beyond the comprehension even of the author of *Timaeus*, and yet, Plato's depiction of God makes such an unfathomable act of love seem almost fathomable. Where else in the non-Jewish world is it even suggested that God does not envy his creation, that he desires to bless and not to destroy, that he wills that we should bear his image?

Starting slowly in the later second century and then picking up speed in the third and fourth, the early church was plagued by a number of Gnostic, Neoplatonic groups that claimed that our world was the aborted creation of a lesser deity and that, as a result, flesh and matter were inherently evil. Early on in his life, Augustine himself was a member of such a group (the Manichaeans); only his conversion to Christianity allowed him to see the flesh as something good and redeemable, though capable of being used for evil purposes (see *Confessions* 7 and chapter ten, below). Granted, the Gnostics *were* influenced by Plato's distinction between the Worlds of Being and Becoming as well as by his tendency to privilege the former as real and downgrade the latter as irredeemable, but their belief that the creation of the material world was itself a fall into corruption is something that does not appear in Plato. Indeed, in *Timaeus*, Plato makes it clear that our world was created by a good God for good purposes and that it was patterned after a model of perfection. Besides, the Bible itself consistently presents heaven as more real and full and perfect than earth, though it also holds out a final promise that transcends Plato's vision: a promise that the earth will be redeemed and transformed into heaven, even as our physical bodies will be transformed into glorious resurrection bodies like the one that even now clothes the risen Christ.

Rightly ordered love. Like Pythagoras before him, Plato believed that he lived in an ordered cosmos. Actually, if truth be told, the phrase "ordered cosmos" is a redundancy. Plato, like Pythagoras, used the word *cosmos* to refer to the universe around us because the word in Greek means order, balance, beauty, and harmony. The heavens are cosmos because they are the ornament, the cosmetic, of the Creator who fashioned it, so *Timaeus* tells us, in accordance with a preexisting model. Within the cosmos there is neither waste nor redundancy: "In order then that the world might be solitary, like the perfect animal [the preexisting model], the creator made not two worlds or an infinite number of

them; but there is and ever will be one only-begotten and created heaven"
(31b). Our world, Plato asserts, is the only world there is, not because
God is a "narrow-minded" Creator, but because he is an economical one.
When God created the cosmos, he quite literally used up all available
matter—that is, all the earth, air, fire, and water that the Presocratics had
posited as the physical building blocks of the universe.

There is, in God's creation, a sort of divine efficiency—he made all
that he could with all that he had. And one of the things that he made
was time itself:

> When the father creator saw the [universe] which he had made moving and
> living, the created image of the eternal gods, he rejoiced, and in his joy
> determined to make the copy still more like the original; and as this was
> eternal, he sought to make the universe eternal, so far as might be. Now the
> nature of the ideal being was everlasting, but to bestow this attribute in its
> fulness upon a creature was impossible. Wherefore he resolved to have a
> moving image of eternity, and when he set in order the heaven, he made
> this image eternal but moving according to number, while eternity itself
> rests in unity; and this image we call time. For there were no days and
> nights and months and years before the heaven was created, but when he
> constructed the heaven he created them also. (37c-e)

As the World of Becoming is an imitation of the World of Being, so
time is an imitation of eternity—not a corrupt or illusory imitation,
but an attempt on the part of the Creator to allow the physical world
to participate, in a lesser manner, in the eternal. Again, the later
Gnostic notion that we and our world fell, not into sin, but into physicality, strongly departs from Plato's *Timaeus*, which presents God as
taking joy in his creation, as God, in Genesis 1, declares his creation
good. Indeed, Plato must mean time to be a good thing, for he links it
very closely to number—and, in the dialogues (especially *Republic*),
math is hailed as the second highest intellectual pursuit, directly under
philosophy, for it is concerned with the Form or Idea of the Right
Triangle, not its earthly approximation.

Time, then, is the natural and proper condition of our world, but
we must be careful not to project our experience of time onto God.

Thus Plato continues his discussion of "days and nights and months and years" by contrasting them with their heavenly Creator:

> They are all parts of time, and the past and future are created species of time, which we unconsciously but wrongly transfer to the eternal essence; for we say that he "was," he "is," he "will be," but the truth is that "is" alone is properly attributed to him, and that "was" and "will be" only to be spoken of becoming in time, for they are motions, but that which is immovably the same cannot become older or younger by time, nor ever did or has become, or hereafter will be, older or younger, nor is subject at all to any of those states which affect moving and sensible things and of which generation is the cause. These are the forms of time, which imitates eternity and revolves according to a law of number. (37e-38a)

Living as we do on this side of the Bible and Augustine, we are likely to overlook the revolutionary nature of Plato's claim that God dwells in the timeless present of eternity. The gods of Homer and Hesiod may be immortal in the sense that they cannot die, but they are certainly not eternal. They, as we saw above, were born out of the primal matter, so that, whether we ascribe to them a spiritual nature (as did the poets) or a material nature (as did the Presocratics, Stoics, and Epicureans), they still have a beginning and thus live within the flow of time. Only in the Bible and in *Timaeus*—and, perhaps, tentatively in some of the teachings of Pythagoras—do we have a God who simply *is*. Thus Yahweh reveals himself to Moses as I AM WHO I AM (Ex 3:14 NKJV); in fact, the Hebrew word Yahweh is closely linked to the verb "I am."

Furthermore, it is only in the Bible and *Timaeus* that we find expressed in philosophical and theological terms a great truth about our world that modern science has only recently discovered: that our universe had a beginning and that that initiating event, known as the big bang, created, in a single moment, matter, space, and time. Or, to quote *Timaeus*, "Time, then, and the heavens came into being at the same instant in order that, having been created together, if ever there was to be a dissolution of them, they might be dissolved together" (38b).

BETWEEN THE ANGELS AND BEASTS

According to the biblical worldview, God made three living creatures to dwell in his cosmos: angels, who are purely spiritual; beasts, who are purely physical; and human beings, whose bodies draw them downward to the beast but whose souls draw them upward toward the angels. The Christian view of man's dual nature should not be confused with gnostic (Manichaean) dualism, which makes the body into a prison house of the soul. Christian theology defines man as a composite creature, whose body is inherently good, though now fallen, and destined, on the last day, to be redeemed and perfected. Plato's view is more closely represented by Gnosticism than by Christianity; certainly, his belief in reincarnation, which is affirmed in *Timaeus*, militates against an incarnational fusion between body and soul. Still, though Plato's dualism is finally incompatible with the Christian view of man as an enfleshed soul, there are hints in *Timaeus*, and only *Timaeus*, of the biblical trichotomy of angel-man-beast—with man taking the middle position.

Despite the efforts of humanist Christians eager to build bridges between Greco-Roman myths and Judeo-Christian teachings, the Olympian gods of Homer, Hesiod, Virgil, and Ovid—with the exception of Hermes (Mercury), who bears the divine word of Zeus (Jupiter) and whose name is the origin of the word *hermeneutics*—simply cannot be reconciled with the angels of the Bible. There is, however, one set of gods who do bear a striking resemblance to that group of immortal, spiritual beings whom God created at the beginning, in the period before he made man or beasts to live on the earth. Those gods are described in *Timaeus* in a way that sets them apart from all the other gods whose presence so enlivens *Iliad* and *Odyssey*. They consist of two types of gods: (1) the anthropomorphic gods of Hesiod and Homer, though stripped of the scandalous behavior ascribed to them by the poets; (2) the planets, stars, and other heavenly bodies whom Plato describes as "divine and eternal animals, ever-abiding and revolving after the same manner and on the same spot" (40b).

In a majestic passage that borders on epic poetry, Plato allows us to eavesdrop on the divine Father's first words to his newly made spiritual creatures:

> Now, when all of them, both those who visibly appear in their revolutions [the stars] as well as those other gods who are of a more retiring nature [the gods of myth], had come into being, the creator of the universe addressed them in these words: "Gods, children of gods, who are my works, and of whom I am the artificer and father, my creations are indissoluble, if so I will. All that is bound may be undone, but only an evil being would wish to undo that which is harmonious and happy. Wherefore, since ye are but creatures, ye are not altogether immortal and indissoluble, but ye shall certainly not be dissolved, nor be liable to the fate of death, having in my will a greater and mightier bond than those with which ye were bound at the time of your birth." (41a-b)

Note that Plato's gods, like the angels of the Bible—who are referred to as "sons of God" (Job 1:6)—do not share in the same absolute eternal existence as the Creator, who alone is the I AM. Their immortal yet still conditional life is bound up in the uncreated, indestructible life of God. Still, Plato makes it clear that the spiritual life of the gods is of a higher order than any other type of life in the cosmos. Though of a lesser intensity than the life of God, their nature is far purer than the animal life that will be shared by beasts and men.

In fact, God's speech goes on to commission the gods to help him shape the life of those very beasts and men whose life will be unto theirs as theirs are unto God:

> And now listen to my instructions:—Three tribes of mortal beings remain to be created—without them the universe will be incomplete, for it will not contain every kind of animal which it ought to contain, if it is to be perfect. On the other hand, if they were created by me and received life at my hands, they would be on an equality with the gods. In order then that they may be mortal, and that this universe may be truly universal, do ye, according to your natures, betake yourselves to the formation of animals, imitating the power which was shown by me in creating you. The part of them worthy of the name immortal, which is called divine and is the guiding principle of those who are willing to follow justice and you—of that divine part I will

myself sow the seed, and having made a beginning, I will hand the work over to you. And do ye then interweave the mortal with the immortal, and make and beget living creatures, and give them food, and make them to grow, and receive them again in death. (41b-d)

From Plato on through the Renaissance, most of the great Western thinkers believed in the principle of plenitude (or fullness). God's cosmos was seen to abound with life, with different creatures inhabiting their proper spheres. Indeed, perfection itself, like justice in *Republic*, rested on a type of completion or wholeness in which each part serves a specific function. The God of *Timaeus* does not call creatures into being lightly or for sport, but because his sense of plenitude demands that all space be filled with its appropriate form of life.

In Genesis, of course, God alone shapes Adam and breathes into him the breath of life (Gen 2:7); however, the God of the Bible does use his angels as mediators in the acting out of his plans for us and our planet. Alike in Christianity and *Timaeus*, God is active in the workings of our world, yet he is willing to delegate power to his creatures. Sovereignty remains with the Creator, but he treats neither angels nor men, who are a little bit lower than the angels (Ps 8:5), as puppets on a string. In his sermon, Stephen accuses his Jewish audience of not having kept the law that they "received . . . by the disposition of angels" (Acts 7:53; see also Gal 3:19). In *Timaeus*, Plato's God assigns to his angels the task of leading men on the road to justice and righteousness. Though the idea of the "guardian angel" is often lampooned in our modern world, there is some biblical basis for it (Ps 34:7; 91:11; Mt 18:10), and, in any case, the Bible makes clear that spiritual warfare is a reality and that our struggles—and, by extension, our succor—"are not against flesh and blood, but against principalities, against powers, against the rulers of the darkness of this world, against spiritual wickedness in high places" (Eph 6:12).

Here is how Plato describes the role of the gods in *Timaeus*: "When he [God] had sown them [human beings] he committed to the younger gods the fashioning of their mortal bodies, and desired them to furnish what was still lacking to the human soul, and having made all the suitable additions, to rule over them, and to pilot the mortal animal in the best and wisest manner which they could, and avert from him all but self-inflicted evils" (42d-e). In Hebrews, a similar role is assigned to the angels: "Are they [angels] not all ministering spirits, sent forth to minister for them who shall be heirs of salvation?" (1:14). In both cases, immortal beings of pure spirit, who, though capable of falling into corruption, rarely do, are assigned to serve creatures who possess both body and soul and for whom the struggle against corruption is intense and ongoing.

MEN AND WOMEN

So much for the angel part of the angel-man-beast trichotomy that is clearly taught in Christianity but that Plato only hints at in *Timaeus*. But what of the other two legs of the triangle? In the long passage quoted above, God gives the following instructions to the gods: "Three tribes of mortal beings remain to be created—without them the universe will be incomplete, for it will not contain every kind of animal which it ought to contain, if it is to be perfect." The fact that God calls on his gods to help him create "three tribes of mortal beings" may at first seem to contradict the biblical trichotomy that I suggested earlier can be discerned, if faintly, in *Timaeus*. But it does not. The three referred to are not men, beasts, and some third species, but human males, human females, and beasts.

Although Plato, in both *Republic* and *Laws*, allows his female guardians to receive the same training as their male counterparts, the overall—and unfortunate—effect of the Platonic dialogues is to assign women a secondary place. Plato's rationale for privileging men over women is identical to his rationale for privileging reason over emotion. For Plato, most women are too strongly tied to their feelings and desires to ascend the rising path of philosophy—an ascent that, in his view, calls for a masculine commitment to pure reason and abstract logic. On account of this masculine-feminine, logic-feeling, reason-emotion dichotomy, Plato places women midway between reason-driven males and appetite-driven beasts. In fact, he explains that a man who gives way to his base desires and forsakes the narrow path of virtuous living would return in the body of a woman, and "if, when in that state of being, he did not desist from evil, he would continually be changed into some brute who resembled him in the evil nature which he had acquired" (42c).

Near the end of *Timaeus*, Plato returns to this image of a descent down the ladder of being from male to female to animal, making it clear this time that men were created first and that "those who were cowards or led unrighteous lives" (90e) were reborn in the next generation as women. In succeeding generations, men and women who were foolish or evil devolved into the irrational animals of land, sea, and air (91d-92c). Note that Plato here agrees with the biblical account of woman being born out of man (Gen 2:21-22); however, whereas the Bible presents Eve as a "helpmeet" to Adam who shares fully in his rational, emotional, and spiritual capacities, Plato sees women as necessarily drawing men away from the philosophical pursuit of truth, virtue, and reason. Still, Plato depicts woman as being far closer to men than to animals, suggesting that the second descent from woman to animal does not happen as a matter of course, but only if the woman completely forsakes her human responsibility to put the appetitive part of her soul under the tutelage and control of the rational.

In any case, as fellow human beings with their male counterparts, women share the same physical form, a form which Plato interprets allegorically:

> And we should consider that God gave the sovereign part of the human soul to be the divinity of each one, being that part which, as we say, dwells at the top of the body, inasmuch as we are a plant not of an earthly but of a heavenly growth, raises us from earth to our kindred who are in heaven. And in this we say truly; for the divine power suspended the head and root of us from that place where the generation of the soul first began, and thus made the whole body upright. When a man is always occupied with the cravings of desire and ambition, and is eagerly striving to satisfy them, all his thoughts must be mortal, and, as far as it is possible

altogether to become such, he must be mortal every whit, because he has
cherished his mortal part. But he who has been earnest in the love of
knowledge and of true wisdom, and has exercised his intellect more than
any other part of him, must have thoughts immortal and divine, if he
attain truth, and in so far as human nature is capable of sharing in immortality, he must altogether be immortal; and since he is ever cherishing
the divine power, and has the divinity within him in perfect order, he will
be perfectly happy. (90)

In *Republic*, Plato forges a link between virtuous-rational-philosophic
behavior and true happiness. Here, he forges a similar link but with
reference, not to politics or morality or aesthetics, but to the form and
purpose of the human body, which was fashioned to hold our soul. As
human beings, male or female, we stand upright, with our head—the
center, for Plato, of both our reason and our soul, as the belly is
the center of our appetite—reaching upward toward the heavens. The
beasts, in contrast, live with their heads close to the ground, a fitting
sign for how their lives are controlled completely by their belly (appetite) and the impulses of their flesh.

In distinguishing between human beings and animals, it is significant that Plato insists that men were created before animals, and not
vice versa as in the biblical account (Gen 1:24-28). By doing so, Plato
posits that we are the pattern for all life on earth, even as the gods
(angels) were the pattern for our own creation—though we, Plato explains, are less purely mixed than the angels and thus subject to dissolution and decay.

Again, Plato does not clearly place man between the angels and the
beasts as Christianity does; however, *Timaeus* does allow for the tripartite soul developed in *Republic* to be read in conjunction with a
struggle between the beast below (appetitive) and the angel above
(rational). Only when aided by the spirited part of the soul can the rational part control the bestial urges of the appetitive part.

This Platonic *psychomachia*, this internal war within the soul to put
down the bestial side of our nature, would exert a profound influence
on early and medieval theologians, giving them a language and

imagery for the struggle that could complement, rather than contradict, the struggle between flesh and spirit that Paul describes in his epistles (e.g., Rom 7:18-25). Indeed, it will be the burden of part two of this book to trace not only that influence but the other and varied influences that Platonic thought exerted on the Christian faith.

PART II

PLATO'S CHRISTIAN LEGACY

THE RISING PATH

I HAVE SOUGHT, in part one of this book, not only to survey, explain, and assess Plato's monumental philosophical legacy in light of some of his best-known works but also to present those teachings in such a way as to appeal to a wide audience of both religious and secular readers. As we turn to part two, I would like to narrow my focus to consider how the teachings of Plato might be received by Christian readers who accept Christ, the Bible, and the creeds of the church (with their focus on the Trinity, incarnation, atonement, and resurrection) as embodying the fullest, most direct form of divine revelation that the world has yet received. Thankfully, in trying to imagine such a thing, I need not press out too far on my own. As we will see in the five chapters that follow this one, many of the greatest Christian thinkers—I will consider specifically Origen, Gregory of Nazianzus, Gregory of Nyssa, Gregory Palamas, Augustine, Boethius, Dante, Erasmus, Descartes, Coleridge, and C. S. Lewis, though a fuller list would include Aquinas, Donne, Milton, Newman, and Chesterton—have been profoundly influenced by Plato and have found little difficulty not only in reconciling the dialogues of Plato to Christianity but also in receiving those dialogues as sources of wisdom that the God of the Bible used to prepare the Greco-Roman world for the coming of Christ.

Such thinkers are generally referred to as Christian humanists—or, to be more accurate, humanist Christians—for they yearn to draw together the confession that Jesus Christ is Lord with the mandate that Socrates and Plato learned from an inscription at the Temple of Delphi: know thyself. They acknowledge the sovereignty of God and the depravity of man while yet believing in the power of human reason and creativity to order human society through the establishment of laws, institutions, and ethical codes and the cultivation of the arts and sciences.

Before considering Plato's influence on the eleven thinkers listed above, I would like first to explore, from a humanist Christian perspective, whether Plato's ethical system, with its body-soul dualism and its belief, at least mythically, in reincarnation, can be reconciled with a Christian view of God, the soul, and salvation. Or to put it another way, I would like to explore to what extent Plato's humanistic faith in the ability of man to ascend toward truth can be integrated into a Christian system that posits man as irredeemably fallen and defines salvation as justification by grace through faith.

Preparing the Road

At the heart of the Platonic-minded, humanist-Christian psyche lies the image of the path, of the golden steps that lead the initiate out of this world of illusion and error into a higher realm of light and truth. A rising path that is also an ex-odus, a road out, a movement from slavery to freedom, ignorance to knowledge, darkness to light, the shadows on the cave wall to the piercing and revealing rays of the sun. The path marks the abandonment of brute animal instinct—what Tennyson (*In Memoriam* 118.28) called the "ape and tiger" but what many moderns embrace as "human nature"—in favor of a higher form of desire that leads us upward toward that purposeful end (telos) for which we were created. It is, yes, a kind of evolution, but it is neither the naturalistic evolution of Darwinism, nor the materialistic evolution of Freudianism, nor the socioeconomic evolution of Marxism. That is to say, it is eschatological without being deterministic. For the path has both an individual and historical telos toward which it is moving, and that telos is good, meaningful, and personal; but the varied steps along the path—the errors and triumphs, the dreams and hopes and fears, the acts of angelic altruism, the bestial lust and gluttony, the demonic pride and deceit—those long and weary steps that make up what I like to call the pathway of choice: these are neither imposed from below by an arbitrary, uncaring nature nor imposed from above by an impassive, puppet-master God.

At the very dawn of the Renaissance, Count Giovanni Pico della Mirandola, musing long and hard on the nature of this rising path and of those "chameleon" creatures who spend their brief but meaningful lives ascending or descending its divers steps, composed a famous oration in defense of his humanist Christian view of man: a speech that has come to be known as the "Oration on the Dignity of Man." For Pico, as for all humanist Christians, man lies somewhere between the angel and the beast. He is, in the words of the great humanist Christian writer Thomas Browne, "that amphibious piece betweene a corporall and spirituall essence, that middle forme that links those two together,"[1] a fusion of body and soul that not only is unique from all other creatures but also represents the crowning achievement (and telos) of all creation.

Near the beginning of his oration, Pico, with both Genesis and Plato's *Timaeus* echoing in his ears, imagines the triune Lord speaking these words to the newly created Adam:

> We have given you, Oh Adam, no visage proper to yourself, nor any endowment properly your own, in order that whatever place, whatever form, whatever gifts you may, with premeditation, select, these same you may have and possess through your own judgment and decision. The nature of all other creatures is defined and restricted within laws which We have laid down; you, by contrast, impeded by no such restrictions, may, by your own free will, to whose custody We have assigned you, trace for yourself the lineaments of your own nature. I have placed you at the very center of the

---

[1] Sir Thomas Browne, *Religio Medici*, in *The Major Works*, ed. C. A. Patrides (New York: Penguin, 1977), 103.

world, so that from that vantage point you may with greater ease glance round about you on all that the world contains. We have made you a creature neither of heaven nor of earth, neither mortal nor immortal, in order that you may, as the free and proud shaper of your own being, fashion yourself in the form you may prefer. It will be in your power to descend to the lower, brutish forms of life; you will be able, through your own decision, to rise again to the superior orders whose life is divine.[2]

Man, for Pico, is a creature in progress. Over our heads there hovers a perpetual question mark: What exactly am I? What shall I become? Unlike the beasts and the angels, who are fixed in their respective spheres, we belong fully neither to the earth nor the sky. We are truly amphibians, with a foot in each world, and so in our breasts there is a perpetual struggle, an agon: down or up; lower or higher; fall or rise.

When Milton set out to write a biblical tragedy after the manner of the great Greek playwright Sophocles—a truly humanist Christian goal—he chose to call it *Samson Agonistes*—that is, Samson the wrestler. By doing so, he placed Samson in a distinctly classical category, along with the many wrestlers that people Sophocles's tragedies: Oedipus and Antigone, Ajax and Heracles, Electra and Neoptolemus. And yet, at the same time, Milton stayed true to his biblical source, for Samson, as a member of the tribe of Dan, is an heir of him who fathered all the tribes of the Hebrews, he to whom God gave the sacred name by which his people would come to be known. That man is Jacob, and the name he was given is Israel: "he who wrestles [or struggles] with God" (see Gen 32:28). The biblical text offers us no commentary as to the angel's tone of voice when he bestowed this new name on Jacob—did he speak with praise, with scorn, with sarcasm?—but the angel does go on to bless the newly "baptized" Israel, and so we must accept that the name is meant, on at least some level, to be a compliment.

Still, given the subsequent history of the tribes of Israel—that is to say, the sons of Jacob—I would suggest that the name is not so much

---

[2]Giovanni Pico Della Mirandola, *Oration on the Dignity of Man*, trans. A. Robert Caponigri (South Bend, IN: Gateway Editions, 1956), 7-8.

a compliment (or insult) as it is a calling, a prophetic challenge to his chosen race to move and grow and shape itself into the people he desired them to be. Even a cursory reading of the Old Testament will reveal that their agon led them more often down than up, that, in sharp contrast to Antaeus (the giant who gained his strength from contact with his mother, the Earth), their defeat lay in their stubborn, stiff-necked insistence on wrestling themselves into the ground, rather than reaching their arms up to heaven. Nevertheless, their struggle was a real one, and it came to define them as a people, even as our own struggles define each of us as individuals.

"The highest spiritual beings," declares Pico, again fusing biblical revelation with Platonic myth,

> were, from the very moment of creation, or soon thereafter, fixed in the mode of being which would be theirs through measureless eternities. But upon man, at the moment of his creation, God bestowed seeds pregnant with all possibilities, the germs of every form of life. Whichever of these a man shall cultivate, the same will mature and bear fruit in him.[3]

Generally speaking, humanist Christians prefer to think of man and the history of man, not in terms of an iron-clad plan, prearranged down to the smallest detail before the beginning of time, but in terms of eschatological possibilities, visions of what we can be when we open our hearts to God's grace, when we heed the inner desire that drives us upward toward God and combat that other, darker impulse that would drag us earthward.

We are not, Pico argues, the prefabricated products of a predetermined fate—or, I would add, of the modern equivalents of fate: natural selection, the subconscious, and dialectical materialism—but precious, marvelous seeds, rich and fecund, bursting with fruitfulness and a thousand potentialities. True, many of those seeds enter our world weighed down by defects of body, mind, or spirit, but these defects are not mandated from above. They are, rather, byproducts of a "mother" nature that is just as fallen as we are, who, like us, is subjected to the

---

[3]Pico, *Oration on the Dignity of Man*, 8.

entropy and final futility of our world. They are, in short, the earthly counterparts of those divine gifts whose giver is God, and, as such, they are as forceful in dragging us down as the gifts are in drawing us up. Of course, as is the nature of this struggle, the defects, when yielded to God in faith, are as able to draw us upward, as the gifts, when abused and perverted, are able to drag us downward.

And with this tug of war between nature-given defects and God-given gifts we return to the image of the agon, of that lifelong struggle, born of our amphibian makeup, between the better angels and the baser animals of our nature. As "seeds pregnant with all possibilities," we can hardly stand still; we must, and will, either ascend or descend. To descend means to surrender oneself to base instinct, to become brutish, to forsake the twin lights of reason and grace that were ignited in us at our birth. To ascend, on the other hand, means to pursue those heavenly lights, a pursuit that, for Pico, is a form of desire, a panting "after higher things." It is not enough that we study the divine form; we must love it and yearn for it as well. We must become true lovers of wisdom, ardent initiates in the mysteries of philosophy. These ideas, of course, are not unique to Pico; indeed, they characterize the core belief, the very reason for being of the many schools of Neoplatonism, all of which share a common source in the dialogues and myths of Plato.

Let us then return to Plato and see what mark his teachings make on the Christian touchstone of wisdom.

THROUGH A GLASS DARKLY

From the point of view of orthodox Christianity, the essential flaw in the Platonic system is its incessant privileging of the spiritual over the physical. A strict adherence to the cosmic scheme of Plato renders any belief in the incarnation—that Jesus was fully divine and fully human; 100 percent God and 100 percent man—both metaphysically un-desirable and logically impossible. Most people today are aware of the early church heresy known as Arianism, which taught that Jesus was the highest of created beings but was not God the Son (the second person of the Trinity). Less known today, however, was a second heresy,

Docetism, which taught that Jesus was a divine being who only seemed to be human, a spirit who "wore" his body like a person might wear a shirt, but who did not actually become a human being. Docetism, a form of Gnosticism that was strongly influenced by Platonism, simply could not fathom that divinity would allay itself with inherently fallen matter and flesh.

Just as problematic, Plato's conception of God as removed, immutable, and wholly untainted by contact with our shifting corporeal World of Becoming cannot, finally, be reconciled with the biblical revelation of a merciful Savior-God who so loves humanity that he willingly leaves the World of Being, takes upon himself the "prison" of human flesh, and suffers a very physical and bloody death. For a Platonist, the thought that the omnipotent, omniscient, omnipresent God would deign to take on human form would have been nonsensical. And the same goes for the Christian teaching that Christ rose bodily from the dead, the firstfruits of a resurrection that we ourselves will some day share in (1 Cor 15:20). This key biblical teaching (and hope) that in the kingdom of heaven we will wear glorious resurrection bodies would have struck Plato as both absurd and distinctly distasteful. Indeed, when Paul spoke in Athens before the Platonic-minded Stoics and Epicureans, they listened very nicely until he mentioned the resurrection; it was then that most of them sneered and stopped listening (Acts 17:32). Christians today often forget that what the Bible looks forward to is not some insubstantial spirit realm of disembodied souls but a new heaven and a new earth. The body, and physicality in general, will not be done away with, but redeemed and perfected. That is not a prospect that would have pleased Plato.

The gap, I must admit, between the dialogues and the Bible is a profound one, and it may seem, at first, that Plato can be of no ultimate assistance in helping Christians to understand their nature, their purpose, and their place in the universe. But then, we must remember that before the age of Christ and the New Testament, no Jew in his wildest imagination could have conceived of an actual incarnation in which deity would allay itself with flesh. I do not imagine that the messianic prophecies that fill the pages of the Old Testament could possibly have meant to them what they now mean to those of us who live on the other side of the cross and resurrection. Those prophecies would have meant that God had not and would not forsake them, that he would continue to lead and guide them, that his covenantal love was eternal, but they could not have dreamed—as no Muslim today could dream—that God would literally take on flesh, dwell among us, and die a painful death on our behalf.

To my mind, it is clear that the leap from "I will make with them a new covenant" (Jer 31:31) to "this is the new covenant in my blood" (Lk 22:20 NKJV), from the promise of a new heart (Ezek 36:26) to the indwelling of the Holy Spirit (1 Cor 6:19), from obedience is better than sacrifice (1 Sam 15:22) to salvation by grace through faith (Eph 2:8) would have been beyond the spiritual discernment of even the greatest of prophets. They may have known, as at least one Pharisee did, that the heart of the law is to love God with all your heart, soul, mind, and strength and your neighbor as yourself (Mk 12:32-33); they may also have known, as did the Virgin Mary, that God exalts the humble and puts down the proud (Lk 1:52); they may even have known, as did Simeon, that to look on the baby Jesus was, in some strangely splendid way, to look on their salvation (Lk 2:30). Still, this knowledge alone could not have opened itself into a full understanding of the truths of the Christian religion.

And yet, and here is the vital point, those who knew such things about God would in most cases recognize, when these Christian truths were actually revealed to them, that those truths were a fulfillment and consummation of the limited knowledge they did possess. Jesus knew full well that, no matter how many times he explained it to them, his disciples would not understand the significance of his crucifixion; indeed, not until after the resurrection and ascension would their ignorance—which, at times, borders on the comical—be transformed into authentic enlightenment. Just so, St. Paul, who devoted his life to studying the Scriptures and thus knew every facet of the law, did not understand the true and full import of the Old Testament until the fullness of Christ was revealed to him. Then, as if a window had opened on the Scriptures, he began to perceive and know, like all Christians after him, that Christ is there in every book of the Old Testament, that all of it, in one way or another, points ahead to the revelation of God in Christ Jesus.

In his *Reflections on the Psalms*, C. S. Lewis addresses directly the messianic prophecies that fill the pages of the psalms, and makes an analogy between these prophetic, and canonical, "second meanings" and those few but choice moments when pagan poets and philosophers hit on something that has a distinct messianic ring to it. One of these moments occurs in Plato's description (in *Republic*) of the perfectly just man who, both despite of and because of his righteousness, is seized by the populace, beaten, and killed—a description that, as we saw in chapter two, sounds uncannily like a prophecy (e.g., Ps 22) of the passion of the Christ. "Plato is talking," writes Lewis, "and knows he is talking, about the fate of goodness in a wicked and misunderstanding world. But that is not something simply other than the Passion of Christ. It is the very same thing of which that Passion is the supreme illustration."[4]

To help his reader understand the concept more fully, Lewis then goes on to use a more familiar analogy:

> If a man who knew only England and had observed that, the higher a mountain was, the longer it retained the snow in early spring, were led on to suppose a mountain so high that it retained the snow all year round, the similarity between his imagined mountain and the real Alps would not be merely a lucky accident. He might not know that there were any such mountains in reality; just as Plato probably did not know that the ideally perfect instance of crucified goodness which he had depicted would ever become actual and historical. But if that man ever saw the Alps he would not say "What a curious coincidence." He would be more likely to say "There! What did I tell you?"[5]

---

[4]C. S. Lewis, *Reflections on the Psalms*, in *The Inspirational Writings of C. S. Lewis* (New York: Inspirational Press, 1991), 184.
[5]Lewis, *Reflections on the Psalms*, 185.

As perhaps the greatest humanist Christian of the twentieth century, Lewis knew well that Plato was made in God's image and that, though fallen, his reason still retained a spark of that divine breath. He knew, too, that Plato's *desire* to perceive and commune with absolute Goodness had its root in God, even if the *execution* of that desire was rendered ultimately futile by the absence of God's grace in Christ.

UNDERSTANDING HUMAN NATURE

Now, please do not think I, or, for that matter, Lewis, am placing Plato on par with the Old Testament or that I am suggesting that Plato's wisdom came, as did that of Moses, Daniel, and Isaiah, from the direct inspiration of the Holy Spirit. But I do mean to suggest that Plato, as if through a glass darkly, glimpsed many truths not only that are compatible with Christianity but that can also instruct and guide the Christian in his spiritual walk. Yes, as we saw above, his view of the body is decidedly docetic; nevertheless, I would argue that there are many truths in Plato that lie deeper than his apparent "flesh-hating" ethic. He understood, for example, that there is something in man that pulls him down and dulls his desire for union with God, and that that something is perpetually at war with a different something that impels him upward toward the divine. Could this Platonic wrestling—this pulling downward by the appetitive horse and pulling upward by the spirited horse that needs to be moderated by the rational charioteer—not be the English mountain that, in the epistles of Paul, becomes the mighty Alps of the continual war between the flesh (letter, law) that killeth and the spirit that giveth life (2 Cor 3:6)?

To speak on a personal level, it has been Plato more than anyone else who has helped me in my own spiritual walk to identify that portion of myself that is heavy and oppressive, that nagging tug of the flesh that pulls us earthward. It has been Plato, too, who has challenged and even convicted me to rise above the lusts of the flesh, not merely for the sake of discipline, nor to merit the applause of others, but because I was created for a higher kind of life. Perhaps in abstract philosophical terms Plato's disparagement of the flesh is gnostic, but in more practical terms it has always meant to me what Paul meant by the flesh: that which is contrary to the spirit. In contrast, legalistic Christians from the first century to today have read Paul's attack on the flesh in terms that are more ascetic and anti-body than Plato could ever have imagined.

After all, Plato's depictions of Socrates are decidedly anti-ascetic. In *Symposium*, for example, Socrates quite literally drinks all the young men under the table before heading back to his home (223b-d). Socrates is never seen to mortify his flesh nor to fast for the purpose of self-abnegation. Indeed, if and when Socrates does skip a meal, it is because he is too busy philosophizing with his friends. True, one should not make a glutton of himself, but the Platonic rationale for such abstinence does not spring from any belief that food or the body is inherently evil, but from a belief that such indulgence reduces our soul, our humanity, to that of a pig or a donkey. One of the main thrusts of Plato and, I believe, the Bible is that man was not made to live like an animal, a statement whose true import is too often limited to clichés like "cleanliness is next to godliness." The true meaning of the statement is that we were made for a kind of freedom denied to animals: the freedom to follow the dictates of our reason and our conscience, even when these contradict our bodily desires. The freedom, that is, not to be controlled by instincts, impulses, or our own fallen human nature.

I have always favored the simple, if somewhat reductive, definition of human nature that was put forth by the humanist Christian psychologist M. Scott Peck: "Human nature is to go to the bathroom in your pants."[6] The child who struggles his way through potty training is doing something that, at first, seems profoundly unnatural. Only once he has attained the dignity of controlling his bowels will the process of restraining his urges seem natural.

BODY AND SOUL

So much in Plato can be reconciled with, and indeed give support and impetus to, the Christian calling to move and grow into the

---

[6]M. Scott Peck, *Further Along the Road Less Traveled* (New York: Touchstone, 1998), 115.

image of God. But there is one aspect of Plato that cannot coexist with a Christian understanding of man: Plato's belief in the transmigration of souls. Just as Christianity teaches that the incarnate Christ was fully God and fully man, so does it teach that we as human beings are incarnational: not half body and half soul, but fully physical and fully spiritual. We are not, as Plato and his heirs thought, souls trapped in a body, but enfleshed souls. Reincarnation, like the belief that when we die our soul merges with, and is lost in, a universal One Soul, ultimately violates our integrity as incarnational beings and the unique, individual purpose for which each of us was made.

How then, we must ask, could a thinker like Plato, who understood so well the telos for which we were made, err on such a cardinal point? The main problem, I would argue, is that Plato did not have access to the first three chapters of Genesis. Had he been given the privilege to read this divinely inspired account of the creation and fall of man, he would have known that the nature of the fall is not physicality—on the contrary, physicality is one of the central aspects of creation itself—but that rebellion and disobedience—that is, sin—is what impedes us from achieving our full potential. I will return in a moment to consider sin and redemption; for now, let us concentrate on the Christian understanding of the relationship between body and soul.

According to Genesis 2:7, God breathed his spirit into Adam, and he became a living soul. In its ideal state, then, our body was not meant to be, nor was it, a prison house for the soul. Even more importantly, the soul and the body were not to be antagonists but, as it were, spouses specially fitted for one another. The body is more than a mere garment; it is linked essentially to the soul, a link that defines our nature as human beings. Indeed, according to 1 Corinthians 15, even in heaven our souls will be clothed, or rather espoused to, resurrection bodies; though we may, at death, shed the flesh, blood, and bones that make up our earthly bodies, we will, throughout eternity, continue to exist in a kind of physicality, a divine corporeality that we cannot now imagine. Just so, when the second person of the Trinity ascended to the Father, he did not return to a purely spiritual state but continued, and will continue for all eternity, to be the incarnate Christ: fully God and fully man.

Having had no knowledge of the incarnation and resurrection of Christ—which, even more than the creation account, forms, or at least should form, the foundation of all Christian understandings of body and soul—Plato could not possibly have conceived of the special, eternal marriage that exists between body and soul. In its absence, theories of reincarnation become not only logical but probable. Given the invisible, indestructible nature of the soul and the visible, ever-changing nature of matter, it is no wonder that Plato, ignorant of the unique fusion that God had effected between the two, arrived at his own spiritual theory of the conservation of energy: souls never die; they just take on one form after another.

Still, if we are willing to "adjust" the dialogues of Plato to square with a more biblical understanding of body and soul, we will, I believe, discover that his theories can, as before, prove extremely useful in assisting humanist Christians who have been saved by grace to ascend the rising path of sanctification toward the Beatific Vision. Better yet, if we "read" Plato as the medieval scholastics "read" the Old Testament, that is, in an allegorical sense, we will find that Plato can be read without even this adjustment.

I am not being facetious here. Plato's musings on reincarnation are always confined to his myths, and, as I explained with regard to his myths, though they should not be dismissed as simple untruths, they should also not be read in a purely literal fashion. They function not as scientific statements but as philosophical poems, meant to provide allegorical explanations to illuminate and authorize his ethical assertions. Coleridge may very well have been correct when he argued, in *Biographia Literaria*, that close readers of Wordsworth's "Ode: Intimations of Immortality from Recollections of Early Childhood" "will be as little disposed to charge Mr. Wordsworth with believing the platonic pre-existence in the ordinary interpretation of the words, as I am to believe, that Plato himself ever meant or taught it."[7]

If we make the attempt to interpret Plato's myths along allegorical lines, we will quickly find emerging a profound psychological truth of what happens internally to those who either ascend or descend the rising path. For, psychologically speaking—and I mean that not in the modern Freudian sense but in the higher, more spiritual sense of Dante's *Inferno,* in which sinners are seen, in part, to create their own torments in hell—Plato's myth of the soul's multigenerational journey up and down what later philosophers would term the Great Chain of Being[8] offers a keen insight into the way in which progressive abandonment to sensual desire first brutalizes, then dehumanizes, then deadens the soul. The steps by which a once moral man can slip into the gravest of sins are gradual ones that chart a successive surrender of spiritual integrity, autonomy, and discernment that bears much resemblance to Plato's "declension" of the soul, through a series of reincarnations, from bird to mammal to reptile to fish. Likewise, the steps by which that same person might, by great effort, reenter the community as a productive citizen are not dissimilar to those of a soul that slowly rises through a succession of nobler animals until it achieves the moral and psychological breakthrough into the human world of ethical decisions and moral responsibilities.

The struggle to ascend Plato's cosmic rungs is a monumental one that involves successive liberations from a series of chains that can, without stretching credulity too far, be linked to the diverse natures of an upward march of animals and "less cultivated" human beings. It is no coincidence that the one called Israel was also the one to whom God vouchsafed the vision of that heavenly ladder on which the angels ascended and descended (Ex 28:10-17).

---

[7]Samuel Taylor Coleridge, *Biographia Literaria,* ed. James Engell and W. Jackson Bate (Princeton: Princeton University Press), 2:147.
[8]See Arthur O. Lovejoy, *The Great Chain of Being* (New York: Harper & Row, 1936).

MALE AND FEMALE

Before I move on to the twin issues of sin and salvation, I feel compelled to discuss a difficult aspect of the Platonic theory of the transmigration of souls that is, I believe, linked to an even more problematic aspect of his theory of the education of the philosopher. According to the final section of *Timaeus* (90e), men "who were cowards or led unrighteous lives" do not always fall directly into the bodies of animals; sometimes they descend first into those of women. That is to say, in contrast to the biblical view, which posits woman as a separate and special creation made to enter into a meaningful bond of mutuality with man (Gen 2:20-24), Plato held both that woman is a lesser man and that women as a group were the near slaves of the physical cravings of their wombs.

Sadly, because his view of the soul and body led him to view women in such negative terms, Plato could not fathom how a woman could play any role in the education of the philosopher. As a result—and here, I admit, I am drawing a somewhat atypical conclusion, especially given the fact that Plato makes some provision for female guardians in *Republic* and *Laws*—Plato's paradigm for the journey of the philosopher up the rising path is masculine in focus. And that leads us to another subject that I have thus far passed over in my analysis of Plato's dialogues: homosexuality. In Plato's account of the education of the lover (in *Symposium*), the lover and beloved are both male. That single beautiful person whom the would-be philosopher-lover begins by loving is always a young boy; the relationship that begins, and often perpetuates, the journey upward is a homosexual one (211b-c).

Indeed, as is well known, Plato, along with all the cultivated Greeks of that time, considered it acceptable for an older man to take a younger man as his ward—for the Greeks, homosexuality nearly always manifested itself in the form of pederasty. And, although Plato insisted repeatedly in his dialogues that the ideal ("Platonic") love between the older and younger man should not be sexual—Socrates, we are told in *Symposium* (219b-d), continually rejected the sexual advances of the handsome and dashing Alcibiades—homosexual activity was clearly a frequent component of these relationships. My point here is not to survey this aspect of ancient Greek life, but to consider whether the male bond of lover and beloved is an essential, inseparable element of the Platonic education of the philosopher. For, given that homosexuality is unambiguously condemned in the Old and New Testament alike (Lev 18:22; Rom 1:26-27), any attempt to reconcile Plato with Christianity must make at least some attempt to broach this subject.

The simplest way to effect this reconciliation is to point to the great monasteries of Christendom as proof that a male community of Christian "wisdom-seekers" need not be homosexual in its orientation, though that is not to deny that pederasty sometimes occurred. Here, the separation of the sexes meant that the monks would not be bound by any obligations to wife or family and could thus pursue their "education" free from any entangling alliances to the mundane concerns of the world. As a humanist Christian I cannot help but affirm the desire of the monk to ascend the rising path—not to mention applaud the fact that it was the monasteries that preserved most of that classical literature that is so central to the humanist Christian creed; still, I am troubled both by the legalistic, ascetic, anti-body ethos that monasticism often fosters and its tendency toward a puritanical separation from the world. I would like therefore to offer an alternate way of addressing Plato's views on homosexuality.

Plato, I would suggest, had he possessed a more positive view of women and had the women of Athens been allowed fuller educational opportunities, might very well have granted women a place and function in the growth of the philosophic mind. Indeed, Plato's liberal program for the education of women, laid out in *Republic*, may mark an attempt on his part to rethink the nature and status of women vis-à-vis the individual and corporate pursuit of justice and wisdom. The tendency in Plato, as it has been throughout much of history, is to identify women solely with their sexuality; viewed as such, women would seem only to drag men earthward and dull their desire to ascend. Had Plato been able to accept the integrity of female spirituality, had he been able to see in the physical beauty of women a deeper Beauty that connected their souls to the divine, had he been able to grant that a man's love for a woman could transcend the lust of the flesh and its innate impulse to propagate, he would, I believe, have modified the "curriculum" of the philosopher-lover in *Symposium* to include heterosexual love.[9] This is not, of course, to say that humanist Christianity favors the "sowing of wild oats"—from a biblical point of view, extramarital heterosexuality is just as sinful as homosexuality—but it does at least move us in the right direction.

What I am suggesting is that if Plato had possessed a higher view of women, he might have seen in the marriage relationship the possibility for a kind of dialectic not dissimilar to the one Socrates employed in his pursuit of truth. Plato's dialectic involves a collision of ideas out of which knowledge emerges. This collision, this rubbing of idea against idea—like raw wood against a lathe—is precisely what occurs in any authentic marriage. One of the chief reasons God created the sexes—and, hence, marriage—was, I believe, so that husband and wife might hone and refine each other. Indeed, in the absence of this grounding relationship, the male philosopher is apt to become too abstract, too divorced from the world.

Tennyson best captures this stoic masculine attitude, an attitude that marks one of the chief dangers of Platonism for the would-be humanist Christian, in his poem "The Lotos-Eaters." Here, Ulysses's men, after tasting the sweet fruit of the lotus, lose all desire to be reunited with their homes and families; their sole wish now is to lie on the hills and eat their lotus, oblivious to the world and the little lives of men. They sing,

> Let us swear an oath, and keep it with an equal mind,
> In the hollow Lotos land to live and lie reclined
> On the hills like Gods together, careless of mankind.
> For they lie beside their nectar, and the bolts are hurled

---

[9]As a possible analogy, Plato, in *Republic* 10, asserts that if poetry could be shown to be both pleasant and useful and to have a legitimate place and function in a well-ordered state, he would be happy to allow the poets to return to the republic from which he had exiled them (607d).

Far below them in the valleys, and the clouds are lightly curled
Round their golden houses girdled with the gleaming world;
Where they smile in secret, looking over wasted lands,
Blight and famine, plague and earthquake, roaring deeps and fiery sands,
Clanging fights, and flaming towns, and sinking ships, and praying hands.
But they smile, they find a music centered in a doleful song
Steaming up, a lamentation and an ancient tale of wrong,
Like a tale of little meaning though the words are strong. (153-64)[10]

PRAEPARATIO EVANGELICA

But, of course, all this talk of climbing and struggling and working our way up the ascending path is not really Christian, is it? The Bible speaks to us of unmerited grace (Rom 11:6), of justification by faith (Eph 2:8-9), of imputed righteousness (Rom 1:17), of the inability of humanity to strive after God (Rom 3:23). The works of the law bring down only condemnation on our heads (Rom 4:15). How then can the Platonic scheme of the education of the philosopher be integrated into a Christian worldview that stresses man's utter helplessness in the face of his desperate need for forgiveness and salvation?

With great difficulty. I already mentioned above that Plato's concept of the fall does not include the concept of sin, that his fall is into physicality rather than disobedience. For Plato, we are prevented from reaching the divine, not by the lust of the eye but by errors of perception, not by the lust of the flesh but by the corporeal weight of the body, not by the pride of life but by lack of self-knowledge. In contrast, Christianity holds that we are fallen people, incapable of achieving righteousness through our own hard work and merit. Indeed, were we not fallen, there would have been no need for God to send his Son to earth to die a painful and humiliating death on our behalf. The essence of Christianity is grace; salvation is not a reward for hard work but a free gift granted to those who embrace the life, death, and resurrection of Christ and who make him their Lord and Savior. If Christ's death on the cross is to be seen merely as an exemplary act on which we are

---

[10]*Tennyson's Poetry*, ed. Robert W. Hill Jr. (New York: Norton, 1971), 51.

to model our lives rather than a divine act of propitiation by which God took on himself the punishment for our sins (2 Cor 5:21), then Christianity becomes merely one of many religions and Jesus himself is reduced to the level of a holy man: just another teacher in the distinguished but solely human line of Moses, Zoroaster, Buddha, Confucius, Socrates, Hillel, and Muhammad.

No, we cannot allow respect and admiration for Plato to divorce Christianity from its most central and essential teaching: justification by grace through faith, offered by the triune God through the person and work of Jesus Christ. If we do, we will eventually end up in the ranks of the Neoplatonic Gnostics with their belief that salvation comes via secret teachings and occult wisdom that can be known and understood only by the elect few.

If we accept, as nearly all Christians accept, that we are granted by God the awesome right and responsibility of accepting or rejecting his grace, then I think the Platonic system may have some relevance: not as a system by which we can be restored to a right relationship with God—apart from the cross, this is impossible—but as an education that has the potential, not only to aid us in the movement from salvation to sanctification, but to prepare us to make the right choice when the grace of Christ is offered us. After all, as we saw in our analysis of the myth of Er, the education of the philosopher that Socrates so carefully lays out in *Republic* turns out, in the end, to be one long preparation for a single, all-important choice: what our next life will be.

Or, to move to a higher, more mystical level, the myths of *Phaedrus* and *Symposium* teach us that to follow the path of the Platonic philosopher is to yearn after truth and reality, to desire to commune with the one who created us and thus knows our proper telos. It is, too, a search for freedom, for the Platonic philosopher, even if he confuses sin with error, recognizes a recalcitrance in his flesh that will not yield itself to being shaped by the divine Forms. He knows that this rebellious stubbornness must be overcome if he is to ascend to the World of Being and achieve the communion he desires. It is true, as I have said above, that this World of Being toward which the initiate strives is finally an impersonal and stoic one; nevertheless, I would assert that anyone who strives with all his heart, soul, and mind to reach such a place, and achieve such a communion, must at some point in his journey wonder if this higher world might not also be a place of love, acceptance, and forgiveness.

Indeed, if only a spark of this wonder is present, there is a very good chance that when such a seeker hears of the love of Jesus, he will feel both joy and recognition in his heart. Plato, as we saw earlier, believed that all higher wisdom is attained, finally, through an act of recollection. I would like to suggest, then, that Christians can accept this teaching without having to accept either reincarnation or the preexistence of the soul. According to orthodox Christianity, we all share in Adam's fall; if that is the case, may we not share as well in his brief experience of living in direct communion with God? May we not, as a human race, all share a collective memory of Eden? If that is so, then I would suggest further that our ascent up the rising path may help us to recapture that special memory, and thus to recognize that the Christ we hear preached to us is one with that God whose footsteps Adam heard in the garden in the cool of the day (Gen 3:8).

In one sense, I am echoing here Augustine's belief that our learning does not proceed merely from study, but from an innate, intuitive knowledge that he referred to (in *De Magistro* 12.40 and *83 Different Questions* 46) as divine illumination. Critics have long debated to what extent Augustine's theory of divine illumination relies on Platonic recollection and the preexistence of the soul, but for my argument, it is not necessary to insist on an ironclad connection. It is enough to argue that Augustine's theory of divine illumination *can* be reconciled with recollection and preexistence (Augustine never specifically denied that it did) and that the ultimate source of that illumination is the mind of God, into which Augustine placed Plato's Forms, and the incarnate Christ.

While I, as a humanist (and Platonic) Christian, agree with Augustine on this matter, I would go a bit further to suggest (1) that our illumination goes back to our collective, prenatal memory of the garden when we gazed, not on impersonal Forms, but, in some unspecified manner, on God himself, and (2) that a Platonic type of yearning for truth and illumination—a yearning to escape from the shadows in the cave—can predispose the soul for the gospel. To put that in classical, pagan terms, might not one who has sincerely sought all his life to know and experience the love of Adonis (one of the "dying gods" of Greek mythology) recognize in Jesus a historical enactment of the myth and thus rejoice at the good news that Jesus is a God who can be known directly and taken into the heart? Such, I believe, was the case with the Gentile Magi (Mt 2:1-12). They, like Plato, lacked the Law and Prophets, but, when they stood before the Christ child, they recognized that this child was the telos of their long yuletide search. Or again, though the Roman centurion with the sick servant and the other Roman centurion named Cornelius lacked direct knowledge of God, their pursuit of virtue (Lk 7:5; Acts 10:2), while not earning them salvation, clearly predisposed them to recognize Jesus' authority and power to save.

CAUTIONS AND HOPE

Such is the shape and nature of my idealistic hope that a Platonic education can prepare the soil of our heart for the seed of the gospel, that it can be, to use Eusebius's pregnant phrase, a *praeparatio evangelica*.[11] Still, lest I stray from the course of virtue, let me qualify my enthusiasm somewhat with two caveats.

First, it must be acknowledged that the Platonic system of education can easily lead to a deadly self-righteousness that is generally quick to deny the claims of the gospel. I would be dishonest if I did not remind myself and my readers that the wisdom of God is foolishness to man and that, to wisdom-seeking Greeks, the cross of Christ is the height of folly (see 1 Cor 1:18-31). Socrates, like the Platonic philosopher, is a lover of truth whose central desire is to rip away the illusions of this

---

[11] Eusebius, *The Preparation for the Gospel* (Aeterna Press, 2015).

world in order to gain a clearer, more direct apprehension of Goodness, Truth, and Beauty. In this sense, the teachings of Plato are neutral: it is *how* we use them and *what* we use them to discover that will determine whether they lead us, in a straight, glorious line, to Christ or in an egocentric circle back to ourselves.

The second caveat to my faith that a proper adherence to the path of philosophy can, like the preaching of John the Baptist, prepare the way for the Lord springs from the simple fact that a person who knows nothing of philosophy can just as readily accept the gospel as one who has glimpsed the nature of the divine. Even more startling, those who have devoted their lives to greed or licentiousness or anger—the thief on the cross, for example—will often respond more quickly to Christ than the lover of wisdom. And this, of course, is as it should be. Were it not, God would be open to the charge of being a "respecter of persons," and the gospel would become the property of the cultured elite.

No, philosophers are neither more worthy nor more able to receive Christ, but they are, I would argue, more equipped to make a smoother transition into the Christian life. If philosophers have already learned to control the lusts and impulses of the flesh, they will usually avoid the difficult period of adjustment that so often befalls Christians who come to the faith without any knowledge or experience of how to conduct themselves "in a way that becometh the gospel" (Phil 1:27). Likewise, the one who comes to Christianity with a disciplined mind that is used to searching after things that cannot be seen will often understand and practice more quickly the spiritual disciplines of prayer and meditation on the Word. What I am suggesting here is simply this: that the Platonic system of education can act, like the law, as a sort of tutor, preparing us for the grace to come (Gal 3:24).

ORIGEN'S MUSINGS

Having outlined the relationship between Plato's philosophy and the Christian faith in broader terms in the previous chapter, I will now begin to trace Plato's influence as it runs through a select number of Christian thinkers who each found unique ways to integrate their Christian faith with the deep, pre-Christian truths that illuminate the dialogues.

I begin, not with Irenaeus or Tertullian or Justin Martyr, but with a heterodox early church father who yearned to honor Plato without compromising basic Christian orthodoxy.[1] Indeed, he established a famous school that enrolled Christians and (Neoplatonic) pagans alike and that sought to use the classical liberal arts as a preparation for the fuller truth of the Bible and the gospel. His name was Origen (ca. 185–ca. 253), and his masterwork, *On First Principles* (ca. 225), offers

---

[1]Although, three full centuries after his death, Origen's writings would be condemned as heretical at the Second Council of Constantinople (553), he nevertheless exerted a profound influence on Christianity. As Henry Chadwick documents in *The Early Church* (London: Penguin, 1975), "Eusebius of Caesarea, the church historian, looked back on Origen as the supreme saint and highest intelligence in the catalogue of heroes in history; and no Greek commentator on scripture could escape his influence. Even Epiphanius of Salamis in Cyprus, who regarded Origen as a heretic who had corrupted Christianity with the poison of Greek culture, admitted that there was excellent stuff in his Bible commentaries. As the monastic movement developed in the fourth century, there were many ascetics who found in Origen's spirituality a theological basis for their personal aspirations" (112).

one of the most intriguing fusions of Plato and Christianity
ever conceived.

THE GOD WHO IS WISDOM

Whereas some Christian theologians have treated sovereignty as the
central attribute of God's nature, while others have posited love or
power or holiness as the key to unlocking the mysteries of God, Origen
suggests that wisdom comes closer than any other attribute to defining
and illuminating the nature of God. His exaltation of wisdom first
emerges in the second chapter of *On First Principles* in the midst of a
discussion of Christ's many titles. In addition to hailing Christ as the
firstborn of all creation and the Logos of God, Origen exalts wisdom
as one of the key messianic titles, and attributes, of God the Son. He
bases this claim on a well-known passage from Proverbs:

> The LORD possessed me [wisdom] in the beginning of his way,
> before his works of old.
> I was set up from everlasting,
> from the beginning, or ever the earth was.
> When there were no depths, I was brought forth;
> when there were no fountains abounding with water.
> Before the mountains were settled,
> before the hills was I brought forth. (Prov 8:22-25)

According to Origen, this passage speaks of the preincarnate Christ,
he through whom all things were made (Jn 1:3), a claim that leads
Origen not only to list wisdom as one of the qualities possessed by the
Son but also to state, quite boldly, that wisdom *is* the Son of God.
Indeed, Origen goes even further to state that, since Christ and God
are one, and since Christ is wisdom, then "wisdom, through which
God is called Almighty, has a share even in the glory of omnipotence.
For it is through wisdom, which is Christ, that God holds power over
all things" (1.2; 24).[2]

---

[2]Origen, *On First Principles*, ed. and trans. G. W. Butterworth (New York: Harper & Row, 1966).
I will provide in the text the book and chapter numbers followed by the page number.

Actually, the above conclusion is a bit more complicated. In terms of wisdom, it is not just their shared Godhead that links Father to Son; it is the fact that, in the beginning, all things were created through Christ—or, rather, that wisdom which is Christ—and, at the end, all things will be put in subjection under Christ, who will himself be in subjection to the Father. Now, Origen argues, since God cannot be truly Almighty unless he has something to rule over, and since it was through Christ (wisdom) that all things came into being, then wisdom is inseparable from the power and rule (sovereignty) of God. Likewise, if that same world that was created by wisdom will someday be subjected by the same means, then it will be primarily through wisdom, rather than power, that God in Christ will subject the world:

> Now if every knee bows to Jesus [Phil 2:10], then undoubtedly it is Jesus to whom all things have been subjected, and it is he who wields dominion over all things, and all things have been subjected to the Father through him; for it is through wisdom, that is, by word and reason and not by force and necessity, that they are subject. His glory, therefore, lies in the very fact that he possesses all things; and this is the purest and brightest glory of omnipotence, that the universe is held in subjection by reason and wisdom, and not by force and necessity. (1.2; 25)

Though Origen's discussion of wisdom may have seemed, at first, to be merely an esoteric exercise, I hope it will be noted that the conclusion quoted above is, in fact, rich with implications.

For, if Origen is right about the role of wisdom in the subjection of the universe, if he is right that God's final victory over the forces of evil and rebellion will be effected not through force and necessity but through reason and wisdom, then the possibility for a real synergy between man's efforts and God's will becomes feasible and even probable. To posit wisdom as God's chief tool for subjecting the universe is tantamount to suggesting that God will accomplish his plan on earth by appealing—in a very Platonic manner—to our reason through a sort of divine rhetoric rather than by terrifying our bodies through the force of his divine wrath.

It suggests further that God's foreknowledge need not necessitate determinism and that our decisions and struggles can play a vital and real part in the fulfillment of God's plan. Above all, it safeguards the dignity of man, by allowing us to view ourselves not as pawns to be swept aside in a game of omnipotent force but as students, and philosophers, of a divine schoolmaster who would educate and refine us through a wisdom that both creates and restores a wisdom that, like the music of Orpheus, has the power to coax even hell to give up its prize. Or, to use Plato's imagery, a wisdom that, when heeded, leads us out of the darkness of the cave into the light of the sun.

As we can see, wisdom for Origen, as for Plato, is more than mere knowledge or understanding: it is a higher kind of harmony that holds the cosmos (Plato's ordered universe) and all that it contains in perfect balance. Later in his book, Origen, in a burst of speculative bravado that recalls the creation myth of *Timaeus*, extends this eschatological wisdom backward to take in the creation of all those souls that would one day be subjected to God in Christ:

> We must suppose, therefore, that in the beginning God made as large a number of rational and intelligent beings [souls], or whatever the before-mentioned minds ought to be called, as he foresaw would be sufficient. It is certain that he made them according to some definite number foreordained by himself; for we must not suppose, as some would, that there is no end of created beings, since where there is no end there can neither be any comprehension nor limitation. If there had been no end, then certainly created beings could neither have been controlled nor provided for by God. For by its nature whatever is infinite will also be beyond comprehension. (2.9; 129)

God, Origen here suggests, does not just do anything he has a mind to and then label his action as wise. There exists a perfection of wisdom and harmony that orders and determines God's actions in the universe. That is not to say that wisdom, therefore, is older or more powerful than God; rather, it is to say that wisdom is a part of God's nature that he always acts in harmony with. In God, there is no waste, no excess; all is in perfect balance. If fulfilling his eschatological purposes for the universe necessitates a fixed number of souls, then God will confine himself to creating only so many: neither more nor less.

Such a view of God is difficult to harmonize with traditional understandings of God's sovereignty. Still, if we follow Origen following Plato and consider wisdom, rather than power, to be the central quality of God, such a view need not rob God of his glory or his prerogatives. On the contrary, it will prove him to be well-suited to rule the universe he has created, since he alone knows the exact number of souls that can provide his universe with the maximum amount of diversity while yet ensuring that all can, in the end, be restored to unity. Read in this light, Origen presents God's plan as a dynamic, evolving symphony whose greater harmonies can accommodate billions of diverse instruments playing the notes of a trillion hopes and choices and dreams.

The God who is wisdom is a God who not only sees all and knows all but also who understands how each part is related to the whole: "For there is one power which binds and holds together all the diversity of the world and guides the various motions to the accomplishment of one task, lest so immense a work as the world should be dissolved by the conflicts of souls" (2.1; 77). In this fashion, God is like a good, earthly manager who, by studying and knowing well both the strengths and weaknesses of all those under him, can coordinate the diverse and at times contradictory activities of numerous workers. Not all of these individuals will work at peak efficiency; many of them will do as little as they can; some may even do things that detract from the success of the company. Still, the good manager will be able to take all of these human factors into account, both the good and the bad, and by carefully arranging, manipulating, and recombining them achieve the overall goals of the company.

Origen did not spin this powerful and compelling vision of the God-who-is-wisdom out of thin air. He learned it from meditating on the philosophical truths put forth in Plato's dialogues. Without denying God's absolute sovereignty, Origen explores those dimensions of God and his cosmos that I surveyed in my reading of *Timaeus*. Not power but balance, order, harmony, and proportion are the hallmarks of that God who created the world out of nothing and gave it shape and form. God shows his perfect wisdom by coordinating contrary parts and forces and wills. He shows it as well in his divine efficiency and plenitude, creating precisely the right number of souls and orchestrating those souls into an anthropological music of the wills to complement the celestial music of the spheres.

Given such a vision of God, the education of the philosopher takes on a deeper meaning. Starting with the early dialogues, Plato had argued consistently that none of the virtues can be practiced apart from wisdom, for without wisdom we cannot understand the true nature of the choices we are called to make and the virtues we are expected to practice. Only wisdom can keep us, and the polis, on track; only wisdom will allow us to perceive the Form behind the imitation. Of course, in Christianity, wisdom apart from faith is insufficient to draw us to God, but we need the wisdom if we are to know what we are putting our faith in. If God is not only to save and regenerate the human soul, but to return it to the proper Edenic balance it once knew, then he must instill in us a vigorous wisdom that can help restore harmony to our disharmonious souls.

THE WAX AND THE MUD

We cannot, Martin Luther once quipped, stop the birds from flying over our heads, but we can stop them from making nests in our hair.[3] Origen makes essentially the same point in book three of *On First Principles*:

> But if anyone should say that those impressions from without that call forth our movements are of such a sort that it is impossible to resist them, whether they incite us to good or to evil, let him who thinks thus turn his attention for a little while to himself, carefully examining his own inner movements, and see whether he does not find that, when the attraction of any desire strikes him, nothing is accomplished until the assent of the soul

---

[3]Although I have been unable to locate the actual source of this saying, it is quoted often by writers and preachers, including at this webpage from the Lutheran Church of Australia (www.lca.org.au/birds-and-nests/) and this one from *Christian History* magazine (www.christianitytoday.com/history/issues/issue-34/colorful-sayings-of-colorful-luther.html).

is gained and the bidding of the mind indulges the wicked suggestion. It is as if an appeal were being made on certain plausible grounds from two different sides to a judge dwelling within the tribunal of our heart, in order that when the grounds have been first stated the sentence to act may proceed from the judgment of the reason. (3.1; 161)

The sin does not lie in the thought or the image that strikes our eye—Jesus himself was tempted three times in the wilderness (Mt 4:1-11)—but in whether we dwell and then speak and then act on it. On this point, Origen and Luther would have agreed; however, Origen, following in the footsteps of Plato, posits a rational part of our soul with the power to judge between two contrary desires that sound quite a bit like the appetitive and the spirited.

For Origen, each time we come on a situation that calls for choice, a Platonic *psychomachia* takes place within us, a dynamic wrestling match between the carnal and the spiritual that is played out in the soul of every individual. To heed too often the demands and impulses of the flesh is to make one's way down Plato's ladder of being toward the brutishness and callousness of the animal and vegetable worlds: "When the sensitiveness of the soul has grown duller through its subservience to the passions of the body, it is weighed down by the mass of its vices and becomes sensitive to nothing refined or spiritual" (3.4; 236). To respond to the call of the spirit is to ascend the rising path out of the cave—both the cave of ignorance, as Plato would have it, and the cave of sin, as the fuller revelation of the Bible makes clear.

This struggle was a real one for Origen, a struggle whose outcome was never certain. And, since it was never certain, then it was imperative for the soul to be trained in the art of making wise judgments: an art best acquired by following, in one way or another, the educational system laid down by Plato. For it is only through such an education that we can train the spirited part of the soul to come to the defense of the rational, so that both together might overcome the demands of the appetitive.

Origen's analysis of spiritual struggle, though true to the Bible, tracks closely with Plato's *psychomachia*. When it comes to the kind of education system that Plato lays out in *Republic*, however, Origen factors in elements that are unique to Christianity.

The first of these factors centers on the Christian belief that God's grace, power, and wisdom must be accepted if they are to assist us in mounting the rising path; indeed, if they are resisted or rejected, they will work against us and actually impede and frustrate our journey. Just so, the rays of the sun are vehicles that allow us to see; yet, if we stare directly at those rays for too long a period, they will destroy our very ability to see. Or, to use Origen's own analogy, "The sun, by one and the same power of its heat, loosens wax and yet dries up and binds together mud" (3.1; 175). In the context of Origen's argument, this analogy serves as an aid in solving that most puzzling of biblical riddles: How could a just and fair God harden Pharaoh's heart? Given his Platonic-Christian allegiance to the reality of human volition, Origen could only answer that Pharaoh, not God, was ultimately responsible for this hardening. But how?

We must agree, Origen reasons, that the heat of the sun is the cause of both the loosening of the wax and the hardening of the mud, and yet, if the sun is the cause, and the sun is one, how is it that such contradictory results (loosening and hardening) could issue from the same source? The answer, of course, lies in the nature of the wax and the mud; figuratively speaking, the wax yields to the power of the sun, while the mud resists it. The former's essential pliancy is revealed and released by the heat, while the stubbornness of the latter is, by the same operation of the sun, exposed and increased.

Having set up so succinctly this paradoxical relationship between sun, wax, and mud, Origen then proceeds to apply it to the case of Pharaoh:

> So therefore one and the same operation of God, which worked through Moses in signs and wonders, revealed on the one hand the hardness of Pharaoh, which he had developed by the intensity of his wickedness, and on the other hand proclaimed the obedience of those other Egyptians who

> were mingled among the Israelites and are said to have gone out of Egypt
> along with them. (3.1; 175)

Origen's point here is a strong one, and it helps to explain why the gospel of Christ can elicit both joy and anger in the same crowd. Indeed, though Origen does not make the connection, I would suggest that his reading of the hardening of Pharaoh's heart can be applied directly to a similar situation in the Gospels: the hardening of the Pharisees' hearts.

For Origen, the education of the Platonic-minded humanist Christian must begin with a softening of the heart, a humble willingness to confess one's faults and seek assistance from God:

> He who does not first understand his infirmity and sickness is unable to
> seek a physician. . . . So, too, if a man has not first learned the defects of his
> soul and the wickedness of his sins and confessed them openly with his
> own mouth he cannot be cleansed and absolved; otherwise he might be
> unaware that what he receives is a gift of grace and might think that the
> divine liberality was a blessing that belonged to him. This would un-
> doubtedly give rise again to arrogance and pride of heart and become once
> more the cause of his downfall, as we must believe happened in the case of
> the devil, who thought that the privileges which he enjoyed when he lived
> blamelessly were his own and not given to him by God. (3.1; 181)

One seeks in vain to find such a passage in the writings of ancient Greece, even in those of Plato himself. Though the Greeks understood well that "pride goeth before destruction" (Prov 16:18), the notion that one must come naked before God, confess both sin and need, and then receive God's grace with thanksgiving would have struck them as alien. True, in their epics and tragedies, they depict heroes and heroines whose strength or beauty or good fortune causes them to "stick out" and be noticed, to their doom, by the jealous gods, but this is not the same as Origen's suggestion that Satan's fall was precipitated by his thanklessness and proud assertions of his own self-sufficiency. The former view posits a tyrannical God who arbitrarily blasts any stalk that raises its head above the others; the latter, a merciful but holy God who pours out his grace freely, yet insists that that grace be received and acknowledged (e.g., Mt 10:32-33).

For Origen, the struggle that leads us to God is, finally, a synergistic one that requires us both to receive and strive after God's grace. Indeed, one of the chief differences between the embryonic, proto-Christian humanism of Plato and the fuller humanist Christianity of Origen lies in the fact that, while Plato saw the philosopher's journey up the rising path as wholly self-initiated and self-propelled—though aided by recollections of our previous existence in the World of Being—Origen taught that human effort alone was powerless unless accompanied by and combined with the assistance of God: "We are not to think that the things which are in the power of our will can be performed without the help of God, nor that those which are in God's hands can be brought to completion apart from our acts and earnest endeavours and purpose" (3.1; 210).

Thus, though Origen insisted that we must cultivate our soul through discipline—according to Jesus' parable of the sower, the seed that is sown is always the same; it is the nature of the soil that determines the success of the crop (Mt 13:1-23)—he also knew that the final source of that divine fire that warms and impels us on our journey lies not within the soul of the initiate but in the soul of the incarnate Christ. While we remain close to that fire, we are inspired and enabled to progress up the ladder; but the moment we move away from it, our souls begin to grow cold, and we lose our passion to climb. Just so, in canto 7 of Dante's *Purgatorio*, we learn that the souls in purgatory can only move up the hill during the hours of daylight. Once the sun sets, their desire for sanctification and glorification wanes, and they fall into a deep slumber from which only the morning rays can raise them again.

THE PREEXISTENCE OF THE SOUL
AND UNIVERSAL SALVATION

Still, despite Origen's deep and passionate understanding of God's mercy in Christ Jesus, he did, like Plato, gravitate toward a system of merits, a philosophical and theological orientation that led him to embrace the preexistence of the soul. According to this Plato-inspired teaching, God created, at some point near the beginning of his creation, all the souls that will ever exist on the earth or in the universe. These souls would then remain in heaven in a disembodied state until the time came for them to be placed in bodies and to dwell on the earth. This teaching was not so much entertained by as thrust on Origen as the only possible way to undergird his firm belief that "the position of every created being is the result of his own work and his own motives . . . not by some privilege of creation but as the reward of merit" (1.5; 47).

Origen's dilemma might be stated thus: If our choices and actions are accepted as the determining factors in what kinds of lives, both heavenly and earthly, we will lead, then what possible choice or action could determine the state and character of our birth? On the basis of what merits are some born rich and others poor, some healthy and others disabled. Neither blind luck, divine election, nor parental actions were acceptable to Origen as explanations for these genetic inequities. The only solution, therefore, was that these infants were judged on the basis of merits accumulated during their preexistence.

Indeed, Origen carries this explanation further to take in even the angels and devils. According to his view, Michael and Gabriel were chosen as archangels, not on the basis of election, but on the basis of merit (1.8; 66). Even more shocking, Origen surmises that the distinction between angel, human, and demon was itself the result of merit, and that, accordingly, we could shift between these three states over the course of our soul's journey. For Origen, the struggles of the initiate to reach the top rung of the ladder are not confined to our short lifespan; they stretch out in both directions, from the beginning of creation to the end and consummation of all things.

I must admit that, though I find Origen's ideas here to be creative and awe-inspiring, I am troubled by the full implications of this curious teaching. Nevertheless, I will not, as many would and have, throw out all of Origen's ideas merely on account of his teachings on the preexistence of the soul. Rather, I will attempt to discern a deeper truth in Origen as I have tried to discern deeper truths in Plato. And I will do so by treating the preexistence the way Origen reads the Old Testament: allegorically.

Paul teaches in Romans that we all share in the sin nature of Adam (Rom 5:12). I would add that we all share as well a collective memory of the joys and perfection of Eden. Perhaps what Origen calls the preexistence of the soul is another way of expressing the same higher truth: that we were all there in Eden, that we shared both in the glory and the tragedy of our primal parents. Just as the Platonic philosopher is able to grow in wisdom by recollecting the glories he experienced and the wisdom he knew during his thousand-year journey through the World of Being, so the initiate of Origen can gain a fuller and richer understanding of his position in the created universe by calling on his intimations of Eden and the fall.

So much for beginnings, but what of endings? Just as Origen's Platonism led him toward a heterodox understanding of our ultimate origin, so it led him as well to a heterodox understanding of our ultimate destination. Throughout *On First Principles*, Origen considers the doctrine of universal salvation, the belief that, in the end, all will be saved: including even the devil. At several points in his work, Origen describes hell not as a place of eternal damnation and punishment but as a sort of divine correctional facility where God, the great physician, uses both knife and fire to remove and purge the sin from our soul (see 2.10; 143). God's ultimate desire for the universe is to draw all things to himself, to return, that is, to that primal state of unity that was disrupted when a large percentage of the souls he had created misused their free will to rebel rather than obey their Creator. Since that time, the universe has been marked by diversity, disunity, and futility; but a time will come when all that was lost will be found, when all shall ascend the rising path, when God shall be all in all.

Though wonderfully optimistic, these Platonic musings of Origen are at best heterodox and, if pushed too far, fall into heresy. Still, I think that they, like the preexistence of the soul, can be partially accounted for if we take them in their overall context. It must be understood that the universal salvation toward which Origen strains his eyes will not occur at the end of our present age. Origen does not dispute the existence of the "lake of fire" as it is described in John's apocalypse (Rev 20:14-15). Rather, he posits that the end of this age will, in turn, give way to a new cycle of history that is beyond our comprehension. And this cycle, in turn, will give way to others, until, at the end of a thousand cycles, all will be reconciled to God.

Origen's suggestion that all will be saved, though it is far from orthodox, need not lead us to reject him as a sincere and powerful preacher of the Christian gospel. Indeed, I would argue that his heterodoxy in this area does not so much rise out of a misreading of the biblical concepts of salvation and damnation as it does out of a misreading of the biblical understanding of time. Origen had a tendency to champion the Hellenic at the expense of the Hebraic: a tendency that, in this case, led him to embrace a cyclical rather than linear conception of history. Though the Bible abounds with typological links that form mini-cycles in the flow of time, the Bible nevertheless presents a view of history that, like a good Aristotelian plot, has a beginning, a middle, and an end.

The "higher" Greek view of Plato gravitated toward a more Asiatic, particularly Indian, understanding of time; in this view, man begins in an age of gold but, over time, slowly degrades through three additional ages of silver, bronze, and iron. At the end of the Iron Age (what the Hindus call Kali[4]), all is destroyed, and a new golden age rises, phoenix-like, out of the ashes. No one can tell how many cycles of ages have preceded our own (Plato himself suggests as much in *Laws* 3; 676b-c), nor how many will follow after. Origen, uncomfortable with the static, literal nature of the Hebraic view of time, chose instead to embrace the dynamism and allegorical richness of the Hellenic view; by so doing, he left himself the daunting task of hypothesizing what had happened and would happen in those multiple eons that predate the Garden and postdate the new Jerusalem.

---

[4]www.britannica.com/topic/Hinduism/Cosmology#ref303701.

But this misinterpretation of the biblical concept of time is not the only source and fountain of Origen's musings on the subject of universal salvation. His musings also spring in part from a crucial misreading of a single verse of the Bible: 1 Corinthians 15:28. According to this verse, when the end comes, all things will be made subject to Christ, who will himself be subject to the Father. By way of a very loose exegesis, Origen treats this subjection as if it were all but equivalent to salvation, as if Paul were saying that this final subjection to God in Christ is a promise that all will share in the blessedness of God (1.6; 58). But, of course, the word *subjection* does not suggest this at all. Slaves are subject to their masters, but they certainly do not share in their blessedness. James tells us that "the devils also believe [in one God], and tremble" (Jas 2:19), yet certainly they are not saved nor do they share in the blessings of God. On this point, I believe, Origen was too optimistic. Like Plato, who could not believe that anyone would consciously perform an activity that he knew would injure him (for knowledge is the greatest virtue), Origen seems to have had too much faith in human rationality.

The Desire of the Soul

Still, despite the misunderstandings of time and of human nature that underlie Origen's theories of universal salvation, meditating on his Platonic-Christian musings can help open our eyes to the incredible vibrancy of the spiritual life. As spiritual beings, we are constantly ascending and descending Jacob's ladder. Our souls are in constant flux, now running after the lusts of the flesh, now striving upward toward the spirit. And what is the ultimate source of all this vibrancy and dynamism? Desire, the desire either to return to our original state of unity with the Father or to rebel against that union and seek fulfillment elsewhere. It is this desire that moves us out of our egocentrism toward one of the twin poles of flesh and spirit; this desire, too, that drives us to seek out completion, consummation, the telos of all our hopes and dreams.

Indeed, so convinced was Origen of the power and necessity of desire that, at one point in his work, he goes so far as to make this shocking statement: "It is better, if it be possible, that [the soul] should attach itself to the spirit and become spiritual. If, however, this is not possible, it is more expedient for it to follow even the wickedness of the flesh than by remaining fixed in the sphere of its own will to occupy the position of an irrational animal" (3.4; 234). Origen's point here is a profound one. At the heart of all action and all motion lies desire. If our desire is only for things of the flesh, then it shall drive us downward, away from God, back into the cave. But if that desire is for higher things, for the things of the spirit, it shall drive us upward to God, to the Form of the Good that dwells in the timeless World of Being. The latter desire is, of course, better than the former, but the former is better than no desire at all.

Standing in the great tradition of Socrates and Plato, humanist Christians like Origen see life in terms of drama, and they thus have little patience for those who would seek, like the legalists, to close it down, or who would content themselves, like the Stoics, with merely observing it from afar. They are enemies of all pretension and hypocrisy, and they balk at those whose desires are too weak for any real engagement with life or the God who is Life.

Desire is good; it is nothing less than the meat and drink of our soul. The desire was put there—perhaps in the preexistence, perhaps at birth—by God, and he alone can fulfill it: "This longing, this love has, we believe, undoubtedly been implanted in us by God; and as the eye naturally demands light and vision and our body by its nature desires food and drink, so our mind cherishes a natural and appropriate longing to know God's truth and to learn the causes of things" (2.11; 149-50). Plato, in his partial wisdom, knew and felt this longing. He heeded it in his life, taught it in his dialectic, and incarnated it in his myths. It remains to us, his heirs, to feel it as well and allow it to impel us to move out of the cave and into the light.

A JOURNEY HOME

But why, we must ask yet again, should a Christian who believes in salvation by grace through faith in Christ devote so much time and energy to ascending the rising path? To this question, Origen offers an answer that is not only profoundly Platonic but also defines a central goal of the humanist Christian. In the paragraph that directly follows the one quoted above, Origen has this to say to those who would follow their God-implanted desire:

> Now we have not received this longing ["to know his truth and to learn the causes of things"] from God on the condition that it should not or could not ever be satisfied; for in that case the "love of truth" would appear to have been implanted in our mind by God the Creator to no purpose, if its gratification is never to be accomplished. So when even in this life men devote themselves with great labour to sacred and religious studies, although they obtain only some small fragments out of the immeasurable treasures of divine knowledge, yet [they gain this advantage,] that they occupy their mind and understanding with these questions and press onward in their eager desire. Moreover they derive much assistance from the fact that by turning their mind to the study and love of truth they render themselves more capable of receiving instruction in the future. For when a man wishes to paint a picture, if he first sketches with the faint touch of a light pencil the outlines of the proposed figure and inserts suitable marks to indicate features afterwards to be added, the preliminary drawing with its faint outline undoubtedly renders the canvas more prepared to receive the true colours. So it will be with us, if only that faint form and outline is inscribed "on the tablets of our heart" by the pencil of our Lord Jesus Christ. This is perhaps the reason why it is said, "To every one that hath shall be given and added." It is clear, then, that to those who have now in this life a kind of outline of truth and knowledge there shall be added in the future the beauty of the perfect image. (2.11; 150)

Origen's answer to the question of why Christians saved by grace should dedicate themselves to ascending Plato's rising path is as rhetorically eloquent as it is simply straightforward: to prepare.

Just as a painter intent on producing a masterpiece will often prepare a canvas by making a faint, sketchy outline, so the humanist

Christian prepares the mind to receive God's divine presence in all its glory by rendering it "capable of receiving instruction." If, for example, I knew that next year I would be given the opportunity to visit the Holy Land, rest assured I would spend considerable time preparing for the journey. I would pour over maps of Israel and brush up on the history, culture, and archaeology of that land on which our Savior trod. By so doing, the joy of my eventual journey would be multiplied many times, for I would experience the twin pleasures of first recognizing the originals of those lesser imitations I had studied the year before, and then of moving beyond what I had studied to an experiential knowledge that is both real and intimate.

But, of course, the prepared journey to heaven will be even more wonderful than this. For not only will God's kingdom *truly* meet and exceed my expectations, but those expectations themselves will be grounded in a longing for God that was (innately) implanted in me before my birth. My desire to visit the Holy Land is of recent origin and is not really linked in any intimate way to the roots and mainstays of my soul; but my desire to "know God's truth and to learn the causes of things" is one that runs deep, down to the very foundations of my being. How glorious it will be on that day when those things for which we yearned, those things that in this life are but faint outlines on a canvas, will be revealed in all their glory, in what Origen calls "the beauty of the perfect image."

Though we cannot follow Origen on every theological point, inspired by him, we can affirm, in the words of Paul, "For now we see through a glass, darkly; but then face to face: now I know in part; but then shall I know even as also I am known" (1 Cor 13:12).

PLATO IN THE EAST

The Three Gregorys

As I FREELY admitted in the previous chapter, many of Origen's Platonic musings are heterodox at best. Although in his other writings—most notably, *Against Celsus*—Origen proved himself to be an effective, fiercely orthodox defender of the Trinity, the incarnation, and the atonement, in *On First Principles* he chose, by his own admission, to let his mind wander free over subjects on which the Bible was either silent or ambiguous. Indeed, in his preface to the latter work, he makes clear the difference between the essential, nonnegotiable doctrines of the faith and those peripheral teachings that are open to speculation:

> The holy apostles, when preaching the faith of Christ, took certain doctrines, those namely which they believed to be necessary ones, and delivered them in the plainest terms to all believers. . . . There were other doctrines, however, about which the apostles simply said that things were so, keeping silence as to the how or why; their intention undoubtedly being to supply the more diligent of those who came after them, such as should prove to be lovers of wisdom, with an exercise on which to display the fruit of their ability. (preface; 2)

It is precisely because the author of *On First Principles* chose to read Plato's dialogues alongside his Bible as he diligently exercised his philosophical powers on those peripheral teachings that I turned to him first.

Still, I would like to turn now in this chapter, and the three that follow, to ten Christian thinkers who, with the (possible) exception of Descartes, succeeded in absorbing the ideas and methods of Plato while remaining firmly within the bounds of orthodoxy. Taken together, these ten philosophers-theologians-critics-poets offer a myriad of ways by which the pre-Christian wisdom of Plato has inspired and guided Christians toward enduring truths.

GREGORY OF NAZIANZUS ON THEOLOGY

Since Origen, and through him Plato, exerted his most direct influence on the Eastern church fathers, it seems only right to begin in the Orthodox East before moving on to the Roman Catholic West. The fourth century marked a flowering of Christian theology in the East, with its greatest mouthpieces being Athanasius and the three Cappadocian fathers: Basil of Caesarea and Gregory of Nyssa (who were brothers), and their close friend Gregory of Nazianzus.

Though he was the son of a bishop, Gregory of Nazianzus (ca. 330–ca. 389), like many young men of his day, received a full pagan classical education, in Athens no less. Ironically, at one point in his studies, he took classes with Julian the Apostate: he who, when he became emperor, would attempt, unsuccessfully, to undo the Christianizing work of Constantine and push Rome back to paganism. While a student, Gregory had planned to become a civil servant, but he chose instead to lead an ascetic monastic life. He was not, by nature, a man suited for public controversy, but he found himself in Constantinople during a revival of orthodoxy and was coaxed to preach five theological orations on the nature of God (380). While cleaving closely to orthodox doctrine, Gregory's orations betray, in a good way, his Platonic education.

After an introductory oration, Gregory devotes his second to God the Father, with the third and fourth focusing on the Son, and the fifth on the Holy Spirit. I will confine myself here to his second oration, for in it, he carries on a conversation with Plato that, far from drawing him away from the truths of the Scriptures, propels him upward toward a fuller and richer engagement with the God who revealed himself to Moses as I AM.

Early in his second oration, Gregory makes an indirect allusion to Plato's allegory of the cave. After explaining that even the most mystical of theologians can only, like Moses, see God's back (Ex 33:21-23)—that is to say, his glory rather than his actual essence—Gregory describes "the back parts of God" thus: those things "which he leaves behind him, as tokens of himself, like the shadows and reflections of the sun in the water, which show the sun to our weak eyes, because we cannot look at the sun himself, for by his unmixed light he is too strong for our power of perception" (2.3; 138).[1] Just as the philosopher who escapes from Plato's cave can only look at reflections in the water until his eyes are strong enough to look at the sun, so Gregory's theologian must be content with reflections (or imitations) of God's direct nature until the soul is prepared to receive what medieval theologians, after Plato, would call the Beatific (or blessed) Vision.

Gregory goes on in the next chapter to assert the difficulty of defining the invisible God by means of a direct allusion to Plato's *Timaeus* (28e): "It is difficult to conceive God, but to define him in words is an impossibility, as one of the Greek teachers of divinity taught, not unskillfully, as it appears to me" (2.4; 138). How then is the philosopher-theologian to proceed? By way of the Socratic-Platonic, two-step process that I argued for in chapter one—that is, by first clearing away false definitions (Socrates), and then moving forward to a definition that squares with the true nature of reality (Plato).

Accordingly, Gregory, using Socratic *eristic* and *reductio*, smashes the pretensions of those who make idols in the form of physical things,

---

[1] Gregory of Nazianzus, *Theological Orations*, in *Christology of the Later Fathers*, ed. Edward Roche Hardy, trans. Charles Gordon Browne and James Edward Swallow, Library of Christian Classics (Louisville: Westminster John Knox, 1954), 128-214. I will provide in the text the oration and chapter numbers followed by the page number.

those who worship passion or beauty or strength as deities, and those who, like the Presocratics, hold up the four elements as the first principles of the cosmos. He carries out this necessary demolition job with Socratic brio, but he does not allow his oration to end with a Socratic aporia. Rather, like Plato, he moves from the negative elimination of the false to the positive affirmation of the true: "He who is eagerly pursuing the nature of the self-existent will not stop at saying what he is not, but must go on beyond what he is not, and say what he is; inasmuch as it is easier to take in some single point than to go on disowning point after point in endless detail, in order, both by the elimination of negatives and the assertion of positives to arrive at a comprehension of this subject" (2.9; 142).

Significantly, in seeking out the true nature of God, Gregory begins by assuring his audience that our difficulty in apprehending God through human reason is *not* the result of God envying us that information, "for envy is far from the divine nature, which is passionless and only good and Lord of all" (2.11; 143). Although the Bible certainly implies that God is not envious—though it does depict him as being righteously jealous of our love and allegiance (e.g., Ex 20:5; Deut 32:21)—it is Plato's *Timaeus*, rather than the Old or New Testaments, that begins its exploration of the nature of the Creator by positing God as being above feelings of envy. Such a starting place is essential for both Plato and Gregory, for both rest their theological musings on their firmly held belief that "every rational nature longs for God and for the first cause" (2.8; 145).

Running Platonic desire through Paul's analysis of sin (Rom 1:24), Gregory then goes on to argue that, when our desires go astray, we fall into worshiping idols of all sorts. Of such people, Gregory says that "though they are of a rational nature, and have received grace from God, they have set up the worse as the better" (2.15; 146). Gregory's phrasing here, I would argue, equates idolaters with those sophists who so misused rhetoric as to make the weaker argument the stronger. However, whereas the pagan Plato laid the fault for this misuse at the feet of ignorance, the Christian Gregory links it to demonic influence:

Satan "laid hold of their desire in its wandering in search of God, in order to distort to himself the power, and steal the desire, leading it by the hand, like a blind man asking a road; and he hurled down and scattered some in one direction and some in another, in to one pit of death and destruction" (2.15; 146).

The devil's wiles are strong indeed, but they can only lead astray a desire that is itself good and divinely implanted. Gregory, through his meditations on *both* Plato and the Bible, is sure of this: "Reason that proceeds from God, that is implanted in all from the beginning and is the first law in us, and is bound up in all, leads us up to God through visible things" (2.16; 147). It is because of this assurance that Gregory can, wonderfully but unexpectedly, restate his doubt as to our inability of conceiving God's true nature and then transcend that doubt:

> What God is in nature and essence, no man ever yet has discovered or can discover. Whether it will ever be discovered is a question which he who will may examine and decide. In my opinion it will be discovered when that within us which is godlike and divine, I mean our mind and reason, shall have mingled with its like, and the image shall have ascended to the archetype, of which it has now the desire. And this I think is the solution of that vexed problem as to "We shall know even as we are known." (2.16; 147)

The move that Gregory here makes from the ascent of the Platonic philosopher (in *Symposium*, *Phaedrus*, and *Republic*) toward the Beatific Vision to Paul's promise (1 Cor 13:12) that a time is coming when we will know even as we will be fully known is breathtaking. Plato, Paul, and Gregory alike depict spiritual growth as an ascent up the rising path toward the Form-Truth-Archetype. For now, we see dimly, as in a mirror, but if we continue up the rising path, we will eventually see and be seen face-to-face.

For the next three chapters, Gregory offers his own version of the roll call of the faithful (Heb 11), a list of biblical figures who caught glimpses of God's true light: Enoch, Noah, Abraham, Jacob, Elijah, Manoah, Isaiah, Ezekiel, Peter, and Paul. He then sums up his point in chapter twenty-one:

The truth then—and the whole world—is full of difficulty and obscurity; and, as it were, with a small instrument we are undertaking a
great work, when with merely human wisdom we pursue the knowledge
of the self-existent, and in company with, or not apart from, the senses,
by which we are borne hither and thither, and led into error, we apply
ourselves to the search after things which are only to be grasped by the
mind, and we are unable by meeting bare realities with bare intellect to
approximate somewhat more closely to the truth, and to mold the mind
by its concepts. (2.21; 150)

Though there is nothing here that contradicts the Bible, Gregory's
warning that our senses can often lead us into error is strongly Platonic,
with its insistence that we move from our physical eye to our mind's
eye, from that which is seen to that which is unseen.

Still, Gregory does not stray past the Bible. Rather than allow the
danger of overtrusting our senses to push him toward a negative,
gnostic view of matter and the body, he uses it to instill humility. That
is why he moves into a lengthy, rhetorically powerful peroration based
on Job 38–41 in which he asks, If we cannot comprehend the mysteries
of God's creation, how can we hope to comprehend the mysteries of
the Creator? Then, putting us in the proper humble state of mind, he
pulls everything together. If we had eyes to see, we would be able to
perceive the Creator in and through his creation; better yet, we would
allow our awe over the power and majesty of the sun to lead us to
reverence for the God who made the sun, and who illuminates the
spiritual realm as his created sun illuminates the physical.

And that leads Gregory back to the allegory of the cave, making an
allusion to Plato's *Republic* that is as direct and clear as the one I identified in chapter three is indirect and ambiguous: "Have you considered the importance of the fact that a heathen writer speaks of the
sun as holding the same position among material objects as God does
among objects of thought? For the one gives light to the eyes, as the
other does to the mind; and is the most beautiful of the objects of sight,
as God is of those of thought" (2.30; 157). Note that Gregory quotes
Plato here, as he does earlier, as an authority, as one through whom

real truths were conveyed by a God whom Plato did not know—or at least only knew in part.

Indeed, Gregory discerns the same kind of Platonic truth that treats the sun as an earthly imitation or figure of God (or the Good) in the link that Hebrews 8–9 makes between the earthly and heavenly temple:

> Shall we pause here, after discussing nothing further than matter and visible things, or, since the Word knows the Tabernacle of Moses to be a figure of the whole creation—I mean the entire system of things visible and invisible—shall we pass the first veil, and stepping beyond the realm of sense, shall we look into the holy place, the intellectual and celestial creation? (2.31; 158)

Buoyed up by *both* Plato's allegory of the cave and the epistle to the Hebrews, Gregory yearns to continue his philosophical-theological ascent up the rising path toward the true cause and origin of the physical sun and the earthly tabernacle. Without treating either matter or our senses as inherently evil, Gregory inspires his readers to transcend the limits of the visible to gaze on the invisible God.

GREGORY OF NYSSA ON MOSES

Gregory of Nyssa (ca. 332–395) shared the desire of his friend Gregory of Nazianzus to transcend the limits of the visible and temporal to gaze on that which is invisible and eternal. Like his friend, he was a fearless defender of orthodoxy—he played an important role in defining and guarding the essential doctrine of the Trinity—who also loved Plato and was eager to learn from him those ideas and methods that would draw him closer to the one, true God. His Christian Platonism runs throughout his work, but it plays a particularly strong role in his allegorical reading of the biblical account of Moses.

In *The Life of Moses* (ca. 390), Gregory indulges a kind of biblical interpretation that would become very popular in the Middle Ages but that has its roots in the influence that Plato exerted on the Neoplatonic Plotinus, the Jewish Philo, the Christian Clement of Alexandria, and Clement's star pupil, Origen. By the time of Aquinas and Dante, every verse of the Old Testament was believed to work, at least potentially, on four separate levels of meaning: the literal (or historical), the alle-gorical (or typological), the moral (or tropological), and the anagogical (or spiritual). Thus, to borrow from a letter Dante wrote to one of his patrons, the verse "when Israel out of Egypt came" (Ps 114:1) can be read in four separate but simultaneous ways: to refer to the exodus (literal); to signify how Christ freed us from sin (allegorical); to de-scribe the conversion of the soul from bondage to sin to freedom in Christ (moral); and to prophesy that glorious moment when the human soul will leave behind the body's long slavery to death and cor-ruption and enter the Promised Land of heaven (anagogical).

Although Gregory's exegesis technically confines itself to the first two meanings, the literal and the allegorical, he is concerned throughout with how his allegorical reading will improve our moral behavior and how it will point us toward final things. Like Plato, and Origen and Gregory of Nazianzus, he strongly affirms free will and choice and wants his readers to make a wise use of it so that they may grow spiritually and ascend toward the truth of God.

After giving a brief historical overview of the life of Moses (book one), he moves on, in the much lengthier book two, to read that history in allegorical terms. The strangeness of his reading greets us immedi-ately in his interpretation of Pharaoh's decree to kill the male, but not the female, Hebrew babies (Ex 1:16). For Gregory, the female repre-sents the physical, the emotional, and the appetitive, while the male represents the spiritual, the rational, and the ascetical. Though we have no control over our physical birth, he argues, when it comes to our moral birth, we are "in some manner our own parents, giving birth to ourselves by our own free choice in accordance with whatever we wish to be, whether male or female, moulding ourselves to the teaching of virtue or vice" (2.3; 55-56).[2] In the manner of Origen, Gregory finds a Platonic *psychomachia* lurking allegorically behind Pharaoh's massacre of the innocents, one that pits not only flesh against spirit but

---

[2]Gregory of Nyssa, *The Life of Moses*, trans. Abraham J. Malherbe and Everett Ferguson, Clas-sics of Western Spirituality (New York: Paulist Press, 1978). I will provide in the text the book and chapter numbers followed by the page number.

also appetite against reason, vice against virtue. He also lends man, as in Plato and Origen, considerable free will in choosing the manner of his spiritual birth.

Does that mean Gregory blindly accepts as true all of Plato's theories? By no means! He makes it clear that there are things the Christian can accept from Plato and things he must reject: "Pagan philosophy says that the soul is immortal. This is a pious offspring. But it also says that souls pass from bodies to bodies and are changed from a rational to an irrational nature. This is a fleshly and alien foreskin" (2.40; 63). No orthodox Christian can accept Plato's teachings on the transmigration of the soul. And yet, though Gregory makes this clear, he finds an allegorical truth in Plato's suggestion, in *Phaedrus*, that souls that turn from the path of virtue will reincarnate as animals. Thus, in his allegorical reading of the plague of frogs that Moses unleashes on Egypt, Gregory discerns a truth about what happens to those who live a carnal life:

> One sees in the sordid and licentious life that which is indeed born out of clay and mire and that which, through imitation of the irrational, remains in a form of life neither altogether human nor frog. Being a man by nature and becoming a beast by passion, this kind of person exhibits an amphibious form of life ambiguous in nature. (2.70; 70)

Later, while considering the allegorical lesson behind the sexual immorality and idolatry that the militarily successful Israelites committed with the daughters of Moab (Num 25:1-3), Gregory combines the rational-appetitive struggle within the tripartite soul in *Republic* with the downward reincarnation of *Phaedrus*:

> By vanquishing by her very appearance those who had not been conquered by weapons, pleasure raised a trophy of dishonor against them and held up their shame to public scorn. Pleasure showed that she makes men beasts. The irrational animal impulse to licentiousness made them forget their human nature; they did not hide their excess but adorned themselves with the dishonor of passion and beautified themselves with the stain of shame as they wallowed, like pigs, in the slimy mire of uncleanness, openly for everyone to see. (2.302; 132)

Gregory understood well the nature of grace and of the atonement, but that did not prevent him from urging himself and his flock to press on morally and spiritually. The Christian initiate, like the lover-philosopher initiate in *Symposium*, *Phaedrus*, and *Republic*, must not allow himself to slide backward into irrationality. He must continue up the rising path.

Although such a view can easily fall into works righteousness, this does not happen to Gregory—in great part because of his embrace of Platonic desire. It is that desire, fused with the uniquely Christian virtue of hope, that draws the soul from the beauty of what is seen to the greater beauty of what is unseen: from the imitations within the cave to the realities that lie outside, illuminated by the sun.

For the Platonic Gregory, God fulfills our desire while filling us with an even greater desire to continue the journey. We must stand still in his presence, even as we continue upward:

> Hope always draws the soul from the beauty which is seen to what is beyond, always kindles the desire for the hidden through what is constantly perceived. Therefore, the ardent lover of beauty, although receiving what is always visible as an image of what he desires, yet longs to be filled with the very stamp of the archetype. (2.231; 114)

And again:

> This truly is the vision of God: never to be satisfied in the desire to see him. But one must always, by looking at what he can see, rekindle his desire to see more. Thus, no limit would interrupt growth in the ascent to God, since no limit to the Good can be found nor is the increasing of desire for the Good brought to an end because it is satisfied. (2.239; 116)

Phrases like the "ardent lover of beauty," reminiscent of *Symposium*, and "the Good," reminiscent of *Republic*, betray Gregory's Platonic orientation; but they also fuel his desire to continue his ascent toward that face-to-face meeting with the ultimate Form/Archetype (the personal, triune God), for whom Paul also longs (1 Cor 13:12).

For a modern Christian, the call to imitate Moses means a call to obey God and to trust his provision. For the Platonic Gregory, it means something more. It signifies nothing less than a perpetual striving to transcend the barriers of our world and achieve the Beatific Vision: "For he who elevates his life beyond earthly things through such ascents never fails to become even loftier than he was until, as I think, like an eagle in all things his life may be seen above and beyond the cloud whirling around the ether of spiritual ascent" (2.307; 133).

GREGORY PALAMAS ON THE UNCREATED LIGHT

Between the two Gregorys of Nazianzus and Nyssa and the great Gregory Palamas (1296–1359), there exists a gap of almost a thousand years. And yet, partly because they share a common heritage in Plato and the Bible, their vision and their desire are remarkably similar. Similar, that is, with a twist. Whereas the two Gregorys happily acknowledged their debt to ancient Greek thought in general and Plato in particular, Palamas, while working within parameters set down by Plato, vigorously denied his reliance on the ancients.

Palamas was not only a monk; he was a hesychast (from the Greek word for peace or quietude): a hermit who sought a deeper communion with God through continual, solitary prayer and contemplation. Although he was raised in Constantinople by a wealthy and noble family, and although he had the same classical education as the two Gregorys, he threw both aside for a strict monastic life in the most remote and severe of Greek Orthodox monasteries, Mount Athos. Like Gregory of Nazianzus, he probably would have preferred to stay out of the limelight, but the religious controversies of his day drove him to write theology.

The work with which he is most associated, *For the Defense of Those Who Practice Quietude* (1338–1341; more commonly known as *The Triads*), was written specifically to defend the worldview and way of life of the hesychasts from those who accused them of being fanatical, anti-intellectual navel-gazers. As a result, its tone is as polemical and one-sided as Luther's *Bondage of the Will*. And yet, ironically, just as Luther's attack of the classical humanist Erasmus is shot through with over two dozen carefully chosen references from such pagan writers as Cicero, Horace, Virgil, Cato, Ovid, and Homer, so Palamas's *Triads* borrow extensively from the very Platonic tradition that they eschew.

Palamas begins his polemic by stating clearly the position from which he will be distancing himself in the *Triads*:

> I have heard it stated by certain people that monks also should pursue secular wisdom, and that if they do not possess this wisdom, it is impossible for them to avoid ignorance and false opinions, even if they have achieved the highest level of impassibility; and that one cannot acquire perfection and sanctity without seeking knowledge from all quarters, above all from Greek culture, which also is a gift of God—just as were those insights granted to the prophets and apostles through revelation. (1.1.1; 25)[3]

I could not have stated better myself the position of the humanist Christian who would unite Athens and Jerusalem and build bridges between Plato and the Bible—except that Palamas subtly inflects it to suggest that Platonic-humanist Christians believe that they cannot attain perfection without the aid of pre-Christian, Greco-Roman philosophers. Such is not my position, or that of Origen, the two Gregorys, or the seven writers I will discuss in the next three chapters. Like Luther after him, Palamas writes in a polemical mood, causing him to gravitate toward an all-or-nothing approach that would dismiss *all* secular philosophy as vain, empty, and deceptive (see Col 2:8).

Several chapters later, Palamas qualifies himself somewhat: "The intellect of pagan philosophers is . . . a divine gift insofar as it naturally possesses a wisdom endowed with reason. But it has been perverted by the wiles of the devil, who has transformed it into a foolish wisdom, wicked and senseless, since it puts forward such doctrines" (1.1.19; 27). With proper discernment, this passage suggests, the Christian can locate some real wisdom in a philosopher like Plato. Indeed, Palamas goes on to concede that, if we take the serpent philosophy and cut off both its head and tail—which he links to the "wrong opinions" and "fabulous stories" of the pagans (1.1.21; 29)—we

---

[3]Gregory Palamas, *The Triads*, ed. John Meyendorff, trans. Nicholas Gendle, Classics of Western Spirituality (New York: Paulist Press, 1983). I will provide in the text the triad, book, and chapter numbers followed by the page number.

can make some good use of it. Nevertheless, he concludes that it is far less dangerous to bypass the philosophers and seek knowledge of God through direct contemplation.

As an Eastern Orthodox theologian writing in the tradition of Athanasius and Dionysus the Areopagite (or Pseudo-Dionysus or Denys), Palamas's ultimate goal is to achieve theosis, or deification. Just as God became like us in the incarnation, so we must strive to become like him. Importantly, that does not mean we will become a god; rather, it means that our proper telos is to participate in the glory of the triune God (2 Pet 1:4). And to do that, we must enter into the uncreated light of God. Although that final transformation will occur in heaven, Palamas catches glimpses of it in the glowing faces of Moses when he came down from Sinai (Ex 34:29), Stephen just before he was martyred (Acts 7:55), and the three disciples who witnessed the transfiguration of Christ on Mount Tabor (Mt 17:2).

In one long, beautiful sentence, Palamas lists what the initiate must do to prepare the soul for the fullness of that vision of light:

> One recognises this light when the soul ceases to give way to the evil pleasures and passions, when it acquires inner peace and the stilling of thoughts, spiritual repose and joy, contempt of human glory, humility allied with a hidden rejoicing, hatred of the world, love of heavenly things, or rather the love of the sole God of Heaven. (3.1.36; 90)

I do not use the word *initiate* here lightly. The step-by-step spiritual progression that Palamas maps out bears a striking resemblance to that of Plato. Palamas has his own divided line, his own pilgrimage from the cave to the outside world that calls on the initiate to slowly separate himself from the vain, temporal things of this world in search of a peace that transcends understanding.

In fact, just one chapter earlier, Palamas, using Platonic imagery, promises his fellow hesychasts that "we too will become luminous if we lift ourselves up, abandoning earthly shadows, by drawing near to the true light of Christ" (3.1.35; 90). As in Plato, this movement from darkness to light is not sensual—it does not, as we would say today, change the rods and cones of our physical eyes—but spiritual. Indeed, Palamas insists that even a blind man can receive the longed-for vision of uncreated light, for it is not with the bodily senses that we see it.

Still, Palamas adds two elements to the journey of the Platonic philosopher/lover that make his vision distinct from that of Plato: the first, I will argue, draws out something that was already implicit in Plato; the second, I will insist, adds a Christian dimension of which Plato, because he lacked special revelation, was ignorant.

Whereas many Christian monks, theologians, and mystics share Plato's mistrust of the senses, Palamas goes one step further. To reach the uncreated, something more than our senses must be transcended: the vision of

> angels and angelic men . . . is not a sensation, since they do not receive it through the senses; nor is it intellection, since they do not find it through thought or the knowledge that comes thereby, but after the cessation of all mental activity. It is not, therefore, the product of either imagination or reason; it is neither an opinion nor a conclusion reached by syllogistic argument. (1.3.18; 35)

In sharp contrast to most Platonic-minded Christians, yet consistent with the Eastern Orthodox apophatic tradition, Palamas asserts that *neither* the senses nor the intellect, the imagination, nor the reason can apprehend the uncreated light of God.

It is true that the movement in Plato is from the sensual World of Becoming to the intellectual World of Being, and yet, as we saw in part one, Plato himself was aware of the limits of reason, logic, and the dialectic. As I argued in chapters three and four, Plato's greatest philosophical statements always give way to a myth or allegory that speaks to the reader on a level that transcends reason without "sinking" into the kind of poetic language that Plato dismissed as an imitation of an imitation. For all his exaltation of the rational part of the soul, there is ever something in Plato's best dialogues that pushes past the limits of reason to a state of pure contemplation.

As for the second Christian dimension that Palamas adds to the Platonic ascent up the rising path, he, quite fairly, bases it on the inability of the pre-Christian Greeks to imagine that our body could play a positive role in our pursuit of the Beatific Vision:

> Do you not see that if one desires to combat sin and acquire virtue, to find the reward of the struggle for virtue, or rather the intellectual sense, earnest of that reward, one must force the mind to return within the body and oneself? On the other hand, to make the mind "go out," not only from fleshly thoughts, but out of the body itself, with the aim of contemplating intelligible visions—that is the greatest of the Hellenic errors, the root and source of all heresies, an invention of demons, a doctrine which engenders folly and is itself the product of madness. This is why those who speak by demonic inspiration become beside themselves, not knowing what they are saying. As for us, we recollect the mind not only within the body and heart, but also within itself. (1.3.4; 43-44)

Though Palamas's language is unnecessarily harsh and condemning, and his invoking of the devil is gratuitous—surely Plato cannot be blamed for having no access to the Bible—he is correct to take the Neoplatonists to task for their dualism and Gnosticism. Just as most of the Stoics and Epicureans of Athens laughed at Paul when he spoke of the resurrection (Acts 17:32), so the Neoplatonists could not conceive that a soul would want to hold on to its body.

But then that is precisely the reason why the would-be Christian Platonist must test and modify the teachings of Plato in accordance with the fuller revelation of Christ and the Bible. The notion that we might be enfleshed souls rather than souls trapped in bodies, and that our bodies could be glorified along with our souls, was simply not thinkable within Plato's worldview. I don't think Plato could have conceived that the spiritual activities of the initiate could transform not only the soul but the body as well. He certainly could not have imagined that God would take on human flesh (Jn 1:14).

And yet, had he lived after the incarnation and accepted, as did the three Gregorys of this chapter, that Christ assumed the fullness of our humanity, might he not have accepted as well the implications of that great doctrine:

> For just as the divinity of the Word of God incarnate is common to soul
> and body, since He has deified the flesh through the mediation of the soul
> to make it also accomplish the works of God; so similarly, in spiritual man,
> the grace of the Spirit, transmitted to the body through the soul, grants to
> the body also the experience of things divine, and allows it the same blessed
> experiences as the soul undergoes. (2.2.12; 51)

In many ways, the Orthodox doctrine of theosis, to which Palamas
refers in this quote, will seem less alien to the Platonist than to the
evangelical Protestant. For the Platonist knows instinctively what the
Protestant too often forgets: that sanctification is a long, slow process
in which salvation gives way to transformation as initiates are slowly
conformed to the image of the Goodness, Truth, and Beauty after
which they seek.

Christian philosophers and theologians need not reject Plato because he did not know that the body participated in that transformation. To the contrary, it should be their task, and joy, to extend
Plato's understanding of the journey of the soul to include the glorification of the body.

PLATO IN THE WEST

Augustine, Boethius, and Dante

IN BOOK TWO, chapter sixty of *On Christian Doctrine* (ca. 397), Augustine of Hippo, borrowing a biblical metaphor that Origen used often, lays out the exact relationship between pagan learning and Christian truth:

> If those who are called philosophers, especially the Platonists, have said things which are indeed true and are well accommodated to our faith, they should not be feared; rather, what they have said should be taken from them as from unjust possessors and converted to our use. Just as the Egyptians had not only idols and grave burdens which the people of Israel detested and avoided, so also they had vases and ornaments of gold and silver and clothing which the Israelites took with them secretly when they fled, as if to put them to a better use. They did not do this on their own authority but at God's commandment, while the Egyptians unwittingly supplied them with things which they themselves did not use well. In the same way all the teachings of the pagans contain not only simulated and superstitious imaginings and grave burdens of unnecessary labor, which each one of us leaving the society of pagans under the leadership of Christ ought to abominate and avoid, but also liberal disciplines more suited to the uses of truth, and some most useful precepts concerning morals. Even some truths concerning the worship of one God are discovered among them. These are, as

it were, their gold and silver, which they did not institute themselves but dug up from certain mines of divine Providence, which is everywhere in-fused, and perversely and injuriously abused in the worship of demons. When the Christian separates himself in spirit from their miserable society, he should take this treasure with him for the just use of teaching the gospel. And their clothing, which is made up of those human institutions which are accommodated to human society and necessary to the conduct of life, should be seized and held to be converted to Christian uses.[1]

I quote this lengthy passage in full, for it provides the key to anyone who would understand how the Christian thinkers of late antiquity and the Middle Ages interacted with Plato. They knew very well the dangers of pagan learning, but many of them had the faith that they could seize hold of the truths latent in Plato, and the other ancients, and convert them for Christian use.

The episode to which Augustine alludes is generally referred to as the despoiling (or plundering) of the Egyptians (Ex 12:36), an episode that Augustine, like Origen before him, allegorizes. In the standard medieval interpretation of the episode, the gold and silver point ahead to "liberal disciplines" and "useful precepts" whose ultimate origin is "from certain mines of divine Providence." God not only allows but *commands* that we plunder that gold so that we may purge it of its demonic elements and make a proper use of it. Christ followers are the lawful possessors of truth, and it is right that they should claim that truth wherever they encounter it.

In this chapter, as we move from the Eastern church to its Western counterpart, we will consider three original-yet-traditional thinkers who made a full and proper use of the gold and silver that they plun-dered from the writings of Plato. I will begin with Augustine (354–430), whose long road to faith, recorded so memorably in his *Confessions* (397–400), took him from a heretical sect of Gnostics known as the Manichaeans to Christian orthodoxy by way of the writings of the Neoplatonists.

---

[1]Saint Augustine, *On Christian Doctrine*, trans. D. W. Robertson Jr. (Upper Saddle River, NJ: Prentice Hall, 1958), 75.

AUGUSTINE'S CONVERSION

As a member of the Manichaeans, the young Augustine believed that the flesh was irredeemably corrupt and had to be escaped from and transcended. The Manichaeans taught that, in his struggle against the dualistic forces of corruption, the incorruptible God had sent forth an offshoot of his substance to do battle. This substance was man's soul; however, in its struggle with corruption, "it had been taken captive, made impure, and corrupted, while the Word of God, which was to come to its assistance, was free, pure, and incorrupt. Yet if this was so, the Word of God must also have been subject to corruption, because it came of one and the same substance as the soul" (7.2; 135).[2]

While Augustine the Manichaean understood the problem that the soul faces if it is to achieve salvation and liberation, he soon came to realize that the teachings of the Manichaeans could not effect the salvation they called for. That is why, in the second sentence of the above quote, Augustine makes use of a Socratic reductio ad absurdum to show that, if the Manichaeans are correct about the inherent corruption of the flesh, then any attempt on the part of God to enter our world and rescue the soul would be doomed from the outset. For the next several chapters, Augustine continues to expose the contradictions at the heart of Manichaeism, until, in chapter nine, he comes to the writings of the Neoplatonists, particularly Plotinus, and there finds the bridge he needs to cross the Tiber.

In "the books of the Platonists," Augustine explains, he found it written that the Logos was God, that the Logos had come to his own, and that the Logos had brought light and life (Jn 1:1-5, 9), but he did not find it written that all those who believed in his name were given the right to be called children of God (Jn 1:12). Likewise, although "in the same books I also read of the Word, God, that his birth came not from human stock, not from nature's will or man's, but from God

---

[2]Augustine, *Confessions*, trans. R. S. Pine-Coffin (London: Penguin, 1961). I will provide in the text the book and chapter numbers followed by the page number.

[Jn 1:13] . . . I did not read in them that the Word was made flesh and came to dwell among us [Jn 1:14]" (7.9; 144-45).

Continuing on in the same chapter, Augustine then makes a third distinction between the teachings of the Neoplatonists and the teachings of the New Testament—namely, that while the Neoplatonists accept the first verse of Paul's great incarnational passage (Phil 2:6) and teach that "God, the Son, being himself, like the Father, of divine nature, did not see, in the rank of Godhead, a prize to be coveted," they deny that the Son "dispossessed himself, and took the nature of a slave, fashioned in the likeness of men, and presenting himself to us in human form [Phil 2:7]" (7.9; 145). What is at issue here is what Paul refers to as the kenosis, the teaching that the divine Logos, in taking on humanity, emptied himself of the full glory and prerogatives he shared as a member of the Godhead and made himself, to quote the author of Hebrews, "a little lower than the angels" (Heb 2:7).

Though Augustine here exposes errors in the Neoplatonists, he does so in a far different manner than he did with the Manichaeans. Whereas the Manichaeans led him astray, the Neoplatonists helped set his feet on the proper road toward truth. Indeed, Augustine ends chapter nine by invoking the same biblical metaphor that he does in the passage from *On Christian Doctrine* quoted above:

> It was from the Gentiles that I had come to you, and I set my mind upon the gold which you willed your people to carry away from Egypt for, wherever it was, it was yours. Through your apostle you told the Athenians that it is in you that we live and move and have our being, as some of their own poets have told us [Acts 17:28]. And, of course, the books I was reading were written in Athens. But your people had used the gold that was yours to serve the idols of the Egyptians, for they had exchanged God's truth for a lie, reverencing and worshipping the creature in preference to the Creator [Rom 1:25], and it was not upon these idols that I set my mind. (7.9; 146)

In a somewhat cryptic manner, Augustine here explains that his pilgrimage to Christ did not proceed by way of the Old Testament (the Jews who misused the gold they despoiled from the Egyptians to make the golden calf), but through the writings of the Greek Neoplatonists (the Gentiles, who had access, through the mines of divine providence, to real truth). To complicate the primary analogy a bit more, Augustine makes a secondary analogy between his own journey to faith and Paul's speech in Athens: just as Paul helped build a bridge between the Stoicism and Epicureanism of the Athenian elite by quoting a verse from the Greek poet Epimenides (Acts 17:28), so Augustine found his own bridge in the philosophical writings of Plato and his heirs.

As Augustine makes his slow transition from the partial truth of the Neoplatonists—who knew the eternal Word (Jn 1:1) but could not conceive of the incarnation (Jn 1:14)—to the complete truth of Christ, the Bible, and the church, he describes the process by way of a Platonic metaphor of ascent from the physical to the spiritual: "So, step by step, my thoughts moved on from the consideration of material things to the soul, which perceives things through the senses of the body, and to the soul's inner power to which the bodily senses communicate external facts" (7.17; 151). In the end, Augustine makes clear, it was his direct encounter with the incarnate-resurrected Christ, and not with Plato, that saved him (7.18). Nevertheless, Plato prepared the way by taking him to the first rung of the ladder and pointing his gaze upward: "By reading these books of the Platonists I had been prompted to look for truth as something incorporeal, and I caught sight of your invisible nature, as it is known through your creatures [Rom 1:20]" (7.20; 154).

Interestingly, as Augustine winds down his discussion of the role that the writings of the Neoplatonists played in his conversion, he suggests that the deeper problem with the Neoplatonists was not their intellectual errors but their spiritual pride:

> How could I expect that the Platonist books would ever teach me charity? I believe that it was by your will that I came across those books before I studied the Scriptures, because you wished me always to remember the impression they had made on me, so that later on, when I had been chastened by your Holy Writ and my wounds had been touched by your healing hand, I should be able to see and understand the difference between presumption and confession, between those who see the goal that they must reach, but cannot see the road by which they are to reach it, and those who

see the road to that blessed country which is meant to be no mere vision but our home. (7.20; 154)

The heirs of Plato knew the goal (the Beatific Vision) for which the soul was to strive, but they did not know the proper road to get there, for they presumed they could get there by their own effort and their own wisdom. Their *desires* were right, but they lacked the humility to see and confess their need.

And something more. Only once he embraced Christ did Augustine realize that the true telos for which he was made transcended Plato's vision of the Form of Goodness. Enlightenment is a good thing, but the proper end for which we were made is far more personal and intimate. The end of the journey is not a universal principle to contemplate but an eternal home to dwell in. So it is that Augustine prays to God in the famous opening paragraph of *Confessions*, "You made us for yourself and our hearts find no peace until they rest in you" (1.1; 21).

BOETHIUS'S *CONSOLATION*

Boethius's *Consolation of Philosophy* rests on the philosophical-theological premise that God speaks to the world through both general and special revelation. Despite the fact that Plato lived and died before Christ and lacked knowledge of the Old Testament, his writings bear witness to the truth to which all people have access through creation, conscience, reason, and our shared human desire to seek after the telos for which we were made. Indeed, *Consolation* marks a hinge point in the dialogue between general and special revelation, paganism and Christianity, Plato and Christ.

For, in his *Consolation*, the Christian Boethius (ca. 480–524) set himself a monumental task: to see how much true wisdom he could gain from the writings of the highest pre-Christian philosophers (Plato, Aristotle, Cicero) and schools (Neoplatonism, Stoicism, Epicureanism). Although Theodoric, king of the Ostrogoths and ruler of Italy, had paved the way for Boethius to become a consul of Rome (510), he later had Boethius thrown in prison (523), most likely because Theodoric, an Arian, disapproved of Boethius's orthodox beliefs.

Before dying a martyr's death the following year, Boethius wrote his *Consolation* in prison as a way of finding what solace he could from the legacy of Greco-Roman philosophy.

In a fluke of history—or as a result of divine providence—*Consolation* became one of the chief conduits through which Greek thought was channeled to medieval Europe during the long years when the Greek language was all but lost in the West (it would return when the Byzantine Greeks fled from the conquering Ottoman Turks, restoring to Europe the classical knowledge that helped spark the Renaissance). The Greek thought Boethius helped preserve included the literary and the ethical as well as the philosophical and the theological; however, in this section, I will focus specifically on how he kept alive Plato's call to ascend the rising path.

Told through a memorable dramatic frame reminiscent of Plato's dialogues, *Consolation* imagines Boethius visited in prison by Lady Philosophy, who first chases away the muses—who have only increased Boethius's grief and self-pity—and then instructs him in the proper method of viewing and handling his misfortunes. As if she were Socrates berating the Athenians for valuing lesser things like wealth and power over greater things like wisdom and virtue, Lady Philosophy challenges Boethius to understand his unique purpose as a rational human being:

> He [the Creator] intended that the human race should be above all other earthly beings; yet you thrust down your honourable place below the lowest. For if every good thing is allowed to be more valuable than that to which it belongs, surely you are putting yourselves lower than them [the animals] in your estimation, since you think precious the most worthless of things; and this is indeed a just result. Since, then, this is the condition of human nature, that it surpasses other classes only when it realises what is in itself; as soon as it ceases to know itself, it must be reduced to a lower rank than the beasts. To other animals ignorance of themselves is natural; in men it is a fault. (2; 33-34)[3]

---

[3]Boethius, *The Consolation of Philosophy*, trans. W. V. Cooper, in *The Great Books: Seventh Year 2* (Chicago: Great Books Foundation, 1959). I will provide in the text the book number and the page number.

Philosophy, so Plato was taught by his master, begins when we pay heed to that all-important two-word command: know thyself. Until we know who we are, we cannot determine our purpose or how far we have advanced in achieving that purpose. We certainly cannot assess the value of things, for we will have no fixed touchstone to measure them against.

To be ignorant of our true nature is to be reduced to the level of an irrational beast that lacks both conscience and consciousness. To come to know ourselves as we are is to rise above that which in us is bestial. As a Christian, Boethius does not believe in the transmigration of souls, and yet, he finds a way to preserve and affirm all those Platonic myths in which an evil soul declines downward through various animal bodies. And that way is the way of allegory, used, as we saw in the previous chapter, by Origen and Gregory of Nyssa alike. Since directly referencing the Bible would violate his decision to limit himself to general revelation, Boethius borrows a myth from Homer and then allegorizes it.

That myth is the well-known story in *Odyssey* 10 when Circe the witch transforms Odysseus's men into swine. By locating an eternal spiritual truth lurking within the pagan tale, Boethius allows Christian readers to access the wisdom of Plato without compromising their belief that we are enfleshed souls:

> As goodness alone can lead men forward beyond their humanity, so evil of necessity will thrust down below the honourable estate of humanity those whom it casts down from their first position. The result is that you cannot hold him to be a man who has been, so to say, transformed by his vices. If a violent man and a robber burns with greed of other men's possessions, you say he is like a wolf. . . . If another is in a slough of foul and filthy lusts, he is kept down by the lusts of an unclean swine. Thus then a man who loses his goodness, ceases to be a man, and since he cannot change his condition for that of a god, he turns into a beast. (4; 89)

Notice that Boethius, while staying true to the spirit of Plato, smuggles in the Orthodox notion of theosis. As in the myths, when we allow our souls to become heavy and sluggish through indulgence in vice and appetite, we only succeed in demeaning ourselves. Violence, greed, and lust drag us down, transforming us into something we were not created to be. We may not literally become wolves or pigs, but we do become wolflike and piglike as our sins cause us to give over our humanity.

It is not our telos to sink into bestiality, but then it is also not our telos to remain merely human. We were made to rise upward toward, and to participate in, the life of the Godhead. Boethius knows that Plato did not know about theosis, that he probably could not imagine men dwelling in intimacy with the Demiurge of *Timaeus*, and yet, once again, Boethius creates a space where Plato's journey of the soul toward the Beatific Vision can touch the pilgrimage of the Christian soul toward the triune God.

To encourage Boethius to seek after that vision of the Forms, Lady Philosophy first extols the Creator in language borrowed directly from *Timaeus*:

> Thou who dost rule the universe with everlasting law, founder of earth and heaven alike, who hast bidden time stand forth from out Eternity, for ever firm Thyself, yet giving movement unto all. No causes were without Thee which could thence impel Thee to create this mass of changing matter, but within Thyself exists the very idea of perfect good, which grudges naught, for of what can it have envy? Thou makest all things follow that high pattern. In perfect beauty Thou movest in Thy mind a world of beauty, making all in a like image, and bidding the perfect whole to complete its perfect functions. (3; 62)

This is not exactly a loving God, and yet, one whose lack of envy allows him to cultivate a desire to see his creatures attain that perfection he designed into his cosmos. Yes, this is the impassive Unmoved Mover of Aristotle (*Metaphysics* 12.7) who sets all in motion but is himself motionless, but he has a Platonic love of Beauty, and he has patterned creation after something very like that Word (or Logos) that Augustine discovered in the writings of the Neoplatonists.

But Lady Philosophy's invocation of the Creator is only the prelude to her request that Boethius, and all other philosophers, be enabled and empowered to ascend the rungs of the ladder to the World of Being:

Grant then, O Father, that this mind of ours may rise to Thy throne of majesty; grant us to reach that fount of good. Grant that we may so find light that we may set on Thee unblinded eyes; cast Thou therefrom the heavy clouds of this material world. Shine forth upon us in Thine own true glory. Thou art the bright and peaceful rest of all Thy children that worship Thee. To see Thee clearly is the limit of our aim. Thou art our beginning, our progress, our guide, our way, our end. (3; 63).

Once again, this is true to Plato and his search for the Sun behind the sun, the Form of the Good; but it also embodies the Christian yearning to gaze on the uncreated light of God and to know, and be known by, the One who is Alpha and Omega, beginning and end (Rev 1:8; 22:13). The Creator is not just an idea; he is a king on a throne. In him, there is more than contemplation; there is rest.

Whether we be a Platonic initiate or a Christian disciple, our goal is to push aside "the heavy clouds of this material world" that we may see the light of Truth.

DANTE'S JOURNEY

Of all the great medieval writers, the one who was most profoundly influenced by Boethius's *Consolation* was the poet Dante Alighieri (1265–1321), who received his Aristotle from Aquinas, but who relied on Boethius (and Augustine) for most of his Plato. His three-part epic poem, *The Divine Comedy*, completed shortly before his death during his long exile from his beloved Florence, maps out a journey of the soul that combines the philosophical insight of Plato's divided line with the awe and wonder of his allegory of the cave. Indeed, one could read the *Comedy* as an extended Platonic myth of the afterlife, a sort of myth of Er writ large.

To understand the shape of Dante's epic journey, one could do no better than to meditate on three passages from book three of *Consolation*, passages that capture the very heart of Plato:

For there is implanted by nature in the minds of men a desire for the true good; but error leads them astray towards false goods by wrong paths. (3; 45)

> But to return to the aims of men: their minds seem to seek to regain the highest
> good, and their memories seem to dull their powers. It is as though a drunken
> man were seeking his home, but could not remember the way thither. (3; 46)

> All things must find their own peculiar course again, and each rejoices in
> his own return. (3; 48)

Although Genesis and Exodus are undergirded by a theme of pilgrimage, of sojourners called to be strangers in a strange land, the
concept of the mystical journey of the soul is far more Hellenic than
Hebraic. Even the New Testament, which uses powerful images of
darkness and light, error and truth, does not really speak the language
of Plato's myths of ascent. Boethius is channeling Plato far more than
he is the Gospels or Paul's epistles, and the same goes for Dante—
though, by the time we get to Dante, Christian theology and philosophy have quite fully absorbed Plato.

I argued above that Hebrews 9 speaks of the heavenly and earthly tabernacle in language that echoes Plato's distinction between the Forms and
their physical imitations. Nevertheless, when Clement of Alexandria or
Origen, Gregory of Nyssa or Augustine finds spiritual meanings in the
stories of the Old Testament, they go beyond Jesus or Paul's use of
typology—"And if ye will receive it, this [John the Baptist] is Elias [Elijah],
which was for to come" (Mt 11:14); "Christ our passover is sacrificed for us"
(1 Cor 5:7)—into a type of analogical thinking whose ultimate source is
Plato. True, Paul writes in mystical-allegorical terms when he compares
Sarah and Hagar to two mountains and two covenants (Gal 4:21-26) or
when he identifies Jesus as the spiritual rock from which Moses and the
children of Israel drank (1 Cor 10:4), but the specific focus on the journey
of the soul toward the light has stronger Platonic than Judeo-Christian roots.

Consider the famous opening lines of the *Comedy*:

> Midway in our life's journey, I went astray
>   from the straight road and woke to find myself
>   alone in a dark wood. (*Inferno* 1.1-3; 16)[4]

---

[4]Dante Alighieri, *The Divine Comedy*, trans. John Ciardi (New York: New American Library,
2003). I will provide in the text the canto and line numbers followed by the page number.

Although Dante pictures himself moving physically and externally through hell, purgatory, and paradise, his journey, in Platonic fashion, is ultimately a spiritual and internal one. Before the epic opens, the lines imply, Dante had thought he was moving along the right road—that is, until he fell off the path to find himself stranded in a dark wood, a dimly lit world of error and illusion that suggests Plato's cave.

Indeed, the link between Dante's wood and Plato's cave is strengthened by the fact that when Dante struggles his way to the edge of the wood, he sees shining above him

> the sweet rays of that planet [the sun]
> whose virtue leads men straight on every road. (1.17-18; 17)

Just as the sun in the allegory of the cave represents the Form of the Good, so here it stands in for the triune God. Unfortunately, Dante soon finds that he cannot ascend directly toward the sun; if he is to find his way back to God, he must take a far longer and more arduous route. Like Er, he must descend, while still alive, into the underworld to see the final state of souls and understand the consequences of our choices on earth.

His guide for two-thirds of that journey will be the pre-Christian Virgil, who stands in relation to pagan poetry as Plato does to pagan philosophy—as the supreme embodiment of the furthest that human reason and virtue can reach apart from divine grace. Dante knows that Virgil (like Plato) can take him far along his appointed road—back, in fact, to the Garden of Eden—but he cannot take him all the way to the true Sun. Virgil's vision, like that of Plato, was limited and must be superseded, *though not canceled out*, by the fuller revelation of God's grace in Christ and the New Testament: symbolized in the *Comedy* by Beatrice.

Virgil and Plato, as it turns out, share an eternal dwelling in the first circle of hell, the realm of the virtuous pagans: those who were essentially sinless but lacked the grace of Christ. First-time readers of *Inferno* 4 are apt to feel great pity for Virgil, Plato, and their fellow virtuous pagans, and may even consider Dante cruel and unfair for placing them in hell, but the answer lies in the details. Dante's description of the final resting place of the most virtuous of the pre-Christian poets, philosophers, and statesman is based directly on Socrates's description of the Elysian Fields at the end of *Apology* (40e-41c; echoed by Virgil in *Aeneid* 6): a grassy plain on which the souls of the righteous walk back and forth discoursing about truth and virtue. That is to say, Dante gives to Plato and Virgil the full extent of their own desires and imaginations.

Dante has access to a knowledge denied to Plato and Virgil, but he also possesses a more capacious yearning for intimacy with God. The pre-Christian Plato sought, through the dialectical method, to trigger recollections of his prenatal experiences with the Forms; the Christian Dante wants to find his true home, a home that transcends Eden. The goal of Plato is to escape from the limits of our decaying World of Becoming; the goal of Dante is to find his proper place vis-à-vis God. Making use of a nautical metaphor, Dante explains that not only he himself but

> every nature moves across the tide
> of the great sea of being to its own port. (*Paradiso* 1.112-13; 600)

Plato's myths are cosmic, as is Dante's epic journey, but Dante's vision expands to take in the placement of every individual human being within that cosmos.

Both Plato and Dante present a hierarchical vision in which some people dwell closer to the truth and others farther away. Dante's universe naturally falls into a Platonic divided line, for his universe runs in accordance with one simple law

> The glory of Him who moves all things rays forth
> through all the universe, and is reflected
> from each thing in proportion to its worth. (*Paradiso* 1.1-3; 596)

In the schemes of both Plato (as filtered through Aquinas) and Dante, there will be some whose experience of the Beatific Vision will be greater than that of others, just as there will be many who will be shut out altogether from that vision. But in Dante, the Platonic emphasis

on knowledge and glory being gained through vigorous effort is transcended by the greater revelation of God's grace.

Thus, when Dante meets Piccarda, the soul of a nun who dwells in
the lowest celestial sphere (the Moon), and wonders whether she
would not rather dwell in a higher sphere closer to the uncreated light
of God, she answers that she is fully content where she is and does not
wish to ascend higher or sink lower:

> Brother, the power of love, which is our bliss,
>> calms all our will. What we desire, we have.
>> There is in us no other thirst than this.
>
> . . . .
>
> And so the posts we stand from sill to sill
>> throughout this realm, please all the realm as much
>> as they please Him who wills us to His will.
>
> In His will is our peace. (*Paradiso* 3.70-72, 82-85; 617-18)

Piccarda has only one desire, and that desire is to be where God would
have her. Were she to move to a higher rung on the Platonic ladder of
beatitude, she would lose the peace and joy she possesses. She is not a
student seeking the highest degree she can; she is a bride who wants
to be exactly where her bridegroom wants her to be. Plato leads us out
of the cave and into the light; Dante leads us out of the dark wood and
into the arms of the one who not only made the light but is himself the
light of the cosmos.

Unlike Socrates, who chose to be put to death rather than be exiled
from Athens, Dante, exiled against his will from Florence, found that
his true and lasting citizenship was in heaven.

FROM RENAISSANCE
TO ROMANTICISM

Erasmus, Descartes, and Coleridge

THOUGH THE EVER-CONTROVERSIAL Dante peppered his *Comedy* with lengthy invectives against the corrupt priests, monks, and popes of his day, he was himself an orthodox Christian who measured his love of classical, pre-Christian writers like Homer, Virgil, Plato, and Aristotle against Christ, the Bible, and the creeds of the church. Such was also the case for another controversial writer who lived at the dawn of the Renaissance and who fought alongside Martin Luther until he felt that Luther had gone too far and was causing unnecessary division. I refer, of course, to Erasmus of Rotterdam (ca. 1469–1536), whose publication of the Greek New Testament was instrumental to the work of the Protestant reformers and whose satirical, anticlerical *Praise of Folly* has led many modern readers to think, falsely, that Erasmus was a proto-Voltaire who used the acid of skepticism to dissolve all faith and tradition.

In fact, Erasmus was a humanist Christian of the highest order who believed that the erosion of classical learning was causing Christian theologians to be *worse* readers of Scripture, though he never left the Catholic Church like Luther:

I find that in comparison with the Fathers of the Church our present-day theologians are a pathetic group. Most of them lack the elegance, the charm of language, and the style of the Fathers. Content with Aristotle, they treat the mysteries of revelation in the tangled fashion of the logician. Excluding the Platonists from their commentaries, they strangle the beauty of revelation. Yet no less an authority than St. Augustine prefers to express himself in the flowing style that so enhanced the lovely writings of the Platonist school. He prefers them not only because they have so many ideas that are appropriate to our religion but also because the figurative language that they use, abounding in allegories, very closely approaches the language of Scripture itself. The great Christian writers of the past were able to treat even the most arid subjects with a beautiful prose. They enriched and colored their sermons and commentaries with the constant use of allegory. Almost all of them were at home with the writings of Plato and the poets, and they used this literary training to the very best advantage in interpreting the words of Scripture.[1]

Luther relied heavily on Augustine in his attempt to reform Christian doctrine and bring it back to its early church roots. Erasmus also looked back to Augustine, but for his classicism as much as for his theology. Both were opposed to the dry scholasticism of the schools, but Erasmus felt that the proper remedy was not to throw out Aristotle but to inject some needed Plato.

The Reformers tended to move away from allegorical readings of Scripture, though they did offer nonliteral readings of the text at times. For his part, Erasmus regarded the aesthetic beauty of the Bible as part and parcel of its message and its truth. But to access that beauty, he, like Augustine before him, needed the help of the Platonist school to properly unpack the figurative language of the Bible. So Erasmus argues in his *Handbook of the Militant Christian* (or *Enchiridion*; 1503), a work that also holds up Dante's virtuous pagans, especially Socrates and Plato, as worthy role models for imitation and guides along the thorny path of virtue: "If the example of the saints is too much for us, we should at least have enough pride not to let ourselves be

---

[1] Erasmus, *The Handbook of the Militant Christian*, in *The Essential Erasmus*, ed. and trans. John P. Dolan (New York: Mentor, 1964), 63-64.

outdistanced by pagans. With little knowledge of God and less of hell many of them have managed to lead clean and upright lives. Some of them even suffered loss of property and of life for this."[2]

While always looking to the Bible as the final authority, Erasmus considered the Socratic mandate to know thyself an excellent launching point for spiritual growth, just as he considered pagan poetry and philosophy a natural doorway to mature meditation on Scripture. Pagan wisdom rightly used can be an effective schoolmaster to lead us to higher truths. After all, did not Moses seek advice for ruling the Israelites from his pagan father-in-law Jethro (Ex 18:19)?

Erasmus on Justice

I could say much more about Erasmus's *Enchiridion*, particularly its focus on the Platonic journey of the Christian up the rising path, but there is another vital work by Erasmus that needs to be better known today, a work in which he updates and Christianizes Plato's *Republic*. Published in 1516, Erasmus's *Education of a Christian Prince* came out one year before Luther posted his Ninety-Five Theses, the same year Thomas More published *Utopia*, and three years after Machiavelli wrote *The Prince* (though he did not publish it until 1532). If Machiavelli proved to be the Thrasymachus of the Renaissance—one who taught that might makes right and that justice is the will of the stronger—then Erasmus hoped to be the Socratic-Platonic counter to realpolitik.

Just as Machiavelli seems to have hoped his political treatise would win him the job of counselor to the Medicis or Borgias, so Erasmus, who dedicated his treatise to the young prince who would become the powerful Holy Roman emperor, hoped it would secure him a post with Charles V or his equally powerful rival, King Henry VIII of England. However, unlike the worldly minded Machiavelli, Erasmus wanted to be to Charles or Henry what Plato tried to be to Dionysus II of Sicily: a tutor to lead him in the path of virtue.

---

[2]Erasmus, *Handbook*, 76.

Erasmus begins *Education* by extolling wisdom as the chief virtue of the Christian prince, and then, in good humanist fashion, quotes Xenophon, Plato, Homer, Plutarch, and Aesop before even mentioning the Bible. In fact, the work reads more like a commentary on the *Republic* than the Bible. Or does it? Again and again, Erasmus draws his readers up from the best of paganism to the higher calling of Christ and his church. After setting forth the pagan understanding of the just prince, Erasmus calls on Christian princes to surpass the pre-Christian ideals of Plato, Aristotle, Seneca, and Plutarch: "It was perhaps sufficient for a pagan prince to be generous towards his own citizens, but merely just towards foreigners. But it is the mark of a Christian prince to consider no one a foreigner except those who are strangers to the sacraments of Christ, and to avoid provoking even these by doing them injury" (5; 78).[3]

Just as Erasmus expects his Christian readers to surpass, not lag behind, the virtues of the ancients, so here Erasmus takes for granted that one who knows Christ and feeds on the sacraments will show greater mercy, charity, and hospitality than the best of pagan rulers. Christian princes are to be held to a higher standard, not only because they have been regenerated by Christ, but also because they have greater and clearer access to the Good, the True, and the Beautiful.

From the outset of *Education*, Erasmus demonstrates that he has a keen understanding of *Republic*. Whereas many today think that Plato advocated philosopher-kings because they were more learned or more clever or more studious than other men, Erasmus zeroes in on the all-important qualification:

> A large section of the masses are swayed by false opinions, just like those people trussed up in Plato's cave, who regarded the empty shadows of things as the things themselves. But it is the role of the good prince not to be impressed by the things that the common people consider of great consequences, but to weigh all things, considering whether they are really good or bad. (1; 13)

---

[3]Erasmus, *The Education of a Christian Prince*, ed. Lisa Jardine, trans. Neil M. Cheshire and Michael J. Heath (New York: Cambridge University Press, 1997). I will provide the section and page number in the text.

This qualification did not change when Platonic insight gave way to Christian revelation; all that changed is the expectation that a Christian prince should possess *more* discernment and a *greater* ability to forsake the shadows of this world for the reality of the truth. Plato was right to make knowledge of the Form of Justice the key criteria for the just prince; he could not imagine that justice would prove to be a person as well as an idea.

Erasmus's Platonic-Christian insistence that princes should enact laws that "conform to the ideals of justice and honour" (6; 79) stands in stark contrast to the sophist-like Machiavellian view that justice—good and evil, right and wrong, virtue and vice—changes from age to age and culture to culture and that the effective prince must therefore adapt himself to the fickle emotions of the crowd and the progressive zeitgeist (*The Prince* 25). In fact, Erasmus, like Plato, was so committed to an absolute standard of justice that he counseled princes to abdicate rather than violate justice: "Stand fast in your resolve and prefer to be a just man rather than an unjust prince" (1; 20).

Such should be the nature of the just ruler, but what of the just state? In that regard, Erasmus also follows closely Plato's lead:

> A kingdom or city is an excellent institution if everyone is assigned a place and performs his proper function, that is, if the prince acts like a prince, the magistrates play their parts, and the people submit to good laws and upright magistrates. But where the prince acts in his own interest and the magistrates simply plunder the people, where the people do not submit to honourable laws but flatter prince and magistrates, whatever they do—there, the most appalling confusion must reign. (7; 91-92)

For Erasmus, as for Plato, the essence of justice lies in a proper balance and harmony—whether in the state or the individual soul—in which each part performs its proper function.

Within that overall Platonic framework, Erasmus—like Plato in his more pragmatic *Laws*—offers a series of practical suggestions on what types of laws, how many, and with what punishments attached should be enacted by the prince. Other utilitarian suggestions are made on treaties and dynastic marriages, peace and war, taxes and welfare, but through them all Erasmus keeps the Platonic-Christian Form of Justice before him as the final measure. In no part of his treatise are unjust means allowed to be justified by supposedly just ends. Absolute standards must be upheld, even if that means the prince must lay down his crown to avoid breaching them.

Truly, the vision of Plato runs throughout *The Education of a Christian Prince*, but Erasmus is perhaps at his most Platonic when he offers his own allegorical reading of the insignia worn by Christian princes:

> What does the anointing of kings mean except great mildness of spirit? What is the crown on his head mean except a wisdom supreme among innumerable people? The interwoven chain put round his neck stands for the harmonious combination of all virtues; the jewels shining with multi-coloured brilliance and beauty mean the perfection of virtue and that every kind of goodness must stand out in the prince; the glowing purple robes signify his intense affection towards his subjects; his official decorations indicate that he will either equal or surpass the achievements of his ancestors. (1; 49-50)

This complex passage reveals an active mind that seeks to see through appearances to the deeper truths lurking within. The world of the Platonic Christian is a world filled with the presence of goodness, truth, and beauty, where every stone, every garment, every ritual—not to mention every cup of wine and loaf of bread—can bear divine meaning and purpose.

DESCARTES ON TRUTH-SEEKING

Though he lived and died in the high Renaissance, René Descartes (1596–1650) laid much of the groundwork for the Enlightenment. In that sense, one might assign to him the blame for cutting philosophy off from its Platonic roots and ushering in a modern worldview that no longer believes in, and therefore no longer seeks after, absolute standards of Goodness, Truth, and Beauty. But the assignation is unfair. Granted, Descartes may have opened a philosophical Pandora's box, but he himself, in his methods and his understanding of the nature of reality, honored Plato far more than he broke from him.

True, in his *Discourse on Method* (1637), he boldly swept away all that had come before him, but he did so in the manner of Socrates-Plato, rather than that of an ancient sophist or modern skeptic. Just as Socrates wiped the slate clean of false definitions so Plato could inscribe on it true definitions, in the same way Descartes's so-called skepticism marked only a preliminary stage in his final goal of accurately identifying that which is true. Descartes was above all a lover of wisdom: the meaning of the word *philo-sopher*. He firmly believed truth existed, but he knew that it could only be found through a vigorous, almost mathematical method of pursuit.

Thus, in his *Meditations on First Philosophy* (1641), he begins by doubting all but what is clear and distinct. Refusing to allow himself to be swayed by the illusions of this world—the shadows on the cave wall—he closes his mind to everything that is not real and actual. In doing so, however, he does not play the part of the modern materialist-empiricist who only believes in physical things that he can see with his eyes, but of a Platonist who privileges the unseen, the unchanging, and the eternal over the tangible, the changeable, and the temporal. That is to say, Descartes, in the manner of Plato, turns everything on its head.

In the face of what passes for "common sense," Descartes argues that our idea of mind in general and God in particular is clearer and more distinct than that of physical objects perceived by the senses. He may not use the exact language of Plato's Forms, but that is what he seeks in his *Meditations*. This becomes apparent in his discourse on wax. When a piece of wax is brought close to the fire, it so changes its physical form that the senses can no longer apprehend it in the way they did before; yet it remains the same wax. That is because, Descartes argues,

> the nature of this piece of wax is in no way revealed by my imagination, but is perceived by the mind alone. (I am speaking of this particular piece of wax; the point is even clearer with regard to wax in general). . . . The perception I have of it is a case not of vision or touch or imagination—nor has

it ever been, despite previous appearances—but of purely mental scrutiny. (2; 21)[4]

What Descartes is perceiving here is very close, if not identical, to what Plato would call the Form of Wax, the true essence of wax that can only be seen with the mind's eye. Our senses, which are based on opinion rather than knowledge, too often deceive us and lead us astray. As in Plato's divided line and allegory of the cave, Descartes gives us a two-tiered cosmos split into two distinct realms: the intelligible realm (World of Being) that is perceived by the mind/soul—what Plato called the psyche—and the physical world (World of Becoming), which we perceive through our senses and imagination. It is the latter, not the former, that is less real and actual.

More than that, the former must be the final cause of the latter, for it is a fundamental, nonnegotiable principle of philosophy that the cause (or source or origin) must be greater and more perfect than the effect; or, to put it another way, the lesser cannot create the greater. This foundational first principle, which lies behind the philosophical proofs for the existence of God put forth by Aristotle, Anselm, and Aquinas, is central to Plato and Descartes's conception of reality. The Platonic philosopher-lover would not continue his journey up the rising path if he did not believe his desire had a transcendent source toward which he could ascend; likewise, Descartes would not continue his *Meditations* if he did not believe his mind had a supernatural source.

Descartes makes perhaps the clearest use of this Platonic orientation toward cause and effect—an orientation that lines up with the revelation of Scripture—in his argument for the existence of infinity, which he lists, alongside immutability, omniscience, and omnipotence, as one of the eternal qualities of God:

> And I must not think that, just as my conceptions of rest and darkness are arrived at by negating movement and light, so my perception of the infinite is arrived at not by means of a true idea but merely by negating the finite.

---

[4]Descartes, *Meditations on First Philosophy*, ed. and trans. John Cottingham (Cambridge: Cambridge University Press, 1996). I will provide the meditation and page number in the text.

On the contrary, I clearly understand that there is more reality in an infinite substance than in a finite one, and hence that my perception of the infinite, that is God, is in some way prior to my perception of the finite, that is myself. For how could I understand that I doubted or desired—that is, lacked something—and that I was not wholly perfect, unless there were in me some idea of a more perfect being which enabled me to recognize my own defects by comparison? (3; 31)

Since Descartes understands the idea of infinity but does not possess it within himself, there must exist an origin of that idea that transcends his finite nature. If the idea (Form) of infinity did not actually exist, then how could Descartes be aware of his own lack of infinity? Just so, we would not be aware of the fact that we are imperfect if the idea of perfection did not actually exist.

But how, it must be asked, do ideas like infinity and perfection find their way into the minds of finite, imperfect mortals? Here too Descartes offers an answer that is as Platonic as it is Christian: those ideas are innate within us, put there before we were born. As such, learning is, in part, a form of recollection, of calling up what is already stored within our soul. Though Descartes does not theorize a preexistence for himself, he speaks of this process of learning by recollection in a way that recalls the scene in *Meno* when Socrates "teaches" a slave boy higher math by drawing out of him the geometry he already knows.

Thus, while discussing the ideas of quantity and extension, Descartes says that "on first discovering them it seems that I am not so much learning something new as remembering what I knew before; or it seems like noticing for the first time things which were long present within me although I had never turned my mental gaze on them before" (4; 44). Then, recalling *Meno* even more directly, he confesses as well to finding within himself the idea of a triangle that is of "a determinate nature, or essence, or form . . . which is immutable and eternal, and not invented by me or dependent on my mind" (5; 45).

Now, I do not dispute that Descartes's *Meditations* played a central role in paving the way for the Enlightenment reduction of the involved, dynamic, triune God of the Bible to a removed deity (the God of the philosophers) whose chief, if not exclusive, functions are to exist and to set the universe and its laws in motion. That is because Descartes (like Boethius in his *Consolation*) relies only on general revelation, especially Plato, in his formulation of God, with the result that he robs God of his agency, his loving and holy nature, and his interactions in human history. In the same Platonic vein he replaces the central Christian doctrine of original sin with a more Hellenic notion of sin as error, ignorance, and a missing of the mark.

Still, the full Enlightenment reduction of God would not occur, I maintain, until Locke first stripped away Descartes's Platonic focus on innate knowledge and then his equally Platonic belief that the cause of a thing must be greater than the effect.[5] Plato may have pushed Descartes in the direction of a static, impersonal God, but he also helped keep him grounded in the biblical truth that God "has put eternity in their hearts" (Eccles 3:11 NKJV).

COLERIDGE ON IMAGINATION

Although Samuel Taylor Coleridge (1772–1834) is best known for his poetry, particularly his mystical, wildly imaginative "Kubla Khan" and "Rime of the Ancient Mariner," he eventually put down his poetic pen to become one of the finest British philosopher-critics of the nineteenth century. More than that, Coleridge, by way of an intense philosophical-theological journey through the "isms" of his day (associationism, idealism, pantheism, and Unitarianism), matured into one of the finest Christian thinkers of the Romantic age. To document, in part, his intellectual pilgrimage of faith, Coleridge wrote his own version of Augustine's *Confessions*, a spiritual autobiography that is also a work of literary criticism: *Biographia Literaria* (1817).

One of the demons Descartes let out of Pandora's box was a nascent form of reductive materialism that reimagined the human mind as a

---

[5]In *Essay on Human Understanding* 1.1-2, Locke rejects innate knowledge; at 2:17, he reverses cause and effect by arguing that we could have extrapolated the idea of infinity from our knowledge of finite numbers by simply adding one number to the next without ever finding an end.

product of random associations that were purely natural and over which we had no control. Beginning with Locke's belief that our minds are blank slates on which sensation and experience leave their marks and climaxing with the elaborately worked out deterministic theories of David Hartley, associationism, Coleridge came to believe, robs us of our volition.[6] It is based, he explains, on a "subordination of final to efficient causes in the human being, which flows of necessity from the assumption, that the will and, with the will, all acts of thought and attention are parts and products of this blind mechanism, instead of being distinct powers, the function of which it is to control, determine, and modify the phantasmal chaos of association" (1.7; 116).[7]

Plato kicked off true philosophy in the West by denying the belief held by most of the Presocratics (but not Pythagoras and Parmenides) that all things should, and can, be explained by efficient, mechanical causes. Final causes that transcend our physical, natural, material world, argued Plato, are necessary to explain many of the effects we see in our world, a philosophical premise that would be elaborated on by Aristotle and Christianized by Augustine and Aquinas. As we saw above, Descartes held to that premise as well, though his unfortunate splitting of mind from body left the body prey to efficient causes and then left the disembodied mind prey to philosophers like Spinoza and Hume who would subject it as well to material associations.

By cross-examining Hartley in good Socratic fashion, Coleridge uncovers the error at the core of his theory: "The mistaking the *conditions* of a thing for its *causes* and *essence*; and the process by which we arrive at the knowledge of a faculty, for the faculty itself. The air I breathe, is the *condition* of my life, not its cause" (1.7; 123). By such Platonic reasoning, Coleridge rescued himself from an aggressive materialism that reduced everything to objective (natural) processes, only

---

[6]See book 2, chapter 2 of Locke's *An Essay on Human Understanding* (1689) and part one, section two of David Hartley's *Observations on Man, His Frame, His Duty, and His Expectations* (1749).

[7]Samuel Taylor Coleridge, *Biographia Literaria*, ed. James Engell and W. Jackson Bate (Princeton: Princeton University Press, 1983). I will provide the book, chapter, and page number in the text.

to fall temporarily into the opposite extreme: a blend of philosophical idealism (Fichte) and mystical pantheism (Jakob Böhme) that posited the subjective conscious mind as the source of all things.[8] From there, he moved into Unitarianism, where he found some religious truth but was prevented from embracing the key Christian teachings of the Trinity, incarnation, and atonement. Neither Platonism nor Unitarianism offered him a way by which to heal the wound between God and man, mind and nature, persons and things, subject and object.

Still, the Platonic vision behind idealism and mysticism preserved him from the gnostic-Arian heresies of Unitarianism, as Coleridge explains by comparing his journey to that of Augustine:

> I cannot doubt, that the difference of my [idealistic-mystical] metaphysical notions from those of Unitarians in general contributed to my final re-conversion to the whole truth in Christ; even as according to his own confession the books of certain Platonic philosophers (*libri quorundam Platonicorum*) commenced the rescue of St. Augustine's faith from the same error aggravated by the far darker accompaniment of the Manichaean heresy. (1.10; 205)

It was the Platonic focus on Ideas (eternal, trans-physical Forms that are the source and origin of our ideas) and intuition (as a vehicle for connecting us, via innate ideas, with the Forms) that helped Coleridge escape the dead ends of both materialism and Unitarianism and that propelled him forward to construct a fuller Christian synthesis. Indeed, as he prepares to state his method for achieving that synthesis, Coleridge invokes Plato at least three times. First, he makes it clear that the system he seeks demands the kind of vision and rigor that Plato called for in his myths of ascension: "A system, the first principle of which it is to render the mind intuitive of the *spiritual* in man (i.e. of that which lies *on the other* side of our natural consciousness) must needs have a great obscurity for those, who have never disciplined and strengthened this ulterior consciousness" (1.12; 243).

---

[8]See Fichte's *Foundation of the Complete Theory of Knowledge* (1794) and Böhme's *Description of the Three Principles of Divine Essence* (1619).

As for the power of such intuition to connect us with the Forms, Coleridge directly alludes to the *Meno*: "Socrates in Plato shows, that an ignorant slave may be brought to understand and of himself to solve the most difficult geometrical problem" (1.12; 251). Finally, in stating the proper starting point for the higher Christian synthesis that he seeks, Coleridge invokes the key tenet of Socrates-Plato:

> The postulate of philosophy and at the same time the test of philosophic capacity, is no other than the heaven-descended KNOW THYSELF! . . . And this at once practically and speculatively. For as philosophy is neither a science of the reason or understanding only, nor merely a science of morals, but the science of BEING altogether, its primary ground can be neither merely speculative nor merely practical, but both in one. All knowledge rests on the coincidence of an object with a subject. (1.12; 252)

By highlighting the Socratic command to know thyself, Coleridge connects the Cartesian "I think therefore I am" to God's self-revelation to Moses as I AM (Ex 3:14). He also draws together practical, scientific, inductive philosophy that begins with concrete, physical observations of nature with speculative, intuitive, deductive philosophy that begins with abstract, metaphysical truths, first principles that are accepted rather than proved.

Though these two philosophical orientations normally stand in opposition to one another, Coleridge, because of his Christian faith in the incarnation, came to believe that they could be pursued as complementary methods for achieving the same incarnational fusion of mind and nature, subject and object—a fusion, or marriage, that does not so much reject Plato as transcend the limits of his imagination. On the one side, explains Coleridge, is the natural philosopher, who begins his journey, his education, with nature (object) and moves upward toward mind (subject). Though his starting point is natural, his final end must be to effect "the perfect spiritualization of all the laws of nature into laws of intuition and intellect" (1.12; 256).

On the other side is the transcendental philosopher who begins his journey-education with transcendent mind (subject) and moves downward toward nature (object). To begin such a metaphysical pilgrimage, the transcendental philosopher must first purge his mind, in the manner of Descartes, of all sensation by assuming "an absolute, scientific skepticism" (1.12; 258). From this point, however, he must move downward toward the sensual realities of the physical world, seeking ever to incarnate the universal in the concrete.

If both philosophers successfully complete their journeys, they will meet in the middle: at a metaphysical nexus point of the general and the specific where the sought-for marriage of subject and object, mind and nature can be realized. But by what power of the mind, what mental faculty can such a marriage be achieved? Coleridge's specifically Romantic answer may at first seem like a slap in the face to Plato, who kicked the poets out of his perfect republic, but I would argue that it represents a fulfillment, a kind of consummation of Plato's highest desires.

For Coleridge, it was the imagination alone that could effect the marriage. Unlike Hobbes and Locke, who tended to treat fancy and imagination interchangeably, Coleridge asserted that they were distinct powers. While the fancy is a lesser, limited power that can only shift images around into new patterns, the imagination is a freer, more vital power that recombines ideas and images at will to create new, higher unities. Only the imagination, like love, has the perceptive power to see similitude lurking within dissimilitude and the synthetic power to fuse and reconcile opposites into one. Imagination can do these things because it is an "esemplastic" power: a word that Coleridge coined himself from three Greek roots meaning "to shape into one" (1.10; 168).

For all the negative things Plato says about the arts and their tendency to focus on the shadows on the cave wall, he himself possessed precisely the kind of esemplastic imagination that Coleridge calls for. His myths draw the physical up into the spiritual but with a concrete reality that tends to fill our world with, not empty it of, meaning and truth. Plato did not see clearly enough to conceive the great marriage of Christ and the church with which the Bible climaxes (Rev 21–22), but he did yearn for a Beatific Vision in which the lover could contemplate for eternity the beloved Form of Beauty.

C. S. LEWIS'S CHRISTIAN PLATONISM

THE MODERN WORLD, with its naturalism, its utilitarianism, and its deep skepticism, has not proven to be a breeding ground for disciples of Plato, whether Christian or secular. Bentham and Mill, Darwin and Freud, Nietzsche and Marx, Sartre and Derrida have so relativized Goodness, Truth, and Beauty as to cut Western man off, not only from Plato's Forms, but from any transcendent origin or source or cause. Worse yet, in the absence of a divine standard or touchstone, not to mention a personal Creator, the goal of ascending the rising path toward the Beatific Vision loses not only its desirability but its possibility as well. Without a real, actual telos to love and to pursue, the ascent can only turn back on itself, fostering ego rather than awe, self-satisfaction rather than gratitude, stoic equanimity rather than life-giving joy.

Thankfully for those who accept both the wisdom of Plato and the fuller truth of the New Testament, the twentieth century bequeathed the world one of its finest Christian Platonists: C. S. Lewis (1898–1963). In his ecumenical Christian apologetics, his accessible academic writings, and his imaginative, multilayered fiction, Lewis, an Oxford and Cambridge don and professor of English language and literature, found innumerable ways to inform and strengthen his faith by way of the timeless insights of Plato. Whether reflecting on our journey up the rising path, on the nature of heaven and hell, or on the role of desire in the Christian life, Lewis seamlessly synthesized Platonic teachings with Christian doctrine. As such, he is the ideal figure to complete a book that would revive Plato's role in Christianity.

LEWIS ON CHOICE

Most of what Lewis says about the practice of virtue in book three of *Mere Christianity* comes straight out of Aristotle's *Nicomachean Ethics*. Nevertheless, his overall vision of the Christian life as a tug of war that moves us in the direction of either God, virtue, and heaven or Satan, sin, and hell is far closer to the *psychomachia* of the Platonist than the golden mean of the Aristotelian:

> Every time you make a choice you are turning the central part of you, the part of you that chooses, into something a little different from what it was before. And taking your life as a whole, with all your innumerable choices, all your life long you are slowly turning this central thing into a heavenly creature or a hellish creature: either into a creature that is in harmony with God, and with other creatures, and with itself, or else into one that is in a state of war and hatred with God, and with its fellow-creatures, and with itself. To be the one kind of creature is heaven: that is, it is joy and peace and knowledge and power. To be the other means madness, horror, idiocy, rage, impotence, and eternal loneliness. Each of us at each moment is progressing to the one state or the other. (4; 81)[1]

Here we have, in a context that is both Christian and biblical, an underlying Platonic vision of a progression that leads us either upward or downward: that leads, if I may mingle Plato's myths, out of the cave into the light of truth or down the chain of being to be reincarnated as an animal. Yes, the vision is very much a Dantean (and Boethian) one, but then Dante's vision was strongly inspired by Plato's myths as filtered through Boethius's *Consolation*.

---

[1] All of my quotes from *Mere Christianity*, *Miracles*, *The Great Divorce*, *The Problem of Pain*, and *The Abolition of Man* will be taken from *The C. S. Lewis Signature Classics* (New York: Harper One, 2017). Which book I am quoting will be made clear in the text; the reference itself will be by the chapter number followed by the page number.

As in Plato, our choices not only carry immediate consequences; they also shape our souls. Plato was himself influenced by the vision of Pythagoras, who believed that our soul would continue reincarnating until it became so attuned to the rhythms of the cosmos that it heard the music of the spheres. In emphasizing how our choices bring us into either harmony or enmity with God, Lewis carries forward a Platonic understanding of the need for a proper balance in the soul. The orthodox Lewis does not seek here to eliminate or even downplay salvation by grace through faith. Rather, he describes the process of sanctification in a metaphorical language that is very Platonic. While Lewis *does* borrow from Aristotle the notion that virtue is a habit, his strong focus on what sin does to our soul carries him back again and again to Plato's dynamic myths of ascent and descent.

Lewis begins book three of *Mere Christianity* by arguing that there are three parts to morality and then rendering those parts concrete by comparing them to a fleet of ships. For the fleet to operate properly, the ships must not collide with one another (social morality that calls on us to follow the golden rule), each ship must be in good shape (personal morality that calls on us to live clean and wholesome lives), and the fleet must have a destination that will keep it on track (spiritual morality that is oriented toward a telos). If we forget the second part, we will reduce morality to the stubbornly held belief that we can do whatever we want as long as it doesn't hurt anyone. If we forget the third, we will find ourselves adrift in an amoral sea without a fixed star or coastline to steer by.

Just as the ships must know where they are headed if they are to make it to their assigned destination, so we must know our telos if we are to make the right choices—or even know the proper nature and stakes *of* those choices. "Does it not make a great difference whether I am, so to speak, the landlord of my own mind and body, or only a tenant, responsible to the real landlord? If somebody else made me, for his own purposes, then I shall have a lot of duties which I should not have if I simply belonged to myself" (1; 68). True morality does not exist in a void, with people committing random acts of kindness in one moment and violence in another, but in relationship to a clear understanding of who we are, why we are here, and what our purpose is. Apart from that knowledge, we have nothing against which to measure our choices.

Thus far, Lewis's points rest heavily on Aristotelian teleology, on determining what the proper end is for each object and, especially, each living thing. Still, Lewis inevitably pushes us back to Plato's myths and to the journey of the initiate. In the allegory of the cave, the bold pilgrimage of the philosopher begins when the true nature of the situation becomes apparent: the seemingly real is but the shadow of a shadow. For Lewis, real Christian growth begins when we realize that "fallen man is not simply an imperfect creature who needs improvement: he is a rebel who must lay down his arms" (*Mere Christianity*, 2.4; 54). Although Plato did not have knowledge of the doctrine of original sin, both Lewis and Plato shared the same keen insight into the nature of choice: that it rests on a proper perception of our potential and our limitations. There is that within us that desires to climb and ascend; yet we live in a world that deceives and leads us astray.

In *The Problem of Pain*, Lewis describes the nature of the fall and the effect it had on our ability to choose by constructing "a 'myth' in the Socratic sense, a not unlikely tale" (5; 593). As Lewis tells it, even before the fall, we were expected to obey God and surrender to his will; in our prelapsarian state, however, that surrender meant only "the delicious overcoming of an infinitesimal self-adherence which delighted to be overcome" (5; 596). After the fall, we were still expected to surrender, but that surrender—that choice to obey God over ourselves— became difficult and bitter. For "to surrender a self-will inflamed and swollen with years of usurpation is a kind of death" (6; 603). To be fair, the resistance Lewis describes here is moral, while that referred to in the allegory of the cave is metaphysical. Nevertheless, both kinds of blindness rest on our refusal to step into the light and the truth and be exposed for who and what we are.

Before the ascent up the rising path can begin in earnest, something has to be shattered: for Plato, it is our false perception that the world below is more real and concrete and eternal than the world above; for Lewis, it is our false sense of self-sufficiency that makes us believe we can become good and virtuous people apart from God. Because we cannot trust our senses alone (Plato) or ourselves alone (Lewis) to provide us with the truth about our predicament, we must learn to see with new eyes. The Socrates of *Apology* and the Jesus of the Gospels both exposed hypocrites who thought themselves to be upright people in possession of the truth and opened the eyes of disciples who were willing to admit their lack of vision and accept the assistance offered them.

Right thinking was as vital for Plato as it was for Lewis, and it should therefore come as no surprise that both wrote perceptively on the subject of education. In Plato's *Republic*, the proper education of the guardians is key to achieving balance in the soul of the philosopher-king and the wider body politic. In Lewis's *Abolition of Man*, which bears the lengthy subtitle *Reflections on Education with Special Reference to the Teaching of English in the Upper Forms of Schools*, a society that jettisons fixed standards of Goodness, Truth, and Beauty from its educational system will bring ruin on itself. And it will do so precisely because a society that relativizes virtue, reducing it to mere sentiment, will eventually instigate a breakdown in the proper functioning of Plato's tripartite soul.

Lewis explains,

> We were told it all long ago by Plato. As the king governs by his executive, so Reason in man must rule the mere appetites by means of the "spirited element." The head rules the belly through the chest—the seat, as Alanus tell us, of Magnanimity, of emotions organized by trained habit into stable sentiments. The Chest—Magnanimity—Sentiment—these are the indispensable liaison officers between cerebral man [the rational part of our soul] and visceral man [the appetitive part]. It may even be said that it is by this middle element that man is man: for by his intellect he is mere spirit and by his appetite mere animal. (1; 704)

The move that Lewis makes here is quite stunning. At the end of chapter six, I suggested that Plato's *Timaeus* comes close to linking the tripartite soul of *Republic* (and the myth of the charioteer in *Phaedrus*) to a proto-Christian understanding of man standing midway between the angel and the beast. Whereas Plato posits the rational part of the soul (or the charioteer) as the mediating figure that holds the reins on the appetitive and spirited parts (or the fiery and noble horses), Lewis exalts the spirited part of our soul, which he links to the chest, as the part that mediates between reason (head) and appetite (belly). By doing so, he asserts something about the human person that Plato did not know: that we are incarnate beings who are fully physical and fully spiritual.

While Christianizing Plato, Lewis remains true to the essential struggle within the soul, which must lead to a proper balance if the individual, and the state of which he is a part, is to achieve justice and harmony.

LEWIS ON HELL

One of the most important things that Lewis borrowed from Plato—both directly and through Augustine, Boethius, and Dante—is the *drama* of salvation and sanctification, the continuum along which our choices lead us as we move closer to or further away from God, from the one who is the Form of the Forms. Though the emphasis in Lewis is ever on human volition, he avoids getting tangled in the age-old controversies between predestination and free will, Luther and Erasmus, Calvin and Arminius. For Lewis, it is less about the divine mechanism than what our choices do to our individual souls as they proceed on their journey. That is why Lewis's Platonism is strongest in his mythopoeic fiction.

In imitation of their masters (Socrates and Jesus), Plato and Lewis both wrote books that rip away the veil and reveal the first and eternal things that really matter. Rather than make the choice for us, they help us understand the nature of the choice we must make. In the myth of Er, all of philosophy leads up to that critical moment when we must choose our lot for the next life; in Lewis's *The Great Divorce*, a sort of combination of the myth of Er and *The Divine Comedy*, the choice toward which all of life is leading is at once moral (will we repent and accept God's forgiveness) and metaphysical (will we accept and obey God's view of reality or our own).

What if, Lewis imagines, the souls in hell could, if they so desired, take a bus ride to heaven? And what if, when they arrived, they were met by the blessed souls of saints whom they knew in life who tried to convince them, even now, to forsake their sin and self-delusion and embrace the mercy and truth of Christ? What would they do? As it turns out, all but one of them willingly chooses to return to hell: not because it is too dull and boring, but because it is too real and over-whelming. They prefer the darkness of the cave to the painful light of the Sun.

When the damned soul of a landscape painter tells the blessed soul of a fellow landscape painter that he would like to paint the beautiful vistas of heaven, the latter tells him not to bother. When the former balks at this reply, the latter, using Platonic language and imagery, ex-plains, "When you painted on earth—at least in your earlier days—it was because you caught glimpses of Heaven in the earthly landscape. The success of your painting was that it enabled others to see the glimpses too. But here you are having the thing itself. It is from here that the messages came. There is no good *telling* us about this country, for we see it already" (9; 510).

Although one expects the damned soul to remain in heaven and feast on the original Forms of which his paintings were only imitations, he refuses the offer and goes back to hell to mount a new exhibition of his paintings. He would rather devote himself to studying and com-peting over the shadows on the cave wall than move out into the Sun and be exposed to (and by) its light and truth. He is a painter who has lost both his ability and his desire to see.

A similar rejection of the Real in favor of the unreal, the Truth in favor of the lie is made in *The Last Battle*, the final novel in the Chron-icles of Narnia, by a group of rebellious dwarves who reject Aslan (the Christ figure of Narnia), give in to despair, and betray Narnia. When they die, they end up in the same geographical space as the good characters who have died. However, whereas those whose chests have remained strong and pure find themselves in a restored Garden of Eden, the dwarves believe they are in a dark and dingy stable surrounded by dirty hay and animal filth. When the good characters try to convince them that they are in a garden, they refuse to believe it: neither their sense of sight, smell, taste, touch, nor hearing can perceive the beauty around them.

Finally, Aslan arrives and lays out for them a feast. But they are incapable of enjoying it. In the end, they reject the help offered to them, refusing to be taken in by any pie-in-the-sky thinking. "You see," Aslan explains, "They will not let us help them. They have chosen cunning instead of belief. Their prison is only in their own minds, yet they are in that prison; and so afraid of being taken in that they can not be taken out" (13; 148).[2] For both Lewis and Plato, moral and mental confusion go hand in hand. In succumbing to sin, the dwarves render themselves incapable of seeing heaven, much less entering it. They prefer to remain in the cave. Though this equating of seeing the truth with participating in it may seem more Platonic than biblical, Jesus himself, in his conversation with Nicodemus, directly equates seeing the kingdom of heaven with entering it (Jn 3:3-5). We can do neither unless we are born again.

LEWIS ON HEAVEN

In making this Platonic-Christian link between seeing and entering, Lewis runs the risk of reducing hell and heaven to mere states of mind. But that is not his intention. Indeed, when he suggests just that to his guide in *The Great Divorce* (George MacDonald, who combines Dante's Virgil and Beatrice), he is sternly hushed: "Do not blaspheme. Hell is a state of mind—ye never said a truer word. And every state of mind, left to itself, every shutting up of the creature within the dungeon of its own mind—is, in the end, Hell. But Heaven is not a state of mind. Heaven is reality itself. All that is fully real is Heavenly" (9; 504).

---

[2]C. S. Lewis, *The Last Battle* (New York: Collier, 1970). I will provide the chapter and page number in the text.

In insisting that heaven is not only more real than hell but also more real than the earth, Lewis offers the supreme Christianizing of Plato's distinction between the World of Being and the World of Becoming. Because Lewis knew that God made the world and called it good (Gen 1:31), he naturally saw the world as far more substantial and real than Plato did. Still, he had no problem (in the final chapter of *The Last Battle*) referring to our world as the "Shadow-Lands" (16; 183); for, *in relationship to* the thundering reality of heaven, we are living in a world of insubstantial shadows.

In sharp contrast to our modern, anti-Platonic world, which tends to use negative terminology whenever discussing God, Lewis, in *Miracles*, insisted that the opposite is the case.

> God is basic Fact or Actuality, the source of all other facthood. At all costs therefore He must not be thought of as a featureless generality. If He exists at all, He is the most concrete thing there is, the most individual, "organized and minutely articulated." He is unspeakable not by being indefinite but by being too definite for the unavoidable vagueness of language. The words *incorporeal* and *impersonal* are misleading, because they suggest that He lacks some reality which we possess. It would be safer to call His *trans-corporeal, trans-personal*. (11; 381)

The same goes for heaven itself, which is not, as many people today imagine it, earth with all the physical matter (the "stuff") thrown out. Heaven, just like the resurrection bodies we will have when we are there, will not be nonphysical but trans-physical.

In *The Great Divorce*, heaven is described as a place of tangible substance and reality. The grass is so hard and real that the damned souls, whom Lewis depicts as insubstantial and ghostlike, cannot even bend it. More shockingly, when we get to the end of the novel, we learn that the bus did not *move* from hell to heaven; it *grew*. That is because, George MacDonald explains, "all Hell is smaller than one pebble of your earthly world: but it is smaller than one atom of *this* world, the Real World" (13; 537).

However, Lewis saves the full glory of his Christian Platonist view of heaven for *The Last Battle*, where the reader gets to accompany the heroes as they make their way deeper and deeper into Aslan's Country. As they move "further up and further in," which is Lewis's title for chapter fifteen (161), they discover that the land through which they are moving looks like Narnia. This confuses them, for they have just seen Narnia destroyed, until they realize that what they are seeing is not the old Narnia but the new Narnia. Actually, Lewis does not quite express it that way. Had he done so, he would have been making a simple biblical allusion to the new heaven and the new earth celebrated in the last two chapters of John's Revelation.

Instead, Lewis mingles Christian and Platonic imagery. Speaking of the Narnia that has just been destroyed, Professor Digory explains to the children, "That was not the real Narnia. That had a beginning and an end. It was only a shadow or a copy of the real Narnia, which has always been here and always will be here: just as our own world, England and all, is only a shadow or copy of something in Aslan's real world" (15; 169). Then, in case we missed the Platonic reference, Digory adds two more things. First, he explains that the real Narnia and the Narnia they saw destroyed are "as different as a real thing is from a shadow or as waking life is from a dream." Then, he exclaims, point blank, "It's all in Plato, all in Plato" (15; 169-70).

Now, as we have seen before, this Platonic concept, that the real Narnia has always existed and that the earthly Narnia was patterned on it, can be reconciled with the link made in Hebrews 8–9 between the heavenly and earthly tabernacle: especially the verse which states that priests "serve unto the example and shadow of heavenly things, as Moses was admonished of God when he was about to make the tabernacle: for, See, saith he, *that* thou make all things according to the pattern shewed to thee in the mount" (Heb 8:5). Still, without the influence of Plato's theory of the Forms, Lewis, and the many Christian Platonists before him, might have missed the full import of that pregnant verse.

The heavenly *precedes* the earthly, for the heavenly is, like Plato's World of Being, real, eternal, and unchanging. Spiritual things don't have meaning because we projected that meaning onto them, as modernists like Freud would have it—or the witch in chapter seven of *The Silver Chair*, who comes close to convincing our heroes that her cave-like Underland is the only real world and Narnia (and Aslan) the childish dream. To the contrary, the spiritual, which is the source of the physical, is what gives meaning to the things of our world. Bread and wine take their final meaning and significance because of the eternal body and blood of "the Lamb slain from the foundation of the world" (Rev 13:8), even though bread and wine existed long before the Last Supper. In the incarnation, Christ became like us, but that is only because we, as enfleshed souls, were made in the image of the eternal, preincarnate Christ. The core of Lewis's apologetics is based on Plato's contention that the cause must be greater than the effect. For Lewis, there must be a divine, supernatural origin or source for such things as morality, religion, and reason.

And one thing more. There must also be an ultimate origin or source for our desires for heaven, as there must be, in Descartes, for our idea of infinity. "Creatures are not born with desires," argues Lewis in book three of *Mere Christianity*, "unless satisfaction for those desires exists. A baby feels hunger: well, there is such a thing as food. . . . If I find in myself a desire which no experience in this world can satisfy, the most probable explanation is that I was made for another world" (10; 114). Of course, our yearnings for heaven do not in and of themselves prove that we will attain heaven, but if nature is a closed system and there is nothing beyond the physical, then where did the yearning come from? How could unconscious nature produce in us a conscious desire for something that is beyond nature?

In a sense, not only the Chronicles of Narnia but all of Lewis's writings lead up to the ecstatic (Platonic) words spoken by Jewel the Unicorn when he arrives in Aslan's Country at the end of *The Last Battle*: "I have come home at last! This is my real country! I belong here. This is the land I have been looking for all of my life, though I never knew it till now. The reason why we loved the old Narnia is that it sometimes looked a little like this" (15; 171). Plato caught a glimpse of the world outside of the cave, and in doing so he also glimpsed, without knowing it, the greater heaven revealed in the New Testament. Lewis, who drew from both Plato and the Bible, caught a glimpse that was more distinct, and thus he had a better sense than Plato of the true and final origin of that desire that they both felt.

And yet, even C. S. Lewis, in his mortal, earthbound state, had his limits. That is why, after attempting to describe the goodness and light and joy of heaven, Lewis concludes book three of *Mere Christianity* with this humble confession: "But this is near the stage where the road passes over the rim of our world. No one's eyes can see very far beyond that: lots of people's eyes can see further than mine" (12; 123).

CONCLUSION

Plato the Sub-Creator

IN HIS PLATONIC-PTOLEMAIC-DANTEAN science-fiction novel *Out of the Silent Planet* (1938), C. S. Lewis, who was far more a man of the medieval age than he was of our own, sends his protagonist, Ransom, on a journey to Mars. Though Ransom, as a modern man educated in the worldview of naturalism, expects to see only empty space when he looks out the window of the rocket, he is shocked to find instead something for which his post-Enlightenment training has not prepared him:

> He had read of "Space": at the back of his thinking for years had lurked the dismal fancy of the black, cold vacuity, the utter deadness, which was supposed to separate the worlds. He had not known how much it affected him till now—now that the very name "Space" seemed a blasphemous libel for this empyrean ocean of radiance in which they swam. . . . He had thought it barren: he saw now that it was the womb of worlds, whose blazing and innumerable offspring looked down nightly even upon the earth with so many eyes—and here, with how many more! No: Space was the wrong name. Older thinkers had been wiser when they named it simply the heavens.[1]

---

[1]C. S. Lewis, *Out of the Silent Planet* (New York: Macmillan, 1971), 29-30.

Whether Lewis, had he lived into the age of space exploration, would have changed this section of his novel makes for an interesting biographical question but is irrelevant to what Lewis is doing as a theologian, philosopher, and artist. Lewis's goal, as a humanist Christian strongly influenced by Plato, is to get his readers to see the universe as the medievals saw it—as a true cosmos, a beautiful, ordered ornament that displayed in its physical splendor the glory of the God who spoke it into being.

Lewis's good friend J. R. R. Tolkien shared his love of the medieval cosmos and of the great Athenian philosopher who played such a major role in shaping it as both a philosophical model and an aesthetic object. Indeed, in his prequel to *The Lord of the Rings*, *The Silmarillion*, Tolkien spins a creation story that reads like a conflation of Genesis 1, Job 38:7 ("When the morning stars sang together, / and all the sons of God shouted for joy?"), and *Timaeus*. Plato's God, desiring to create new and unique beings to live on the earth, invites the gods to perform the actual shaping of those beings, though he orders them to do so in accordance with his intentions (41b-d). In a similar manner, Tolkien's God (whom he names Eru or Ilúvatar) first sings a group of gods/ angels (the Ainur) into being and then allows them to participate in the shaping of the earth and the nurturing of the elves and men. However, as in *Timaeus*, Ilúvatar sets parameters for Middle-earth and its inhabitants by first imagining them in song, a song that the Ainur are given the privilege of adding to, and then realizing them in the physical world of time and space. Thus, although God/Ilúvatar is the supreme Creator, the gods/Ainur are allowed, to borrow a phrase from Tolkien, to be sub-creators. "Fantasy," Tolkien believed, "is a natural human activity . . . [as well as] a human right: we make in our measure and in our derivative mode because we are made: and not only made, but made in the image and likeness of a Maker."[2]

---

[2]J. R. R. Tolkien, "On Fairy-Stories," in *Tree and Leaf* (Boston: Houghton Mifflin, 1965), 54-55. Tolkien coins the word sub-creator in a poem that precedes the passage quoted above and that depicts man as a natural myth-maker who refracts through himself the pure creative light of God: "Man, Sub-creator, the refracted Light / through whom is splintered from a single

It is my belief that Plato was one of the greatest sub-creators of the ancient world. He may not have written epics like Homer or tragedies like Sophocles or histories like Herodotus—or, for that matter, fantasies like Lewis and Tolkien—but he did construct myths that brought to shimmering life his vision of a two-tiered cosmos in which the unseen World of Being is more real and substantial than the World of Becoming that we perceive, day by day, through our senses. Just as importantly, his myths have inspired generations upon generations of philosophers, theologians, and poets—both pagan and Christian—to journey from the lower world to the higher.

Those who truly love Plato have not been satisfied merely to study him. They have yearned to see the things-that-are with the clarity that he saw them, to perceive behind the shifting shadows of our world the eternal things that do not fade or decay or die. They have sought to defend the Good, the True, and the Beautiful as real things and justice as an absolute to which we must conform ourselves. And they have struggled mightily to resist the downward pull of the appetitive part of their soul lest they grow dull, languid, and brutish. Plato the sub-creator makes us want to do these things, even as Lewis and Tolkien make us want to visit Narnia and Middle-earth or look up and see the heavens, not as our house, but as our home.

There is an old tradition that says that Paul wept at the tomb of Virgil because he could not share with him the gospel of salvation. In the twenty-second canto of *Purgatorio*, Dante invents a story that the first-century Roman poet Statius was converted from paganism to Christianity when he realized that the preaching of the apostles lined up with Virgil's Fourth Eclogue: a poem that reads, remarkably, like a messianic prophecy out of Isaiah. Though Virgil's poem led Statius into the light of Christ, it could not save Virgil, who died in 19 BC. The lamp that Virgil held out to those who came after him, Statius explains, helped lead him into the light, but it proved useless for Virgil himself.

White / to many hues, and endlessly combined / in living shapes that move from mind to mind" (54).

Though I weep in the manner of Paul and lament in the manner of Dante and Statius that Plato, like Virgil, was denied the special revelation of Christ and the New Testament, I celebrate the legacy he left behind and how greatly it has enriched the church. Plato's works proved to be milestones on the road to faith of Augustine, Coleridge, and Lewis. For Origen and the three Gregorys, Boethius and Dante, Erasmus and Descartes, their reading of, and wrestling with, Plato's dialogues helped hone their theology, philosophy, and poetry and teach them to see and wonder and desire more clearly and passionately.

For myself, I can attest that reading Plato has made me want to be a better man, a better teacher, and a better Christian, to ascend the rising path and so find my true telos, the higher purpose for which I was born.

BIBLIOGRAPHICAL ESSAY

CHAPTER ONE

It is most fortunate that the student or general reader who wishes to study the early dialogues of Plato need purchase only one book: *Early Socratic Dialogues*, edited with a general introduction by Trevor J. Saunders (Penguin, 1987). This excellent edition is fully annotated and boasts not only a top-notch introduction to the dialogues as a whole but detailed introductions to each individual dialogue. It really is the only book you need.

But if you want more, a standard study can be found in Richard Robinson's *Plato's Earlier Dialectic*, second edition (Clarendon, 1966). This book is out of print, but it appears in *The Philosophy of Socrates: A Collection of Critical Studies* (University of Notre Dame Press, 1991), edited by Gregory Vlastos. Vlastos, who is not an easy read and who has his biases, but who has devoted his life to studying Socrates and his methods, has also authored *Socrates: Ironist and Moral Philosopher* (Cornell University Press, 1991) and *Socratic Studies* (Cambridge University Press, 1994).

The standard textbook edition of the writings of the Presocratics, with selections given both in Greek and English, is G. S. Kirk and J. E. Raven's *The Presocratic Philosophers: A Critical History with a Selection of Texts*, second edition (Cambridge University Press, 1984). However, I would encourage the beginning reader to purchase Philip Wheelwright's

The Presocratics (Prentice Hall, 1966). This is the best one-volume treatment; it is more accessible in format and presentation than Kirk and Raven and is filled with excellent introductions and analyses.

In 2000, I contributed a lecture on the Presocratics to a massive, eighty-four-part lecture series titled "Great Minds of the Western Intellectual Tradition." The series is published by The Great Courses and is available online at www.teach12.com. I also put together my own twenty-four-lecture series, "Plato to Postmodernism: Understanding the Essence of Literature and the Role of the Author," which includes a lecture on Plato's *Republic*. Other Great Courses that readers of this book may find useful include "Plato's *Republic*, Masters of Greek Thought: Plato, Socrates, and Aristotle, and Plato, Socrates, and the Dialogues."

I devote a chapter each to Plato's early dialogues and to the *Apology* of Socrates in my *Ancient Voices: An Insider's Look at Classical Greece* (Stone Tower Pres, 2020). I also include a chapter that gives historical background for Socrates and Plato.

CHAPTER TWO

To my mind, the best, most accessible translation of Plato's *Republic* is the one by Richard W. Sterling and William C. Scott (Norton, 1996). While still staying faithful to the Greek, this translation renders Plato into modern, idiomatic English; indeed, it is so well done that though the translation was done in the 1980s, it continues to be fresh and "undated" today. Unlike the very fine Penguin Classics edition translated by Desmond Lee (2nd ed.; reissued in 2003), which is loaded with helpful notes and explanations of each section, the Sterling and Scott edition is very lightly annotated; it does, however, include a helpful essay on the divided line. Though I am a fan of the University of Chicago (especially their editions of the Greek tragedies), and though I am a fan as well of Alan Bloom, I find his translation (2nd ed., Basic Books, 1991), in which he seeks to be exceedingly faithful to the original text, difficult to read. Still, Bloom's notes are worthwhile, as are the things he has to say about Plato and *Republic* in his justly celebrated *The Closing of the American Mind* (Simon and Schuster,

1988). Needless to say, there are many, many other translations of *Republic* available; one that has garnered much critical praise is the Oxford World's Classics edition by Robin Waterfield (Oxford University Press, 2008).

A very helpful resource is *The Cambridge Companion to Plato's "Republic,"* edited by G. R. F. Ferrari (Cambridge University Press, 2007). Some other helpful resources are Nicholas P. White's *Companion to Plato's "Republic"* (Hackett, 1979), *The Blackwell Guide to Plato's "Republic,"* edited by Gerasimos Santas (Blackwell, 2006), Stanley Rosen's *Plato's "Republic": A Study* (Yale University Press, 2008), C. D. C. Reeve's *Philosopher-Kings: The Argument of Plato's "Republic"* (Hackett, 2006), and *Plato's "Republic": Critical Essays*, edited by Richard Kraut (Rowman & Littlefield, 1997).

One of the most influential criticisms of Plato's *Republic* continues to be Karl Popper's classic work *The Open Society and Its Enemies*, volume one, *The Spell of Plato* (Princeton University Press, 1971). Popper exposes the dangers of social engineering and lays part of the blame at Plato's feet. In the second volume, Popper goes on to study Hegel, Marx, and totalitarianism. One need not agree with Popper's full thesis to recognize the dangers inherent in a planned society like that described in *Republic*. In contrast to Popper's thesis, Gene Fendt and David Rozema's *Platonic Errors: Plato, a Kind of Poet* (Greenwood Press, 1998) attempts to read Plato as literature, and the dialogues as dialogues, a method that helps the authors get around Plato's supposed hatred of the arts and championing of totalitarianism.

Those interested in Plato's view of the arts might want to consult Morriss Henry Partee's *Plato's Poetics: The Authority of Beauty* (University of Utah Press, 1981) and *Plato: On Beauty, Wisdom, and the Arts*, edited by Julius Moravcsik and Philip Temko (Rowman & Littlefield, 1982). For a somewhat technical but still accessible study of Plato's theory of the Forms, see David Ross's *Plato's Theory of Ideas* (Oxford University Press, 1951).

Throughout my *Atheism on Trial: Refuting the Modern Arguments Against God* (Harvest, 2018), but particularly in chapter five, I treat

Plato as an apologist who defended the reality of the Good, True, and Beautiful against the sophists and the Presocratics.

CHAPTERS THREE AND FOUR

My preferred translation for *Protagoras* and *Meno* is the Penguin Classics edition by W. K. C. Guthrie (Penguin, 1956). Although all the introductions and notes to the Penguin Classics editions of Plato's dialogues are good, the ones written by Guthrie for *Protagoras* and *Meno* are excellent. They make a good introduction not only to these dialogues but also to the distinction between Plato and Socrates and the general teachings of Plato. I also strongly favor the Penguin editions of *Phaedrus* (translated by Walter Hamilton and including Plato's seventh and eighth *Letters*, 1973), *Phaedo* (part of *The Last Days of Socrates*, translated by Hugh Tredennick, 1969), and *Symposium* (translated by the always reliable Walter Hamilton, 1951). The Penguin *Gorgias* is good, but I also like the Library of Liberal Arts edition translated by W. C. Helmbold (Bobbs-Merrill, 1952).

A good overview of the development of Plato's thought with reflections on the myths can be found in J. E. Raven's *Plato's Thought: A Study of the Development of His Metaphysics* (Cambridge University Press, 1965). For a study that helps evaluate the *Meno* myth and the role it plays in Plato's thought, see Roslyn Weiss's *Virtue in the Cave: Moral Enquiry in Plato's "Meno"* (Oxford University Press, 2000). For two close studies of *Phaedrus*, see Graeme Nicholson's *Plato's "Phaedrus": The Philosophy of Love* (Purdue University Press, 1999) and G. R. F. Ferrari's *Listening to the Cicadas: A Study of Plato's "Phaedrus"* (Cambridge University Press, 1987). Lovers of *Symposium* may want to consult a collection of essays on the dialogue put out by the Center for Hellenic Studies in Washington, DC, *Plato's "Symposium": Issues in Interpretation and Reception*, edited by J. H. Lesher, Debra Nails, and Frisbee C. C. Sheffield (Harvard University Press, 2006).

Also, on Plato's myths the great German Catholic philosopher Josef Pieper has much insight to offer: see his *Divine Madness: Plato's Case Against Secular Humanism* (Ignatius, 1995) and *The Platonic Myths* (St.

Augustine's Press, 2011). In my *The Myth Made Fact: Reading Greek and Roman Mythology through Christian Eyes* (Classical Academic Press, 2020), I analyze closely seven of Plato's myths, interpreting them from a Christian point of view and providing study questions for families, classrooms, Sunday schools, book clubs, and personal devotions.

Chapter five of Thomas Cahill's entertaining, informative, and often thought-provoking *Sailing the Wine-Dark Sea: Why the Greeks Matter* (Doubleday, 2003) includes a retelling and partial reinterpreting of Plato's *Symposium* that is worth a look.

CHAPTER FIVE

My preferred edition of Plato's *Laws* is the Penguin Classics edition translated by Trevor J. Saunders (1970). Saunders offers an excellent introduction that sets the dialogue in its proper context. I should mention here that, for the sake of space and to help keep this book accessible to the general reader, I have chosen not to explore some of the other later dialogues that Plato wrote in the same time period as *Laws*: *Parmenides, Theaetetus, Sophist, Statesman,* and (the earlier written) *Cratylus.* These more difficult and more technical dialogues explore Plato's theory of knowledge and of language and are generally less accessible than the better-known dialogues. Also, I find that Plato's greatest contributions can be garnered in full from *Republic, Laws,* and the other shorter dialogues discussed in this book.

Still, for those interested in these lesser-known dialogues, I would suggest Kenneth Dorter's *Form and Good in Plato's Eliatic Dialogues: The "Parmenides," "Theaetetus," "Sophist," and "Statesman"* (University of California Press, 1994), and Jacob Klein's *Plato's Trilogy: "Theaetetus," the "Sophist," and the "Statesman"* (University of Chicago Press, 1977). Two other studies that delve deeply into Plato's theory of knowledge, including reflections on *Republic* and *Laws,* and that are difficult but still accessible, are J. C. B. Gosling's *Plato* (Routledge, 1983) and F. M. Cornford's *Plato's Theory of Knowledge: The "Theaetetus" and the Sophist* (Dover, 2003).

A classic overview of Plato's thought that covers such topics as the soul, the gods, the arts, education, and statecraft can be found in

G. M. A. Grube's *Plato's Thought* (Hackett, 1980). For a more aesthetically rich overview of Plato's thought, including his interactions with the Presocratics, Socrates, and the sophists, by a Victorian sage, see Walter Pater's *Plato and Platonism* (Greenwood Press, 1969). Two other reliable guides to Plato's thought can be found in chapter one of Will Durant's highly readable *The Story of Philosophy* (Pocket Books, 1991) and the slightly more difficult volume one (*Greece and Rome from the Pre-Socratics to Plotinus*) of Frederick Copleston's *A History of Philosophy* (Image, 1993). Chapter four of A. E. Taylor's *Platonism and Its Influence* ("Plato the Theologian," Cooper Square Publishing, 1963) offers an excellent overview of *Laws* 10 as well as arguing convincingly, as I attempt to do several times in this chapter, that many of the ideas we associate with Aristotle find their true origin in Plato.

CHAPTER SIX

My preferred edition of *Timaeus* and *Critias* is the Penguin Classics edition translated by Desmond Lee (Penguin, 1977). This edition includes not only an excellent introduction but also a fine appendix on the myth of Atlantis.

For a classic study of the cosmology of *Timaeus*, see F. M. Cornford's monumental *Plato's Cosmology: The "Timaeus" of Plato* (Routledge, 1971). For another more recent study of the subject that factors in modern developments in science, see the intriguing *Inventing the Universe: Plato's "Timaeus," the Big Bang, and the Problem of Scientific Knowledge* by Luc Brisson and F. Walter Meyerstein (State University of New York Press, 1995).

My favorite study of the persistence of Plato's cosmological model, which was passed down to the Middle Ages via Ptolemy, is C. S. Lewis's *The Discarded Image* (Cambridge University Press, 1964). For a quicker, easier overview of this model, which persisted through the Renaissance and even up to the dawn of the Enlightenment, see E. M. W. Tillyard's *The Elizabethan World Picture* (Vintage, 1959). For the most exhaustive look at the model, see Arthur O. Lovejoy's *The Great Chain of Being* (Harvard University Press, 1964).

CHAPTER SEVEN

I more or less branch off on my own in this chapter but would like to suggest some helpful books. A. E. Taylor's *Platonism and Its Influence* (Cooper Square Publishing, 1963) offers a brief but classic study of Plato's influence on philosophy, ethics, and theology that also assesses with precision Christianity's debt to Plato. In his monumental *Plato: The Man and His Work* (Dover, 2001), Taylor offers a full overview of Plato's work. Paul Elmer More's *The Religion of Plato* and *Hellenistic Philosophies* (Princeton University Press, 1921; 1923) are also very good. For a more difficult, but thoughtful study of the religious implications behind Plato's dialogues and myths, see Eric Voegelin's *Plato* (Louisiana State University Press, 1966).

Two lesser-known books that offer much insight into Plato and his influence on Christianity are Constantine Cavarnos's *The Hellenic-Christian Philosophical Tradition* (Institute for Byzantine and Modern Greek Studies, 1989) and Jerry Dell Ehrlich's *Plato's Gift to Christianity: The Gentile Preparation for and the Making of the Christian Faith* (Academic Christian Press, 2001). The focus of the former book is summed up nicely in its long subtitle: *Four Lectures Dealing with Philosophy in the Greek East from Antiquity to Modern Times, with Special Reference to Plato, Aristotle, Stoicism, and the Greek Church Fathers.* The first lecture looks at the impact on the Hellenic East of Plato's view of the Forms, the soul, and the unity of the virtues. The latter book offers a very thorough and highly accessible overview of those elements of Plato's thought that profoundly influenced the early church. This book, however, is flawed by his overly zealous attempt to personalize Plato's God and his anti–Old Testament (but never anti-Semitic) perspective— a perspective that, quite shockingly, is similar to that of the early church heretic Marcion. Rather than confine himself to arguing that God used Plato to prepare the Greco-Roman world for the full revelation of Christianity, Ehrlich argues that Jesus' concepts of sin and salvation are more grounded in Plato than the Old Testament. He also argues that the early church fathers only linked themselves to the Old Testament to avoid Roman persecution, since the Romans accepted

Judaism as an ancient religion, but were suspicious of new religions. Still, his overview of Plato *is* helpful and often quite insightful. For a more accurate understanding of how the early church selected from Plato those elements that squared with the Bible, both Old and New Testament, stick with Cavarnos—whose *Plato's View of Man* (Institute for Byzantine and Modern Greek Studies, 1975) is also very good.

Readers interested in the allegorizing of pre-Christian writers might consult Robert Lamberton's *Homer the Theologian: Neoplatonist Allegorical Reading and the Growth of the Epic Tradition* (University of California Press, 1986) for its look at how Plato and his successors (both pagan and Christian) "adjusted" Homer to get at his spiritual essence. After Plato and Aristotle, the pre-Christian writer who was perhaps most thoroughly Christianized was Virgil; for a classic study of this process, see Domenico Comparetti's *Virgil in the Middle Ages*, translated by E. F. M. Benecke (Princeton University Press, 1997).

In my own book, *From Achilles to Christ: Why Christians Should Read the Pagan Classics* (IVP Academic, 2007), I develop a theme central to this chapter: namely, that the God of the Bible used Homer, Virgil, and the Greek tragedians—as I try in this book to show that he used Plato—to help prepare the classical world for the coming of the fuller Christian revelation. One of the first books to trace this preparation is by the great historian of the early church Eusebius of Caesarea's *Preparation of the Gospel* (*Praeparatio Evangelica* in Latin).

Another source of insight into Christian Platonism can be found in the writings of Simone Weil, particularly her *Intimations of Christianity Among the Ancient Greeks*. E. Jane Doering and Eric O. Springsted have edited a collection of essays on this aspect of Weil's thought, *The Christian Platonism of Simone Weil* (University of Notre Dame Press, 2004).

Finally, I must mention that one of the finest books ever written on man as enfleshed soul is Pope John Paul II's *The Theology of the Body* (Pauline Books & Media, 1997). I believe this book is destined to become a theological standard; its firmly biblical and orthodox understanding of the body, of the sexes, and of identity in general makes for essential reading in our increasingly gnostic modern world.

CHAPTER EIGHT

My preferred edition for Origen's *On First Principles* is edited and translated by G. W. Butterworth (Harper & Row, 1966). Aside from this text, I pretty much push off on my own. Still, those wishing more information on Origen would do well to consult Joseph W. Trigg's *Origen* (Routledge, 1998), which offers both a biography and some of his selected works. I would also strongly recommend Henri de Lubac's *History and Spirit: The Understanding of Scripture According to Origen* (Ignatius, 2007).

CHAPTER NINE

Henri de Lubac also wrote the definitive study of the late classical and medieval allegorical approach to Scripture: *Medieval Exegesis: The Four Senses of Scripture* (Eerdmans): volume one was translated by Mark Sebanc (1998); and volumes two and three, by E. M. Macierowski (2000–2009). This book will help give background for some of the strange exegesis that one encounters in Eastern fathers like Gregory of Nyssa (in this chapter) and Western fathers like Augustine (in the next chapter).

My texts for the three Gregorys, all of which have good introductions that set the work in its historical and theological setting, are cited in the notes to the chapter, but it should be added here that my text for Gregory of Nazianzus, *Christology of the Late Fathers*, also includes Athanasius's *On the Incarnation*, a seminal read for anyone wanting to trace Platonic influences in the East, along with two shorter works by Gregory of Nyssa. For a good overview of the three Cappadocian fathers, see Patrick Whitworth's *Three Wise Men from the East: The Cappadocian Fathers and the Struggle for Orthodoxy* (Sacristy Press, 2015).

John Meyendorff's *St Gregory of Palamas and Orthodox Spirituality* (St Vladimir's Seminary Press, 1974) offers the relevant background along with much insight into the Orthodox soul. For a good, highly accessible, one-volume overview of Orthodoxy, see Timothy Ware's *The Orthodox Church: An Introduction to Eastern Christianity* (Penguin, 2015). To learn about the Jesus Prayer, the central prayer of the hesychast movement, pick up one of the many editions of *The Way of the Pilgrim*, the autobiography of a medieval Russian monk who devoted himself to the prayer. Finally, if you want to immerse yourself in Orthodoxy, pick up one or more of the four volumes of *The Philokalia* (Faber and Faber, 1979), a collection of writings by medieval Orthodox monks and mystics.

Those who enjoyed this chapter and the previous one may also want to read works by the following Fathers: Justin Martyr, Irenaeus, Clement of Alexandria, John Chrysostom, Dionysius the Areopagite, John Climacus (the title of whose *Ladder of Divine Ascent* betrays its strong debt to Plato), John of Damascus, Photios, and Symeon the New Theologian.

Chapter Ten

Although I have used the Penguin Pine-Coffin translation of Augustine's *Confessions*, I know a number of Latinists who find this translation unsatisfactory. Those who share this caution would do well to consult the excellent translation by Henry Chadwick (Oxford, 2009). One of the best ways to experience *Confessions*, especially its focus on desire, is to read Peter Kreeft's *I Burned for Your Peace: Augustine's Confessions Unpacked* (Ignatius, 2016), which affords the pleasure of reading Augustine over the shoulder of one of the most accessible Christian philosophers writing today—one who knows well how to fuse the insights of Socrates and Plato with the greater truths of Christ and the Bible.

One of the best studies of Plato's influence on Augustine is Phillip Cary's *Inner Grace: Augustine in the Tradition of Plato and Paul* (Oxford, 2008). Cary has also done an excellent audio/video course on Augustine for The Great Courses that treats Augustine's faith fairly and honestly: "Augustine: Philosopher and Saint." For a classic study of how Augustine helped preserve Plato's legacy, see Raymond Klibansky's *The Continuity of the Platonic Tradition During the Middle Ages* (Warburg Institute, 1939). See also his *Plato's "Parmenides" in the Middle Ages and Renaissance* (Ulan Press, 2012).

Although I use the older translation of W. V. Cooper for Boethius, I would encourage readers to pick up the excellent modern translation by Scott Goins and Barbara H. Wyman (Ignatius, 2012). This Ignatius Critical Edition includes a number of accessible essays on the *Consolation*, including one in which I offer an overview of the entire work. In his précis of the medieval cosmological model, *The Discarded Image* (Cambridge, 1964), C. S. Lewis makes the clearest argument for the *Consolation* being written by a Christian in a pre-Christian mode.

I have always preferred the Ciardi translation of Dante; however, the translations (and notes) by Dorothy Sayers (Penguin) and Anthony Esolen (Modern Library) are also well worth consulting. In my *Heaven and Hell: Visions of the Afterlife in the Western Poetic Tradition* (Wipf & Stock, 2013), I devote two chapters to Plato and nine to Dante. Rod Dreher's *How Dante Can Save Your Life* (Regan Arts, 2015) offers a close, accessible, highly personal look at how Dante's epic directs us toward our true home.

CHAPTER ELEVEN

The Essential Erasmus, from which I quoted Erasmus's *Enchiridion*, contains many key works, including *Praise of Folly* and *An Inquiry Concerning Faith*. My edition of *The Education of a Christian Prince* has a helpful introduction and excellent textual notes. For two good, accessible biographies, see Johan Huizinga's *Erasmus and the Age of Reformation* (Benediction Books, 2009) and Roland Bainton's *Erasmus of Christendom* (Hendrickson, 2016).

My edition of Descartes's *Meditations* has a helpful introduction, but few explanatory notes. Readers should consult Peter Kreeft's *Socrates Meets Descartes* (St. Augustine's Press, 2012) for a vigorous and entertaining dialogue that helps get to the core of Descartes. A fun way to experience the history of philosophy, with Descartes in a pivotal role, see Jostein Gaarder's engrossing *Sophie's World: A Novel About the History of Philosophy* (Farrar, Straus and Giroux, 2007).

My edition of Coleridge's *Biographia* (Princeton University Press, 1983) is one of the best of its kind. The introduction and notes offer a wealth of information that set author, book, and ideas in their historical context. The coeditor, James Engell, published his own accessible book on Enlightenment and Romantic theories of the imagination: *The Creative Imagination: Enlightenment to Romanticism* (Harvard University Press, 1981). My lecture series "From Plato to Postmodernism" (also cited above) covers various theories of the imagination, with a full lecture devoted to Coleridge.

CHAPTER TWELVE

I offer an overview of Lewis's life and writings in my twelve-lecture series with The Great Courses: "The Life and Writings of C. S. Lewis." In *Lewis Agonistes: How C. S. Lewis Can Train Us to Wrestle with the Modern and Postmodern World* (B&H, 2003), I offer a biography of Lewis followed by chapters on how Lewis, often with the help of Plato, wrestled with science, the New Age, evil and suffering, the arts, and heaven and hell. I devote seven chapters to Lewis's apologetics in *Apologetics for the 21st Century* (Crossway, 2010) and then cover his fiction and academic writing in *Restoring Beauty: The Good, the True, and the Beautiful in the Writings of C. S. Lewis* (Biblica/InterVarsity Press, 2010). In *C. S. Lewis: An Apologist for Education* (Classical Academic Press, 2015), I discuss Lewis's view of education; in *On the Shoulders of Hobbits: The Road to Virtue with Tolkien and Lewis* (Moody, 2012), I discuss virtue and vice in the Chronicles of Narnia. Plato plays a role in all four books.

Among the many excellent books on C. S. Lewis, here are five that will help elucidate some of the points in this chapter: Michael Ward's *Planet Narnia: The Seven Heavens in the Imagination of C. S. Lewis* (Oxford, 2008; reissued as *The Narnia Code*) argues that Lewis keyed each Chronicle to the seven medieval planets, a worldview that is essentially Platonic. Armand Nicholi's *The Question of God: C. S. Lewis and Freud Debate God, Love, Sex, and the Meaning of Life* (Free Press, 2002) compares and contrast the opposing worldviews of Lewis and Freud (who was as anti-Platonic as he was anti-God). Will Vaus's *Mere Theology: A Guide to the Thought of C. S. Lewis* (InterVarsity Press,

2004) offers an accessible overview of Lewis's theological beliefs. Marsha Daigle-Williamson's *Reflecting the Eternal: Dante's Divine Comedy in the Novels of C. S. Lewis* (Hendrickson, 2015) traces the direct influence of Dante on Lewis, and, by so doing, much of Plato's indirect influence. Peter Kreeft's *C. S. Lewis for the Third Millennium: Six Essays on "The Abolition of Man"* (Ignatius, 1994) offers an analysis that draws heavily on Plato, as did Lewis himself.

SCRIPTURE INDEX